Responsibility and
Atonement

Responsibility and Atonement

Richard Swinburne

90-2152

CLARENDON PRESS · OXFORD
1989

Oxford University Press, Walton Street, Oxford OX2 6DP
Oxford New York Toronto
Delhi Bombay Calcutta Madras Karachi
Petaling Jaya Singapore Hong Kong Tokyo
Nairobi Dar es Salaam Cape Town
Melbourne Auckland
and associated companies in
Berlin Ibadan

Oxford is a trade mark of Oxford University Press

Published in the United States
by Oxford University Press, New York

British Library Cataloguing in Publication Data
Swinburne, Richard
Responsibility and atonement.
1. Christian Doctrine. Man
I. Title
233
ISBN 0–19–824839–3
ISBN 0–19–824849–0 (pbk.)

Library of Congress Cataloging in Publication Data
Swinburne, Richard.
Responsibility and atonement / Richard Swinburne.
Bibliography: p. Includes index.
1. Responsibility. 2. Atonement. I. Title.
BJ1451.S9 1989 241—dc19 88–34613
ISBN 0–19–824839–3
ISBN 0–19–824849–0 (pbk.)

Set by Hope Services, Abingdon
Printed and bound in
Great Britain by Biddles Ltd,
Guildford and King's Lynn

Preface

Responsibility and Atonement is based on the Edward Cadbury Lectures which I gave in the University of Birmingham in the autumn of 1987. I am grateful to the University for inviting me to give the lectures, and to all who entertained me so hospitably during my weekly visits to Birmingham. Previous versions of the lectures were used for graduate seminars at the University of Oxford and at Syracuse University; and a paper based on ideas contained in Chapters 4, 5, and 10 has been read at a number of universities. I am grateful for the friendly and helpful criticism which I received on these occasions, and from colleagues who have read written versions of some of the lectures. Some of the material of Chapters 5, 7, 8, 9, and 10 has been published in two papers—'Original Sinfulness', in *Neue Zeitschrift für Systematische Theologie und Religionsphilosophie*, 1985, **25**, 235–50; and 'The Christian Scheme of Salvation' in T. V. Morris (ed.), *Philosophy and the Christian Faith*, University of Notre Dame Press, 1988. There is also an overlap of some of the material of Chapter 1 with material used in my *The Evolution of the Soul* (Clarendon Press, 1986), and of some of the material of Chapter 12 with material used in my *Faith and Reason* (Clarendon Press, 1981). I am grateful to the publishers involved for permission to reuse this material. And finally I must thank Mrs Bernadette O'Reilly for her most patient typing and retyping of many drafts of the book.

Contents

Introduction

When I benefit or harm you there are often consequences for my moral status and for what I and you and the world should do about it. I may acquire merit or guilt; it may be appropriate for you or others to reward or punish me; or I may need to make atonement for what I have done, and it may then be good that you should forgive me. The first and longer part of this book is concerned with such moral notions, with merit, guilt, praise, blame, reward, punishment, mercy, gratitude, atonement, resentment, and forgiveness; with their logical relations to each other and with the conditions for their correct application to people in their dealings with one another. They are notions to many of which, with the obvious exception of punishment, moral philosophers of recent centuries have given relatively little attention. All these notions, and especially praise and blame, may appear to have application only on the assumption that in some sense people are responsible for their actions; and so I shall need to investigate anew the well-worn question of whether people are responsible for their actions if and only if they are not causally necessitated (e.g. by their genes or their environment) to act as they do. Further, praise and blame are appropriate to actions in so far as the agents do what is morally good or morally wrong or what they believe to be morally good or morally wrong. So I shall need also to investigate what moral goodness and obligation consist in (not what actions are morally good, but what moral goodness in an action amounts to), and how it is that agents can fail to do what they believe to be morally the best thing to do.

Such is the scope of Part I. I hope that it will be of interest to moral philosophers and students of moral philosophy, quite apart from the consequences which I seek to draw in Part II from the results of Part I. Nevertheless, the results of Part I do have consequences for theology, and I seek to draw those out in Part II. Once we have got clear about how such notions as merit and reward, guilt, atonement and forgiveness apply to dealings between people in general, we can then go on to examine how they would apply to dealings between humans and God. (I shall in future sometimes use the short English word 'man' as a synonym for the cumbersome and occasionally ambiguous 'human' or 'human being', to denote a member of the human race.) I introduce a theological assumption that there is a God with certain characteristics who became incarnate as Jesus Christ and did certain things, including allowing himself to be crucified by men. I then examine what follows when all this is added to the results of Part I, for the traditional Christian doctrines concerned with the moral relations between man and God; concerned, that is, with sin and original sin, with our redemption by Christ and our sanctification through the means of grace provided in the Church, with Hell as an eternal punishment for the wicked, and Heaven as an eternal reward for the good.

It would be misleading to talk of '*the* Christian doctrine' on any of these matters. The original New Testament matrix of parable and teaching gave rise, through subsequent theological reflection, to a whole spectrum of rival doctrines on all of these matters. It is my hope that the moral principles elucidated in Part I will enable us to choose between some of the rival theological doctrines. On each of the doctrinal issues there is a recognizable 'hard' position and at least one significantly more 'liberal' alternative to it. A hard position on one issue fits naturally with a hard position on other issues to form a recognizable uniform hardline approach. For the consistent hardliner, every man suffers from a total depravity, guilt for his own sins and the sins of Adam, and a total inability to do other than sin; he deserves everlasting pain as a punishment, but God in Christ bore the punishment in his stead; those who have explicit faith in Christ will be excused the eternal punishment, made capable of doing good, and given an eternal reward. The only good actions are those which seek intentionally the glory of God. All those without explicit faith in Christ will suffer torment in Hell for ever; God predestines in advance who will be saved and who will be damned. For each of the issues, however, there are recognizable more liberal positions in Christian thought, and on many of the issues I would judge that the more liberal position is the majority position. A liberal position on all the issues looks something like this. Every man finds it difficult but possible to avoid sin; and although in some way something is wrong with him as a result of the sins of others, he is not guilty for those sins himself. Christ redeemed us by his suffering (which was not a substitute for the punishment which we would otherwise suffer, but in some way God taking our sins seriously), and made available to us a means of sanctification; but it is up to us whether we choose to avail ourselves of this redemption and sanctification, and God has not predestined how we will choose. However, if we choose to follow the good as we see it, we shall be saved (even if we do not on earth acquire Christian convictions). Although those actions which seek intentionally the glory of God are supremely good, so many other actions (including many actions of seeking one's own happiness, mundane or eternal) are good too. Only if we do not follow the good as we see it shall we be damned. But there may in the end be none of us in the latter category, or, if there are, this damnation will not consist of eternal pain.

Christian thought, I believe, started off in the first three centuries AD with a substantial liberal component. Irenaeus, Origen, and Gregory of Nyssa were clear examples of a basically liberal approach. But the hard line was there too, reaching its climax in the work of Augustine, who fastened his views on the Western Church for centuries to come. The Eastern Church, however, was never bound by the views of Augustine, and very gradually the Western Church began to detach itself from those views. Many medieval thinkers made their contribution to the liberalizing process (among them Anselm, Aquinas, and especially Duns Scotus), and then the Council of Trent, and later the Second Vatican Council, gave official Catholic approval to many liberal positions. Although classical Protestantism took a firm hardline position, more moderate Protestants have always been more liberal. There have, indeed, been within liberal Protestantism occasional exponents of a position far more liberal than the recognizably mainstream position which I have called the liberal position.

I shall argue that when the moral conclusions of Part I are conjoined to my theological assumption there follows a form of the liberal position. Modern secular man will need little convincing to recognize the moral unacceptability of the hardline position. The need is rather to persuade him of the moral acceptability of the liberal position, and that task I will attempt. A more traditional Christian sometimes needs to be persuaded that the liberal position is compatible with the majesty of God and with Christian tradition, and that task too I will attempt.

Some years ago now I wrote a trilogy on the philosophy of religion—*The Coherence of Theism* (1977), *The Existence of God* (1979), and *Faith and Reason* (1981). Its major themes were the coherence and justification of the belief that there is a God (of the kind worshipped in Judaism and Islam, as well as Christianity) and the rationality of living by that belief. It was concerned largely with issues common to various theistic creeds, except in the final volume, where it began to investigate specifically Christian issues.

With the present volume I move further in that direction. This volume will, I hope, prove to be the first of four volumes on specifically Christian doctrines. Subsequent volumes will deal with the aspects of the doctrine of God peculiar to Christianity (the doctrines of the Trinity and the Incarnation); with revelation (with how God could reveal himself to man, and how such revelation could be recognized); and with providence and the problem of evil (giving a larger consideration to this issue than was possible in *The Existence of God*, in the light of specifically Christian doctrines). Some of these doctrines clearly make, at least to a small extent, historical claims, or need to be supported by historical evidence. I shall be concerned only with the philosophical issues of the meaning and inner consistency of the doctrines, with the amount of a priori evidence which can be marshalled for or against them, and with the force which historical evidence of different kinds would have in supporting or opposing them. The philosopher can consider, for example, what it means to say that God became incarnate as a man and whether this claim is coherent; whether a priori in view of the nature of God, he is likely to become incarnate; and what sort of behaviour by a certain man would show that he was God incarnate. The philosopher cannot show that a certain man did exhibit that sort of behaviour; that is a task for the historian. But what the philosopher can show is how strong the historian's evidence needs to be. If your background knowledge of what the world is like shows some detailed historical claim to be quite likely, then you will need little in the way of historical evidence in order rationally to believe it. Conversely, if your background knowledge shows some detailed historical claim to be rather unlikely, then you will need a lot in the way of historical evidence in order rationally to believe it. If you have strong reason to believe on the basis of some biological theory that there are Abominable Snowmen living in the Himalayas, you may reasonably take some rather unclear marks at some place as good grounds for believing that Abominable Snowmen were at that place. But if you have no background reason for believing that there are such creatures, you would need a lot of detailed footprints and a few sightings before you could reasonably believe that the footprints were theirs. This simple point about evidence is sometimes forgotten by modern biblical theologians who feel that the whole weight of establishing the truth or falsity of central Christian doctrines depends on their detailed critical work on the books of the New Testament. It does not. There are larger considerations to be taken into account.

The present volume, however, is concerned only with what follows from the existence of God together with other Christian doctrines for the Christian doctrine of man. I assume those other Christian doctrines; other volumes will consider their justification, and historical evidence has its part to play in establishing or refuting those other doctrines. But historical evidence is not directly relevant to the doctrines considered in the present volume. However, I start my examination of Christian doctrine at the point at which proclamation of the Christian gospel traditionally has started—with man's sin and need for salvation.

PART I

Responsibility

I

Moral Goodness

Objective Moral Goodness

Many things are good, and their goodness is diverse and hard to compare. There is the goodness of the beauty of galaxies, rivers, and paintings, of the litheness of form and power of birds and tigers. And men are to be valued for many aspects of their being—for their shape and power of limb and mind, for their sense of humour, and their sense of colour. But there is a special species of goodness, moral goodness, which can belong to agents and to their actions. The primary variety of this species is objective moral goodness, the moral goodness possessed by an act of paying one's debts or visiting the lonely, quite apart from whether some particular agent considering doing such an action believes of it that it is morally good. We do, all of us, believe that certain particular actions, as done in certain circumstances, are morally good. But what do we believe when we believe that an action is morally good? What is it for an action to be morally good as opposed to good in other ways? My question is, not which actions are morally good, but what is one saying when one says that an action is morally good, what is moral disagreement disagreement about?

The expression 'morally good' is used in English (and expressions normally so translated are used in other languages) in very vague ways, and different philosophers have distilled from different aspects of usage rival and incompatible accounts of the nature of moral goodness.[1] One account presents the moral as the overall, the important, and the overriding.[2] If an action is morally good, then, even if there are bad aspects to it, it is overall good. It is important, it matters that it should be done. And it is better, it matters more that

---

[1] See the introduction to and the various views represented in G. Wallace and A. D. M. Walker (eds.), *The Definition of Morality*, Methuen, 1970.

[2] For an example of such a view, see Neil Cooper, 'Morality and Importance', ch. 6 of Wallace and Walker, op. cit. (revised version of an article in *Mind*, 1968).

it be done than that any action that is not morally good be done; moral goodness, that is, is overriding goodness. To believe that an action is morally good is to believe that it is of overriding importance (in comparison with actions which are not believed to be morally good) that it should be done. The trouble with this account is that it allows the egoist dedicated to the pursuit of his own pleasure to have a moral belief that he ought to steal, murder, seduce, or whatever, simply because he believes such actions to be overall good and of overriding importance. He may have no beliefs that these actions are good because they benefit others in some way, or that similar actions done by others to benefit themselves would be good. He sees the goodness of his actions as arising solely from their benefit to himself. It seems well out of line with ordinary usage to call the egoist's beliefs 'moral beliefs'.

The second account of the moral adds to the previous account in terms of the overall, the important, and the overriding, that the goodness of the action proceed from its possession of universal properties. Moral beliefs are 'universalizable' beliefs. That was the view of Kant[3] and of Hare.[4] I understand by an action deriving its goodness from its universal properties, that it derives it from being an act of a certain kind, where the description of the kind makes no reference to named persons (or other objects), only to persons (or other objects) of a certain kind. For example, we think an act to be valuable in so far as it is *an* act of feeding *a* hungry person, or *an* act of saving *a* dying man. The 'persons of a certain kind' may be picked out by their relations to the agent, for example, as a child or parent of the agent or a person to whom the agent made a promise; and we think of acts as valuable in so far as they are acts of 'educating one's own child' or 'keeping a promise made by oneself' (whoever one is or one's child is). Seeing actions as good in virtue of their universal properties is to be contrasted with seeing actions as good in virtue of their particular properties, properties the description of which involves an uneliminable reference to individuals, e.g. the agent himself or someone loved or hated by him (picked out by a name whose application does not depend on the possession by the person of some relational or other universal property). Thus Jones, seeing

    [3] See *The Groundwork of the Metaphysic of Morals*, trans. H. J. Paton under the title *The Moral Law*, Hutchinson, 1953.
    [4] See his *The Language of Morals*, Clarendon Press, 1952, and *Freedom and Reason*, Clarendon Press, 1962.

an action as good in so far as it promotes Jones' ease or achievement or popularity, sees it as good in virtue of a particular property. This is to be contrasted with Jones seeing an action as good in virtue of promoting 'one's own ease, achievement, or popularity', which would be seeing it as good in virtue of a universal property. If Jones sees an action as good for the latter reason, he will see not merely Jones promoting Jones's ease as good, but Smith promoting Smith's ease as also good. Whereas if he sees an action as good only in virtue of providing Jones's ease, etc., he will see Smith promoting Jones's ease as good, but he will not see Smith promoting Smith's ease as good. A belief that an action has overall, overriding importance which it derives from its possession of universal properties is a belief that the action is morally good—on this second account. This account does, of course allow it as a moral view that certain individuals—for example, the king, parliament, or pope—are entitled to special treatment; so long as that view holds that the special treatment is due to the individual because of universal properties which he or it has—'having been elected by democratic suffrage' or 'being Head of the Universal Church'—not because parliament is those people or the Pope is Karol Wojtyla.[5]

The difficulty with this account, however, is that it does seem logically possible that someone could believe that an action was important to do because of the universal properties which it possessed; and yet think that it derived that importance from universal properties in no way connected with the kind of universal

---

[5] In *Fear and Trembling*, Kierkegaard emphasizes that the ethical is the 'universal'; but claims that man's 'absolute duty towards God', which is a higher duty, is not 'universal'. The exact content of this claim is none too clear. But if he is claiming that we have a 'duty' towards God which does not depend on God's unique possession of certain properties, it would be a very odd claim. It is surely because God is the creator of the universe (or omnipotent, or whatever) that we owe him what we do. Kierkegaard also holds that 'religion involves a teleological suspension of the ethical'. If we understand 'the ethical' as 'the moral', Kierkegaard's view is incompatible with my first account of the moral—for on that nothing could be more important than morality; and with my second account—for on that nothing which derives its importance from universal properties (as does our duty to God) could be more important than morality. His view is compatible with some versions of my third account (yet to be presented); but not with the final account which I shall advocate subsequently, since the grounds of religious obligation are of a kind with the grounds of obligations to humans—e.g. we owe worship to our creator, because there is a general duty to pay respect to benefactors, and so a duty to pay respect to human benefactors also. From that it will follow, on the final account, that religious obligation is a moral obligation. See S. Kierkegaard, *Fear and Trembling*, trans. R. Payne, OUP, 1939, esp. Problems 1 and 2.

properties which we normally suppose contribute to the overall goodness of actions. Thus, to take over an example of Philippa Foot's,[6] someone might think it good in itself to clap one's hands three times an hour, and that its being an action of that sort gave an action overall overriding goodness. By 'in itself' I mean that he supposes that the action derives its goodness solely from the fact that it is an action of that kind, and not because, for example, in his society clapping one's hands three times an hour is a way of showing approval of those near to one, or because the psychological stimulus of clapping one's hands three times an hour prevents the agent from going off to sleep when he is performing some vital task. Yet this belief that clapping one's hands three times an hour is good in itself seems so disconnected from the kind of consideration which we usually suppose to be morally relevant that we would hesitate to call the belief a moral belief.

The third account of moral goodness analyses an action being morally good in terms of it forwarding or exemplifying goodness of a certain kind. Moral goodness is a species of goodness, it need not be important or overriding, but it does arise from the possession of universal properties. There can be different versions of this account, according to the kind of goodness picked out; but the most common version of this view, held by Philippa Foot and G. J. Warnock, and more recently by Peter Railton,[7] claims that moral goodness is the goodness of general human well-being. A belief that an action is morally good is a belief that it forwards general human well-being. On this account it would be a moral view that we ought to feed the starving; but not a moral view that we ought to worship God, nor that artists who can paint great pictures ought to do so even if those pictures will be seen only by themselves. If you use 'moral' in this limited sense, you can say without contradiction, 'I think that religion is more important than morality' or 'I don't think that morality matters much'. The trouble with this account is just this,

---

[6] See pp. 118ff of her 'Moral Beliefs' in her *Virtues and Vices*, University of California Press, 1978. She argues there (with a little hesitation) that the suggestion that such an action is good is incoherent. There are logical limits to what anyone can regard as good, and clapping one's hands three times an hour falls outside these. I am not committed to that strong thesis. I am merely pointing out that it would be odd to call a belief that it is good a 'moral' belief.

[7] See Philippa Foot, op. cit.; G. J. Warnock, *The Object of Morality*, Methuen, 1971; and Peter Railton, 'Moral Realism', *Philosophical Review*, 1986, **95**, 163–207 (see pp. 189f.).

that it has the consequence that there is nothing as such wrong in acting contrary to your moral beliefs; for, as far as this account goes, morality may be and you may think it to be of little importance. This does seem to jar with our normal understanding of 'morality'.

Moral badness on these three accounts is, of course, the opposite of moral goodness, in the sense that on the first account the morally bad is the overall bad, which it is of overriding importance should not be done; and on the second account it is the overall bad which it is of overriding importance should not be done, where that badness derives from universal properties; and on the third account it is badness of a particular kind (e.g. arising from harm to humans).

A study of the ordinary use of English would, I believe, reveal that 'moral' is used in various senses, including both the three delineated by my three accounts and ones intermediate between these. One interesting variant on the third sense prevalent in ordinary talk is that in which 'moral' goodness is the kind of goodness involved in personal relations. The propriety of sexual conduct is a 'moral' matter in this sense, whereas war is not. Thus, one local politician was reported on TV recently as saying in connection with the AIDS crisis that we couldn't afford to consider mere 'moral' issues when it was a matter of saving human life.[8]

Although usage is thus unclear, it seems to me that we do think that many of the actions open to humans are good in a special kind of way, and we often (though not always) use the expression 'morally good' to try to capture that special kind of way; and although philosophers have been over-simple in their account of that kind of way, they have been basically on the right lines. I am therefore going to give a slightly more sophisticated account, which does, I believe, capture what we see as special about the actions many of us call 'morally good'. One test of the correctness of my account is provided by the fact that we believe, if humans do what they believe to be morally good, that is connected with their being worthy of praise and, if they do what they believe to be morally bad, that is connected with their being worthy of blame. (To be guided by one's moral beliefs is to be guided by one's conscience; and to act against them is

[8] With this unclarity in the sense of 'moral' I find unhelpful some recent claims of a purportedly evaluative kind claiming that 'morality' is not automatically overriding; i.e. claims which assume that we know what 'moral' goodness is, and then assert that that sort of goodness does not necessarily make for overriding goodness. See e.g. the discussion in Michael Slote, *Goods and Virtues*, Clarendon Press, 1983, ch. 4; and Philippa Foot, op. cit., chs. 11 and 13. It all depends on what we mean by 'moral'.

to act against one's conscience.) I shall give a detailed account of the connection between these notions in Chapter 2. If the reader comes to agree that that account is correct, given the understanding of 'morally good' which I am about to give, that will be evidence that my account picks out the special feature of actions in virtue of which we often call them 'morally good'. In giving my definitions of moral goodness and badness, let me emphasize that I am concerned with giving a clear sense to claims that actions are morally good or bad; even when we have given clear senses to these terms it will remain a matter for lengthy dispute which actions are morally good (or bad), for people will still have different beliefs about which actions are morally good (or bad) in my sense.

To be 'morally good' as I shall define the term, an action must minimally have goodness of the second kind—that is, overall goodness, of overriding importance, deriving from universal properties; and to be 'morally bad' as I shall define the term, an action must minimally have badness of the second kind. After this paragraph I shall often call goodness and badness of these kinds simple overall goodness and badness. An agent is only culpable for acting contrary to his beliefs about what is of overriding importance to do, and only praiseworthy if he acts in accordance with those beliefs. But such action or failure to act is further only something recognizably to do with conscience if actions are seen as good not because, for example, they benefit the agent, but because of some universal property they have—and not just any universal property, but one which has some connection with what many others of us recognize as making actions importantly worth doing or not doing. A belief that it is of overriding importance to clap your hands three times an hour is so disconnected from normal human beliefs about what is of overriding importance that we would not label an agent's acting or not acting on such a belief action in accord with or against conscience. It would not have to it the sort of quality of action in accord with or contrary to the normal deliverances of human conscience which we find praiseworthy or blameworthy.

Now there is, of course, in the world a wide diversity in beliefs about the overall goodness of actions. Some believe euthanasia on balance good, others believe it bad. People disagree about the overall goodness of capital punishment, corporal punishment, abortion, strict parental discipline, marital fidelity in all circumstances, etc., etc. But such disagreement conceals much underlying agreement.

First, there is the fact that many who disagree about one such issue will often agree about others. And there will normally be a chain between any groups of persons who are diametrically opposed on many such issues, of groups who agree with one extreme group on most issues, groups who agree with the semi-extreme group on most issues, and so on until we come to the group at the other extreme. Between the extreme liberal and the extreme conservative there are so many who share many views with each other and with one or other extreme. Secondly, when two people disagree about the overall goodness or badness of some action, often both of them think that its overall goodness or badness arises from its possession of various universal properties, each of which is in itself good or bad as the case may be; they agree on the whole which universal properties make for its goodness and which make for its badness, but disagree only as to which group of properties outweighs the other group. Each disputant agrees that the considerations adduced by his opponent have some force; that is, would show the action, for example, as overall good but for the considerations which he adduces on the other side. Thus the opponent of the euthanasia involved in helping a depressed man to commit suicide argues that such an act is overall bad because of the sanctity and value of human life, the possibility of helping a depressed man to recover from his depression, the value of his overcoming that depression, and so on. The advocate of euthanasia argues that helping a depressed man to commit suicide is helping him to do what he clearly and firmly wants to do and what hurts no one else in any way; the fact that the act has this character has the consequence that it is an overall good act, despite its other features. Both disputants appeal to considerations which the other will naturally admit to have some weight, although each holds that the considerations which he adduces outweigh those which the opponent adduces. There is a very wide agreement between different groups as to the moral relevance of various considerations, even if not as to the weight to be given to each.[9]

[9] W. D. Ross (*The Right and the Good*, Clarendon Press, 1930, 29 ff.) claimed that it was self-evident what are the 'prima-facie duties', i.e. what considerations tend to make an action obligatory to do or obligatory not to do, although not self-evident how these considerations were to be weighed against each other to determine what is a particular man's duty in particular circumstances. I am claiming only that it is *often* the case that disputants agree about what are in his terminology prima-facie good acts, and so among them about prima-facie obligations. For the distinction between good acts and obligations, see later in the chapter.

Despite much disagreement about overall worth, there is an overlapping and criss-crossing of beliefs about the worth of actions in respect of their universal properties. Other things being equal— causing pain and killing are bad, causing pleasure and saving life are good, keeping promises and telling the truth are good, breaking promises and lying are bad. But then different groups will put different qualifications on these bold assertions—killing is good if it is deserved for wrongdoing, pleasure is good only if it is pleasure at what causes others no pain; and so on. And from there argument begins. But the vast extent of disagreement about what is of overriding importance must not obscure the fact that the disagreement takes place within a network of considerations about which there is very considerable agreement.

Let us call all those universal properties which many humans consider to contribute to the overall goodness or badness of actions and which many of them take into account along with other universal properties taken into account by yet many others, such as (paradigmatically) causing pleasure or pain, in assessing the overall goodness or badness of actions, 'standard moral properties'. Those among them which are supposed to make for an action's overall goodness (e.g. its causing pleasure) I will call positive properties, and those which are supposed to make for its overall badness (e.g. its causing pain) negative properties. By no means everyone thinks all the standard moral properties to be relevant to assessing overall goodness, and certainly they do not attribute the same importance to each; but there is, I have been emphasizing, a continuity between the kinds of property thought relevant by different men to assessing overall goodness. My proposed criterion for the goodness of an action being moral goodness is now that it have overall goodness arising from universal properties belonging to the set of standard moral properties, the positive ones counting for and the negative ones counting against its overall goodness; a belief that an action is morally good is a belief that its goodness is of this kind. Conversely, the badness of an action being moral badness is a matter of it having overall badness arising from a balance of negative properties over positive properties. By this criterion even beliefs that suttee or duelling (to avenge insult to one's relatives) are overall good actions often count as moral beliefs. Those who believe that such duelling is good often believe that this arises from the importance of defending the reputations of those near to one such as relatives who cannot defend it themselves. They defend that reputation by showing how important they regard it, and by deterring others from insulting their relatives further, by being prepared to put their life at stake by fighting those who insult their relatives. Many opponents of duelling would agree that it is important to defend the reputation of one's relatives; but they would argue that it is also important not to kill, and that the latter consideration outweighs the former in importance. The belief that duelling is good is a moral belief if it depends on considerations which its opponents think also to contribute to the overall goodness of actions and which belong to a set of standard considerations by which the overall goodness of actions is assessed, including the paradigm ones of causing pleasure or pain. By this criterion, however, a belief that clapping one's hands three times an hour is an overall good action would not count as a moral belief unless it was supported by considerations from the standard moral set.

The existence of this continuity of agreement about the overall goodness or badness of actions, and the much wider range of agreement about the kinds of considerations which make for overall goodness or badness, makes it appropriate to give a name to these kinds of considerations and to that overall goodness or badness of actions which is founded upon them and which, so many of us believe, is far more important than other kinds of goodness or badness. My proposal to use the word 'moral' to pick out goodness or badness of this kind gives the word a use, I suggest, very close to the centre of the vague spectrum of ordinary uses of the word. I stress again, however, that giving a clear sense to the notion of 'moral goodness' leaves a vast range of disagreement about which actions are morally good, arising in part from disagreement about which features of actions contribute to overall goodness and in part from disagreement about how to weight those features. Similarly, when I come to divide the class of morally good actions into the obligatory and the supererogatory, it will become apparent that clarifying what 'moral obligation', etc. is will leave vast scope for disagreement about which actions are morally obligatory, arising from similar factors.

Most of us, at any rate in our non-philosophical moments, clearly have moral beliefs in my sense—beliefs that it matters that certain actions be done or not, an importance which derives from their possessing properties of the kinds which I have mentioned. Our moral beliefs are beliefs that objectively certain things matter,

whether or not we admit it; in other words, we believe that actions
have objective properties of mattering which exist independently of
our recognizing them. Our moral beliefs are not mere principles
which we *decide* to follow; but convictions which nag at us and to
which we often in part conform. We who believe it wrong to torture
children, believe it would still be wrong if we had been brought up to
think otherwise. We who believe it our duty to help the starving, feel
the force of a moral obligation from without.

It is nevertheless a matter of philosophical dispute whether actions
ever really do possess moral goodness or badness in the sense
defined; whether moral beliefs conform to objective moral facts; or
whether we are merely 'conned' into thinking thus. Because this
book has a different focus, I do not have the space to argue this
central question of metaethics. So I shall have to take it for granted
that some actions are morally good and others are morally bad; that
there are truths about which moral beliefs correspond to the moral
facts. However, I point out in justification of this assumption that
this is the way it seems to most of us, when we are not consciously
philosophizing. We do have moral beliefs.[10]

Obligation and Supererogation

The class of morally good actions is not, I now wish to suggest, as
unified as I have represented it so far. Among those actions which
are overall good, which it is of overriding importance be done, whose
goodness arises from universal properties of the kind discussed,
some are obligatory (or duties), such as (at any rate, barring
exceptional circumstances) keeping one's promises and feeding
one's children; and some go beyond obligation, such as giving
all one's possessions to feed the starving in Ethiopia or one's life to
save the life of a comrade. The latter are supererogatory acts.
Likewise, the class of bad acts includes both wrong acts (i.e. acts
which we are obliged not to do) such as killing or promise-breaking;
and bad acts which are not breaches of obligation. An example of the
latter might be misusing one's talents by slouching in front of the TV

---

[10] I have argued in favour of this assumption in 'The Objectivity of Morality',
Philosophy, 1976, **51**, 5–20; see also my *The Coherence of Theism*, Clarendon Press,
1977, ch. 11.

all day. We may call such acts infravetatory acts.[11] There are also, no doubt, actions which are neither morally good nor morally bad—it does not matter whether you do them or not; these I shall call morally indifferent actions. An example might be strumming your fingers on a desk, when alone.

I begin my defence of the claim that there are both obligatory and supererogatory good acts by drawing attention to the fact that among the moral systems commended to men, we find two kinds—limited moralities and total moralities. A limited morality thinks it important that we fulfil certain limited obligations. It matters that we fulfil our limited set of obligations—that we provide food, education, and company for our children, and care in limited ways for others close to us, that we obey the law of the land (if it is reasonable in its demands for tax and service), that we keep our promises and tell the truth—at any rate on important matters, when there are not rival obligations. But beyond that, according to a limited morality, what someone does or fails to do has no moral importance. His actions at particular moments and life-style in general are his for choice, and no fault is his however he chooses. The advocate of a limited morality tends to see the importance of morality in its providing a minimum social framework which allows men to do as they please and become what they please without hurting others.[12]

A total morality, by contrast, tells one what to do in all circumstances. It asks for everything—though it may offer a choice of ways of fulfilment. Kierkegaard is an obvious example of an exponent of a total morality (though he would be reluctant to call it a 'morality'). He wrote: 'The demand on each is exactly the same; to be willing to do all;'[13] though the 'all' that a man must do will vary

---

[11] Discussion in recent moral philosophy of whether there are works of supererogation was sparked off by J. O. Urmson, 'Saints and Heroes' in A. I. Melden (ed.), *Essays in Moral Philosophy*, University of Washington Press, 1958; repr. in J. Feinberg (ed.), *Moral Concepts*, OUP, 1969. For a history and full-length defence of the doctrine, see David Heyd, *Supererogation*, CUP, 1982. The stern view that there are no supererogatorily good acts was held by Kant. He wrote: 'Be a man never so virtuous, all the goodness he can ever perform is still his simple duty'—I. Kant, *Religion Within the Limits of Reason Alone* trans. T. M. Greene and H. H. Hudson, Harper and Row, 1960, 44. For Kant's reasons for his advocacy of this stern view and for a partial defence of it, see Marcia Baron, 'Kantian Ethics and Supererogation', *Journal of Philosophy*, 1987, **84**, 237–62.

[12] For a defence of a limited morality, see P. F. Strawson, 'Social Morality and Individual Ideal', *Philosophy*, 1961, **36**, 1–17.

[13] S. Kierkegaard, *Purity of Heart*, trans. D. V. Steepe, Harper Torchbooks, 1956, 125.

with who he is—'at each man's birth there comes into being an eternal vocation for him, expressly for him'.[14] But the utilitarian who holds that all men have a 'duty' to forward 'the greatest happiness of the greatest number' is also the exponent of a very demanding morality, for that duty demands all of a man's time and energy. A satisfactory theory of ethics should try to take on board, albeit in a modified form, as many human intuitions about moral matters as it can. The distinction between the obligatory and the supererogatory enables us to take on board the conflicting insights of the two kinds of moral system. We can recognize the point made by a limited morality, as the point that these are limits to human obligations, and the point made by a total morality, as the point that there are no limits to the scope for good actions.

The original meaning of 'obligation' is something owed, and of 'duty' a debt. Though 'owed' and 'debt' are to be understood in senses in which things quite different from money may be owed or constitute a debt, these original senses remain. The paradigm case of an obligation is one undertaken voluntarily. By our words or actions, we undertake to do certain things. Our obligations to spouse and children are of this kind; in choosing to get married and have children, we take on responsibilities of care, nurture, and education. But there are also obligations to our benefactors—our parents and our community (who through schooling and policing keep us alive and bring us to maturity)—to return some lesser benefit to them; to care for parents in old age and to contribute to the community. Such obligations are instances of what have been called special obligations. Special obligations are obligations to particular persons (or other animate beings or corporate bodies) arising from a causal relation (of a universal kind) between them and us.

Such obligations arising from what we undertake or the benefits we receive are, though not undemanding, normally clearly limited, and there is plenty of time during the day when they do not impinge. I must take trouble to see that my parents live in comfort and with company, and that my under-age children are well fed and clothed, well educated, and have opportunities for happy recreation. But there is a limit to the trouble which I'm obliged to take over this; and some people don't have living parents or under-age children. And although I may undertake large obligations voluntarily by making extensive promises, I need not do so, and most people don't.

[14] Kierkegaard, *Purity of Heart*, p. 140.

Obligations are more extensive and intrusive, as James Fishkin has argued recently,[15] if there are general obligations. By general obligations I mean obligations on a subject to any one in some situation, quite independently of his having a particular causal relation to the subject. One example of such general obligation might be that stated by the principle which Fishkin calls the principle of minimal altruism:[16] 'If a person knows that he can prevent great harm, such as the loss of a human life, he is morally obligated to do so if the costs to him (and to anyone else) are minor.' We must not let a person drown if we are passing by him in a boat and can pick him up out of the water without much trouble, etc. Normally, in the past, the opportunity for such life-saving at minimal cost has occurred rarely. But in the present world of starving refugees and rapid communications, the opportunities for such life-saving are great. Fishkin claims that each gift to a refugee charity of a few dollars will keep some poor person alive for a week. But each such gift will not in itself prove a great sacrifice for any Westerner. So he ought to keep on giving. But very many such gifts will mean that he gives away most of his income to help the starving. Such a work we would normally regard as supererogatory; but the principle of minimal altruism has the consequence that it is obligatory. So even admitting such a superficially undemanding principle of general obligation as the principle of minimal altruism has the consequence that the limits to obligations are a lot less narrow than we might suppose.

Even if we accept the principle of minimal altruism, there still are limits to obligation. That is, I may have a duty to give two-thirds of my income, but after that giving a few dollars means a considerable sacrifice for me. Here supererogation begins. More demanding general principles make the limits of obligation yet wider. Fishkin points out that a 'strong principle' suggested by Peter Singer requiring us 'to prevent bad things from happening unless in doing so we would be sacrificing something of comparable moral significance' has the consequence that 'we ought to give until we reach the level of marginal utility—that is, the level at which, by giving more, I would cause as much suffering to myself and my dependants as I would relieve by my gift. This would mean, of course, that one would

---

[15] James S. Fishkin, *The Limits of Obligation*, Yale University Press, 1982.
[16] Ibid. 65.

reduce oneself to very near the material circumstances of a Bengali refugee.'[17]

It seems to me perfectly plausible to recognize general principles of obligation without extending the limits of obligation anywhere near as far as Singer does. One could suppose that the extent of obligation to save life or whatever depends on how much one has done for one's fellows recently at what cost to oneself. Perhaps I have an obligation to save one life by paying $5, a second life by paying $5; but after a time, when I have given a certain proportion of my income over that time, I have done my bit.[18] More than that is supererogatory. That seems to conform to common-sense morality better than Fishkin's principle, let alone Singer's principle. Alternatively, one could suppose that the obligations to save life or relieve poverty are proportional to the number of people in a position to fulfil them. If n is needed, and m wealthy people are under some obligation to contribute, perhaps the extent of the obligation on each is limited to n/m. Anything I do beyond my share (because others fail to do their bit) is supererogatory. Finally, one could argue (though I would not myself wish to argue this) that the obligations to rescue the drowning man or feed the starving refugee are not cases of general obligation at all. They are merely cases of a special obligation, to the human community which has nurtured us and nourished us, to help its members in trouble. So construed, one might see these obligations as a lot more limited in their scope than Fishkin does.

However, even if we do admit principles of general obligation, we may reasonably hesitate to acknowledge ones anywhere near as stringent as that which Singer suggests. Marvellously good though it is that I should sell my house and give the proceeds to Oxfam to feed and clothe the poor in Ethiopia, it does not look as if I *owe* it to the Ethiopians to do so; and good though it is that I should work to promote a higher standard of education and health care in this country, I do not owe it to my fellow-countrymen to devote *all* my time to such causes. I do not fail in obligations if I get married and have a family of my own and spend a few hours playing golf. However, even if we do admit such a strong general obligation as

[17] Peter Singer, 'Famine, Affluence, and Morality' in P. Laslett and J. Fishkin (eds.), *Philosophy, Politics and Society*, 5th ser., Basil Blackwell, 1979, 33, cited and discussed in Fishkin, *The Limits of Obligation*, p. 4 and pp. 71 ff.

[18] Fishkin discusses such principles, op. cit., pp. 160 ff.

that suggested by Singer's principle that everyone should give to others until he has reduced his standard of living to the 'level of marginal utility' (i.e. 'to very near the material circumstances of a Bengali refugee'), there is still much scope for good actions beyond the scope of obligation. You could reduce your circumstances to worse than those of a Bengali refugee; you could even give your life to save the life of another. The strictest utilitarian must treat his own happiness as something to be sought equally with the happiness of his neighbour. To sacrifice your happiness so that your neighbour gains an equal amount of happiness is not required by Utilitarianism. But who can deny that such acts of self-sacrifice are among the best acts which humans have ever done? Whether you draw the line so that the class of obligations is comparatively small (as, I have suggested, common-sense morality wishes to), or so that it is a broad one, some good acts still lie outside it and they are acts of supererogatory goodness. By any reasonable criteria, selling one's all to feed the poor in Ethiopia, throwing oneself on a grenade about to explode to save the life of a comrade, giving up marriage and career to care for aged parents are acts of supererogatory goodness. Obligations are limited, but there is no end to the number of good actions open to humans, if only we had the time and energy to do them. Beyond the finite limits of obligation the scope for supererogatory goodness stretches without a visible limit.

Supererogatory acts, as I have defined them, fall into two groups. There are those which benefit directly other individuals or groups of individuals, and those which directly benefit no one or at most the agent himself and only indirectly benefit others in the position of parents or teachers or the community in general, in the sense that their work of educating the agent has borne fruit. Acts of the first kind I shall call favours, acts of the second kind creative acts. Favours include acts of providing food, clothing, health, and employment for refugees and the poor (beyond the call of duty) and also helping others to live a life of higher quality—giving one's pictures to the nation, or running a local history society. But there are other acts which it is good should be done, but which do not consist in conferring a direct benefit on anyone except perhaps the agent himself. It is good that a man should write poetry or study philosophy rather than merely watch the television even if no one else reads the poetry or receives the philosophy from him, good that the old take trouble to keep themselves active rather than slump in

front of the fire, perhaps sometimes (even if there is no God) good
that a man vow celibacy and spend his time in silent meditation.
Such acts I shall call creative acts. In so far as there is an immediate
beneficiary of creative acts, it is of course only the agent himself, but
I shall claim in a later chapter that the agent's parents and educators
and the community as a whole benefit by such things being done, in
the sense that their work of educating the agent has borne fruit.
Favours are often acts of giving more to individuals or doing more
for them than some amount which the agent is obliged to do. They
are therefore the acts which etymology would suggest are most
naturally called 'super-erogatory' (beyond what is required'). But I
find it useful to use the word 'supererogatory' in the wider sense
which I have defined, to give a name to the class of all good acts
which lie beyond obligation.

Other Varieties of Moral Goodness

My concern so far has been with the objective moral goodness of
actions (divided into the obligatory and the supererogatory) and
their objective moral badness (divided into the wrong and the
infravetatory). Objective moral goodness or badness belongs also,
we may say, to an agent who does an action of the kind in question,
in virtue of his doing it. There are, however, other kinds of moral
goodness, which I shall call kinds of moral goodness in virtue of their
relation to this primary kind of moral goodness, the moral goodness
of the objectively good action and of the agent who does it.

While it is good that objectively good actions be done, it is
additionally good if they are done naturally, readily, spontaneously,
without ulterior motive. It is good that I help the starving naturally,
spontaneously, tell the truth readily and gladly—because I want to
do these things. In other words, it is good that an agent do the
actions which are good because he desires to do them for their own
sake—'desires' in the sense of 'is naturally inclined to'; doing these
things comes naturally, requires no effort of will, the agent is subject
to no temptation to act otherwise.

But also it is good that an agent do the objectively morally good
action for the reason that it is morally good; and indeed we value
such pursuit of the morally good the more if it is done despite
contrary desire. We value both the spontaneous act of generosity and

the act of generosity despite temptation. True, as a recipient of a benefit, we prefer to receive it from someone who loves us rather than from someone who is merely doing his duty. But that is looking at the matter only from the point of view of the selfish recipient. Looked at impartially, we can see the noble self-sacrifice of one who pursues the good as he rightly sees it despite contrary temptation. If we value the good at all, we must value the effort of the agent who forwards it despite difficulty.

The goodness which belongs to one who forwards the good for the reason that it is good, surely belongs also to one who tries to forward the good, but fails due to circumstances beyond his control. For the agent's intentional contribution is the same in both cases. The most he can do intentionally is to try; the rest is not up to him. He who tries but fails to rescue his dying companion, or who sends a large cheque to Oxfam which is lost in the post, has just as much value in respect of his intentional contribution to what is done as one who succeeds.

But if so, then, I think, we must also value the act of the agent who does the action which is not in fact good in the false belief that it is; we must think it good that an agent should do what he believes to be good even if it is not. For again, his intentional contribution of forwarding the good is the same. An agent cannot help his beliefs about which actions are good—at a given time he is saddled with his beliefs. All he can do is to act on them in pursuing the good as he sees it, or fail to do so. There are two kinds of case here. First there is the agent who has true moral beliefs about which universal properties would make some action morally good, bad or whatever, but has a false non-moral belief that some action has those properties. We may say that he has true moral principles but false factual beliefs. I think truly that one ought always to give to a starving friend, if one can; so, believing that you are starving, I give you money, poor though I am myself. But you are not starving, and the money will be spent on whisky. Surely in giving to you, I have done what is in one way a good thing—even if under a misapprehension. Secondly, there is the goodness of the action of the agent doing what he believes to be good, where his belief derives from false general moral beliefs, i.e. false moral principles. Consider the loyal Stalinist henchman who believes it his duty to root out and execute any who do not share his Stalinist convictions; and he does so, resisting in the process his desires to show compassion, his natural human sympathies. Is it really a good thing that he should follow his conscience? The answer is in that respect, again, 'Yes', I suggest—the Stalinist's action of persecuting opponents is good in the respect that he is following his conscience (if indeed that is what he is doing). Our reluctance to admit this is, I suggest, due to two considerations. The first is that (we suppose) his action is clearly a bad one by objective standards, and that fact may lead us to ignore the fact that there is nevertheless something good about it. The second consideration is that we reasonably suspect that the public claim of most Stalinists to be doing what they believe to be their duty is mere lip-service. Either they do not understand what conscience or moral duty are, or deliberately or subconsciously they are lying about what are their moral beliefs. Most Stalinists, we suspect, have other or no moral beliefs, and are not following their consciences.

Our reason for suspecting this arises from the logical limits to what can count as a moral belief. If the Stalinist does have a concept of moral belief, he has been introduced to it, as we all have, via some of the list of overlapping and criss-crossing universal properties which many humans consider it important should be instantiated— such as talking to the lonely, feeding the hungry, educating one's children, and keeping one's promises; and others which many humans think it important should not be instantiated—such as hurting or killing people unless they have done wrong (legal or moral), and not punishing them (i.e. hurting or killing them for having done wrong) without due process of law. Persecution of opponents seems to be closely connected with many actions on the latter list and to have little connection with actions on the former list. One who acquires moral beliefs at all is very likely to acquire a belief that persecuting opponents is morally bad. We rightly suspect someone who says that he does it from duty, of giving us and perhaps himself also, a false account of his moral beliefs. Still, a man could come to hold a belief that pursuing a Stalinist purge was morally good. For he could come to give great weight to actions such as promoting the material well-being of many men, and righting wrongs done to groups of men (which are on the list of standard facets of action which make for goodness of action), and less weight to such actions as causing short-term pain to individuals (which is on the list of standard facets of action which make for badness of action). In that way a Stalinist could indeed come sincerely to believe that it was on balance his duty to conduct a purge (to root out

and execute those who do not share his convictions); for thereby he
would be forwarding the material well-being of the proletariat and
their just triumph over those who have oppressed them, despite the
unfortunate way in which this has to be done. His belief is then
located within a recognizably moral framework, and so is a moral
belief. In that case, I suggest, if, despite contrary desires, he tries to
act in accordance with his moral belief, that is in itself a good thing.
More generally, if an agent is trying to do the morally good action as
he sees it, even though in this respect his belief about moral
goodness is not ours, surely we must say that it is good that he is
doing this. For he has a conception of moral goodness which we
share, and he is doing his best to realize that conception on Earth
and that is good, even though we disagree with him about what is
morally good in this particular case.

I have now distinguished three kinds of goodness which belong to
actions and to the agents who do them. There is objective goodness,
there is what I shall call spontaneous goodness (i.e. the goodness of
doing gladly for its own sake what is objectively good), and there is
subjective goodness (i.e. the goodness of doing or trying to do what
the agent believes to be good, which exists despite any error in the
agent's factual beliefs or moral principles, the goodness that is of
following one's conscience). An action is the better for having both
objective goodness and subjective goodness than it would be if it had
either separately—i.e. for being in fact good and done for that
reason.[19]

But the moral goodness of agents arises not only from the
intentional actions which they actually perform, but also from their

[19] The philosopher who above all stressed the value of subjectively good action was
of course Kant (though Kant tended to assume that a man's general moral beliefs
would not be in error). Although he emphasized the value of 'duty for duty's sake', he
did not in my view hold that an action was morally good only if the agent had no
natural inclination or reason other than duty to do it. For he claims (*Groundwork of
the Metaphysic of Morals*, op. cit., p. 64) that the 'good will' can acquire 'its own
peculiar kind of contentment—contentment in fulfilling a purpose which in turn is
determined by reason alone, even if this fulfilment should *often* involve interference
with the purposes of inclination' (my italics). The word 'often' implies that sometimes
exercise of the good will need involve no 'interference' with inclination. The crucial
thing which gives an action moral worth is that it be chosen for the reason that it is in
accord with duty, and it still has moral worth even if the agent also has a natural
inclination to do it. I thus follow Barbara Herman ('On the Value of Acting from the
Motive of Duty', *Philosophical Review*, 1981, **90**, 359–82) rather than Richard
Henson ('What Kant Might Have Said: Moral Worth and the Over-Determination of
Dutiful Action', *Philosophical Review*, 1979, **88**, 33–54) in her interpretation of Kant.

character. I understand by an agent's character his system of desires, a matter of what comes naturally to the agent: and his most general beliefs, including his moral beliefs about which actions are good or bad. Goodness of character is a kind of moral goodness in so far as it is a matter of which actions an agent believes morally good and which morally good actions he is naturally inclined to do. We value a good character (e.g. a man being naturally loyal or generous or honest) quite apart from the actions to which that character naturally leads. An agent's generous nature would still be something of great value, even if circumstances prevented it from ever being exercised (e.g. because the agent is stranded on a desert island).

I distinguish three kinds of goodness of character. There is the goodness of the agent naturally inclined to do for their own sake the actions which are in fact good—the naturally generous, loyal, honest, or whatever man. It is good that an agent have strong desires for the well-being of family and neighbours, for the relief of famine throughout the world, for education, and the conservation of natural beauty, and the creation and preservation of great works of art and literature. Then there is the goodness of the agent whose moral beliefs are correct. We value an agent for having the right outlook on life (e.g. we value a man who believes that honesty is a good thing) even if he finds it difficult to put it into practice. It matters in itself that one should have true beliefs on important matters. But it is of course also crucial for conduct, for beliefs about what is good and how to attain it crucially affect what we do (which is why the slogan 'it doesn't matter what you believe, it's what you do that counts', was a very foolish one). And finally we value the agent who is naturally inclined to do the good as *he* sees it, who has a strong desire for the good as such (whether or not his beliefs about it are correct, and whether or not he is naturally inclined to do the actions which are in fact good for their own sake), the agent with the naturally 'holy will'.[20] Let us call these three kinds of goodness of character goodness of desires, goodness of beliefs, and goodness of will.

Why is it good that an agent should desire to do for their own sake actions which are in fact good? Why is it not enough to have just a

---

[20] The agent with a perfectly good or holy will naturally does the good as he sees it, and (though Kant might not have been happy at this description) we may describe him as having a natural inclination to the good. Kant held that the good will was 'the highest good' though not necessarily 'the whole and complete good'; and that the goodness of other things depended on how they were related to the good will. See *Groundwork*, op. cit., pp. 61 and 64.

desire for the good as such which together with true beliefs about which actions are good will lead to the good actions? What is the point of a desire to promote the well-being of my neighbour for its own sake, *as well* as a desire for the good and a belief that promoting my neighbour's well-being is good, since the latter desire and belief will lead to my promoting my neighbour's well-being? My answer is that a natural love for particular people and things, for parents and children, country, home, and hobby, is good in itself. The saint with a desire only for the good as such, or even only for God, is open to the charge of being an ill-rounded personality.[21] Why is a desire for the good as such a good thing, so long as the agent desires for their own sake to do the particular actions which are good? Because it is good that the agent desire particular good things not only for their own sake but for that quality which they share with other good things; a desire for the good gives a right unity to the agent's motivations. Also, a desire for the good provides a means whereby an agent who loses the desires to do particular good kinds of actions or true moral beliefs about which kinds of action are good is under pressure to reacquire correct desires and continue to search for true moral beliefs. Goodness of will prompts us to seek correct moral beliefs and ensures that if through misinformation we come to desire what is not good and then come to believe that it is not good, we already have a natural inclination to adjust our desires to our newly acquired belief. There are many altruistic people with desires to make others happy, who find it hard not to indulge those desires even when they come to realize that it is not good to do so. They spoil their children, while realizing that it is bad to do so, because of a strong desire to make their children happy (here and now). If they had a stronger desire for the good as such, they would find it easier to rein in such generally good desires on the few occasions when they come to realize that it is not good to indulge them.

So we have distinguished three kinds of goodness of action, and three kinds of goodness of character. Goodness of each kind belongs

---

[21] See Susan Wolf, 'Moral Saints', *Journal of Philosophy*, 1982, **79**, 419–39. Butler's Sermon 5 'Upon Compassion' argues that joy in the prosperity of others is good in itself and that compassion for their ill fortune seems inseparable from that. He also argues that rational considerations (i.e. moral beliefs) provide but weak influence on action and need to be backed up by good desires. This is certainly true but only in so far as sometimes man is subject to desires for the imperfect. On such desires, see ch. 7. My claim is that desires for particular goods (e.g. the well-being of particular friends) are good in themselves, quite apart from their influence on conduct.

to an agent in so far as he does an action of that kind, or has that kind of character. For reasons which will become apparent in the next chapter, actions and character are bad in ways which are not always the exact opposite of the ways in which they are good, and so we must wait until the next chapter for distinctions of kinds of badness.

Different moral systems may stress the value of actions or of character. Systems which stress the value of actions see goodness belonging to an agent in virtue of the good actions which he does. By contrast a morality of aspiration concentrates on the character of the agent. Aristotle's morality had a list of the virtues, including the moral virtues such as courage, generosity, and integrity, all of which would characterize the ideal man. The possession of the virtue would be shown by the agent practising it in appropriate circumstances.[22] Other moralities of aspiration stress the equal value of each of a number of different kinds of character—of the generous man, the truth-seeker, the brave man, and so on. According to a morality of aspiration, what matters is the sort of person you are, the character you have.[23] My suggestion is that the positive intuitions of both kinds of moral system are right; all the six kinds of goodness of action and character which I have listed are good.

So much unnecessary argument has taken place along the lines 'what is of moral importance is not what you do, but what you try to

---

[22] *Nicomachaean Ethics, passim.* In order to 'exhibit' a virtue, actions 'characteristic of the virtue' have, according to Aristotle, to be done for their own sake and to 'proceed from a firm and unalterable character' (*Nicomachaean Ethics* 1105a). Thus an action will only exhibit the virtue of truthfulness if it is an act of truth-telling, done from love of truth, and springing from a character naturally prone to tell the truth. J. D. Wallace (*Virtues and Vices*, Cornell University Press, 1978) defends a basically Aristotelian view of the nature and value of the virtues, but there seems to me to be a slight difference between Wallace's account and Aristotle's. For Wallace an action exhibits a virtue if it springs from a character naturally prone to do such actions, and if the action is done, despite contrary temptation, because the agent thinks that he 'should' do it. The latter requirement brings a touch of duty-flavoured ethics into the basically Aristotelian account. See Wallace's ch. 2. Aristotle's account of the virtuous man is an account of one who exhibits my first kind of goodness of character, viz. goodness of desires. Wallace also has a chapter on 'conscientiousness', i.e. goodness of will, which is goodness of character of my third kind. For Wallace (p. 127) 'virtues that are forms of conscientiousness are reasonably regarded as traits necessary in a truly good person, though it is reasonable to expect that other sorts of virtue are required too'; but he does not give conscientiousness the priority which Kant ascribes to it.

[23] For valuable commentary on the history of virtue-orientated moral systems, see Alisdair MacIntyre, *After Virtue*, Duckworth, 1981, chs. 9–14.

do', or 'what matters is love, not duty'.[24] All of these things matter; each has its own kind of goodness. There are obvious connections between some of these kinds of goodness, which I have listed, such that one who thinks that goodness of one kind is good will have in consistency to think that goodness of another kind is good, at any rate as a means to it or a consequence of it. For example, if you think that objective goodness is good (i.e. that it is good that agents do the objectively good action, with whatever motive and belief), or that spontaneous goodness is good (i.e. that it is good that agents do spontaneously and gladly the objectively good actions) then you must think that goodness of desires is good (i.e. that it is good that agents are naturally inclined to do the objectively good action). If you think that both objective and subjective goodness are good (and so plausibly that it is better that an action has both—i.e. be objectively good and done for that reason), you must think good goodness of beliefs and goodness of will—since these together will make agents naturally inclined to do those actions which they correctly believe to be good. However, I have been arguing that all six kinds of goodness of action and character have each their own intrinsic goodness in addition to their goodness as means to or as necessary consequences of what is good. Having certain desires is good whether or not their possessor ever has the opportunity to indulge them in action; and, contrary to a view discussed by Parfit, 'acting morally' is not 'a mere means'.[25]

However, although all these six kinds of goodness are intrinsically good, there are some which necessarily cannot be coinstantiated to the maximum degree. I noted that we think subjectively good action the better in so far as effort is needed to perform it, i.e. in so far as the agent has contrary desires. If I give to Oxfam, when, having little money of my own I want to keep it for my own needs (and so desire not to give), the action is better than if I give, when I have plenty of money and little desire not to give. Or if I have to struggle against physical tiredness and weakness (i.e. against my desire to give up), in order to get my wounded friend to the hospital, then my action is better than if it's no problem for me to take him in my car. Although all action in accord with conscience is good, it is better (*qua* subjectively good action) if it is done contrary to desire. Hence

---

[24] 'The man who does not enjoy performing noble actions is not a good man at all'—Aristotle, *Nicomachaean Ethics* 1099a.
[25] See Derek Parfit, *Reasons and Persons*, Clarendon Press, 1984, 46–9.

an objectively good action cannot have both maximum spontaneity (in the sense that it comes naturally without a contrary thought) and maximum subjective goodness (in the sense that it is done despite a very strong contrary desire). The agent with good desires and beliefs, although he will do the action which he believes to be good, will do it so naturally and readily, that it is in no way difficult for him and his action does not have the worth which belongs to the action done despite great temptation. And, perhaps even more paradoxically, for the agent with the naturally 'holy will', who is naturally inclined to seek to do the action which he believes to be good, the subjectively good action will come so naturally that it cannot have the goodness of the action done contrary to very strong temptation. So not merely are there different kinds of goodness, but some kinds cannot coexist when instantiated to a maximum degree.

As well as these necessary connections between goodness of the various kinds, there are extremely important contingent connections which hold for men (and also for many animals), but which are in no way necessary connections, and may well not hold for any other rational beings there may be in the Universe. One such connection is that, other things being equal, each time one does something, the more natural doing it becomes. Doing an action of a certain kind frequently gives one the character of one who is naturally inclined to do actions of that kind. Telling the truth despite a contrary desire makes it easier to tell the truth next time, and gradually, by weakening the contrary desire, makes one into a naturally truth-telling person.[26] And so by causing goodness of desires objective good action leads to spontaneous good action. Similarly, frequent subjectively good action (trying on a particular occasion to do the good as you see it) gradually causes goodness of will. But note that these processes are very slow ones; there are obstacles of circumstance and (in particular agents) of character which may prevent their operation. And, finally, goodness of will, in so far as the agent has diverse experiences of his human environment, is intelligent, and is exposed to moral beliefs of various kinds, will lead to goodness of beliefs (or, more precisely, lead the agent to have more true moral beliefs than he had before). For in so far as an agent tries to do what is good, his experience of the effects of his actions and those of others and his exposure to moral beliefs different from his own will show

---

[26] See *Nicomachaean Ethics* 1103b. 'We become just by doing just acts, prudent by doing prudent acts, brave by doing brave acts.'

him any weaknesses in his moral beliefs, and so, to the degree to which he is intelligent, will lead him to doubt some of them. Having a good will, he will therefore examine whether what he believed to be the morally right action really is, and again to the extent to which he is intelligent and seeking the true answer, he will make progress in his moral beliefs. This contingent connection, like the earlier ones, depends on a contingent facet of human nature, in this case that the agent remembers and recalls the relevant experiences; there may be intelligent agents without sufficient personal memory to enable this process to take place.

2

Moral Responsibility and Weakness of Will

Moral Responsibility

An agent is held to be morally responsible for what he does intentionally, for what he chooses to do; for doing certain actions he is praiseworthy, for doing other actions he is blameworthy.[1] He deserves praise for actions which are good in a certain respect, and blame for actions which are bad in a certain respect. I shall assume in this chapter that agents are indeed morally responsible, that is praiseworthy or blameworthy for some of their actions, and on that assumption I shall consider for which of their actions praise and blame are appropriate. In the next chapter I shall consider attacks on the applicability of the notion of moral responsibility, doubts about whether agents could ever be morally responsible for their actions.

So, in the categories of the last chapter, is an agent to be praised for actions which are objectively good, for actions which are spontaneously good, or for actions which are subjectively good; or for actions which are both objectively and subjectively good, or for some sub-class of these? My answer is basically the traditional one that an agent is praiseworthy for his subjectively good acts, i.e. in so far as he tries to do what he believes to be good. There is, however, given the notion of supererogation, the asymmetry that blame is appropriate to the wrong act rather than the morally bad act; and

---

[1] The view that praise and blame are appropriate only to actions or omissions to act is opposed by Robert M. Adams, 'Involuntary Sins', *Philosophical Review*, 1985, **94**, 3–31. Adams holds that we are to blame for wrong desires and false moral beliefs, which we can in no way control, for the occurrence of which in ourselves we were in no way responsible, and of the presence of which we may be quite unconscious. He rightly points out that we often do reproach people for their attitudes as well as their actions. But it seems to me that what we are doing in such cases is either to tell people that their attitudes are objectively wrong or to blame them for past omissions to act which allowed such attitudes to develop. His examples seem best interpreted in one or other of these ways; and he has no more general argument to oppose the widely held and intuitively appealing view that praise and blame are appropriate only to actions or omissions to act.

that praise is appropriate basically to the supererogatory good act and only to the obligatory act in so far as it is done despite a substantial balance of contrary desire (i.e. in the face of great temptation). However, I shall argue later in the chapter, praise is appropriate even to the supererogatory good act only in so far as the agent is subject to some (however small) balance of contrary desire (i.e. the net balance of his desires is not to do the act). Refraining from obligatory acts is as blameworthy, and from wrong acts in the face of great temptation as praiseworthy, as actually doing positive acts. An agent is not blameworthy for not giving away his own possessions,[2] but he is blameworthy for stealing or not paying his debts. He is not, however, praiseworthy for paying his debts (that is to be expected of him), unless he is subject to much contrary desire—and in that case we do praise him for resisting such desire. So, with these qualifications written in, the traditional view now becomes: an agent is blameworthy for trying to do what he believes to be wrong (and failing to try to do what he believes to be obligatory); and praiseworthy for trying to do what he believes to be supererogatorily good (in the face of contrary desire), and also for trying to do what he believes to be obligatory (and for failing to try to do what he believes wrong) in the face of strong contrary desire. (I understand 'try' in such a sense that an agent tries to do an action both if he tries in the normal sense and fails, and also if he intentionally does the action.)[3]

There is now a further qualification which I need to make to this traditional account. There are two kinds of case in which an agent is not culpable for failing to try to fulfil his (believed) obligations. The first is where he is subject to two (or more) conflicting obligations, only one of which can be fulfilled. That he is in this situation may

[2] Gregory Trianosky ('Supererogation, Wronging, and Vices: On the Autonomy of the Ethics of Virtue', *Journal of Philosophy*, 1986, **83**, 26–40) discusses the point that people make excuses not merely for failing to perform obligations, but also for failing to do supererogatory acts. He sees, however, that this is not because wrong is done and apology owed for such failure. In my view, people make such excuses because they wish to be thought to have good characters, and so they try to show that conduct which suggests that they do not is not really indicative of a lack of good character.

[3] My account of moral responsibility so far is of course, with qualifications, that of Kant who held (e.g. *Groundwork of the Metaphysic of Morals*, 1.10 and 1.11) that actions have moral worth only in so far as they are done from the motive of duty. The qualifications are that (see ch. 1, n. 11) Kant equates the good with the obligatory (the duty), and seems to have taken little account of the possibility of erroneous moral belief.

not be the agent's fault at all (a woman may owe it to her sick child to stay at home and look after him, and simultaneously to her sick mother to visit her and look after her). Or it may be the agent's fault that he is in this situation (as when he has promised to be in each of two different places at the same time). It is clear that everyone is under an obligation not to place himself under obligations that he cannot fulfil and so in my second example the agent is culpable for getting himself in this situation. But having got himself in such a situation, or, as in my first example, having got there by bad luck, he cannot fulfil both his then existing obligations. It follows that he will be in some sense at fault for failing to fulfil an obligation, whatever he does. That this conclusion is correct can be seen by the fact that he owes reparation and apology to the person to whom he owed the obligation which he does not fulfil.[4] The existence of a conflicting obligation no more removes the fault of failing to fulfil a different obligation than the bad luck of having money stolen removes an obligation to repay it.[5] But, although failure to try to perform an obligatory act through trying to perform a different obligatory act, leaves the agent objectively at fault (in a sense which I shall fill out more fully in Chapter 4), the agent is surely not culpable if he does his best in the situation, i.e. tries to fulfil the obligation which he believes to be the greatest (or at least as great as any other).

---

[4] This is the reason why 'conflicts of obligation' cannot be represented as really only conflicts of 'prima-facie obligation' such that performing the most binding obligation makes it the case that you were not under any other overall obligation which you failed to fulfil. For two recent philosophers who also hold that 'conflicts of obligation' cannot be represented merely as conflicts of prima-facie obligation, see Bernard Williams, 'Ethical Consistency', in his *Problems of the Self*, CUP, 1973, and Ruth Marcus, 'Moral Dilemmas and Consistency', *Journal of Philosophy*, 1980, **77**, 121–36, and (less committedly) Bas Van Fraassen, 'Values and the Heart's Command', *Journal of Philosophy*, 1973, **70**, 5–19. These writers reject the 'agglomeration principle' (that it follows from 'S ought to do x' and 'S ought to do y' that 'S ought to do x and y'). For argument on the other side, see W. D. Ross, *Foundations of Ethics*, Clarendon Press, 1939, 83–8; and Earl Conee, 'Against Moral Dilemmas', *Philosophical Review*, 1982, **91**, 87–97. All these papers, together with the paper referred to in n. 5 are reprinted in C. W. Gowans (ed.), *Moral Dilemmas*, OUP, 1987.

[5] Alan Donagan ('Consistency in Rationalist Moral Systems', *Journal of Philosophy*, 1984, **81**, 291–309) has suggested that genuine conflicts of obligation only arise through the agent's own fault, e.g. that the fireman who can only save some of those in a burning building, does not fail in his obligation to save one group by saving another group. His obligation is only to save as many as possible; that he fulfils. In other words, conflicts, other than those incurred through the agent's fault, are really only conflicts of prima-facie obligation. That does not seem plausible for cases such as those in the text of conflicting obligations to both mother and child.

But is an agent to blame if he fails to fulfil any of his (believed) obligations? Normally, certainly yes. But there is an exception where the obligations are not too great and cannot be fulfilled at the same time as a *very* demanding and worthwhile supererogatory act; he would not then be to blame for failing to try to fulfil the obligations, if he tried to do the supererogatory act. Such an exceptional case might be when the agent has made a promise to meet someone for lunch, and then has the opportunity to save a life at great cost to himself (for example, perhaps by sacrificing his own life). In such a case obviously he is not culpable for failing to fulfil his obligations.[6] These two considerations lead me to a final version of the traditional account, obtained by adding to the account given at the end of the last paragraph but one the clause 'except that any failure to try to do what he believes to be obligatory is excused if he tries instead to do an act which he believes to be at least equally of obligation or otherwise better (i.e. that it is of such supererogatory goodness that it outweighs obligation)'.

Praise and blame in the sense with which we are concerned with them are appropriate to chosen intentions, the direction an agent knowingly sets himself; they are appropriate to good and evil in the soul, not to good and evil which belong to an agent by accident. To blame an agent is to say that there is something evil in his intentional contribution to what was done. And the only evil intentional contribution which an agent can make is to try to do what he believes to be wrong (or to fail to do what he believes to be obligatory). And to praise an agent (in the kind of way that is the opposite of blame) is to say that there is something greatly good in his intentional contribution to what was done; and the only greatly good intentional contribution which he can make is to try to do what he believes to be supererogatorily good when he has some inclination to do otherwise (or to refrain from doing what he believes to be wrong when that is difficult). Such is the intuition of the traditional account.

When men first ascribed praise and blame, they no doubt did so on the basis of the objective goodness or wrongness of the outward action. But soon the more morally sensitive communities must have realized that there was a difference between eating a grape which you believe to belong to your neighbour, and eating a grape which (because the boundary posts separating vines have been moved by

[6] I owe this point to F. M. Kamm, 'Supererogation and Obligation', *Journal of Philosophy*, 1985, **82**, 118–38.

vandals) you believe to be your own but in fact belongs to your neighbour. Only in the former case when the agent intentionally does what he believes to be wrong is blame of the kind at stake appropriate. The Book of Numbers distinguished between sins against God done 'with a high hand' (i.e. knowingly) and sins done 'unwittingly', and though it asserted that the latter required some kind of reparation, only the former showed evil of soul and required substantial punishment.[7] The kind of ignorance the Book of Numbers had in mind was ignorance of a simple factual kind which my example illustrates. Yet what blame belongs to the man who eats his neighbour's grape in the belief that it is no man's property because he believes that the property laws of the society (or indeed all property laws of all societies) are unjust? It is clear enough to us today that men can differ very considerably in their moral principles; and so it would seem the natural extension of men's judgement about the kind of example just discussed to hold that a man is to praise or blame for acting or failing to act in accord with his own moral beliefs, however different those beliefs are from ours.

After all, an agent cannot change his beliefs at will in an instant. Over time he can seek out more accurate moral beliefs (or neglect to do so), but at any given instant he has the beliefs he does; and all that lies within his power at that instant is to act or fail to act in accord with them. He has no other access to moral truth, or possibility of conforming his actions thereto except via his own beliefs. Any intentional evil can only lie in failure to conform to his own moral beliefs; and any intentional good can only lie in such conformity. So it is to following or failing to follow conscience that praise or blame would seem to belong.

Aquinas was very much more alive to the possibility of false moral beliefs than many later moral philosophers. In medieval terminology an agent's *conscientia* informed him of which actions were instances of conformity to or failure of conformity to general moral principles (e.g. that taking this grape is stealing, and purporting to marry that woman is bigamy, and so that both actions are wrong), and *conscientia*, Aquinas held, could err. It was a different faculty, *synderesis*, which in medieval terminology informed one about moral principles, and that according to Aquinas could not err. But the examples which Aquinas gives of these moral principles about

[7] Num. 15: 22–31.

which we cannot be in error are so general as to look like simple tautologies—e.g. 'evil ought not to be done' and 'God is to be loved'. And he certainly held that *conscientia* can err over some pretty fundamental matters. Thus:

To believe in Christ is good in itself and necessary for salvation; all the same this does not win the will unless it be recommended by reason. If the reason presents it as bad, then the will reaches to it in that light, not that it really is bad in itself . . . Every act of will against reason, whether in the right or in the wrong, is always bad.[8]

Aquinas is unclear about where the exact boundary lies between *synderesis* which cannot err, and *conscientia* which can. But his view is not far from the view which I have advanced that there are logical limits to the possibility of erroneous moral belief, because beliefs which have no connection with paradigm moral beliefs are not moral beliefs at all; that within a very wide range, there is enormous scope for erroneous moral belief; and that praise and blame belong to an agent in so far as he conforms to his own moral beliefs.[9]

Blameworthiness is greater in so far as an agent's purpose in action continues over a period of time. The quicker the choice, the less the blame. A sudden unpremeditated burst of anger, though culpable, is far less culpable than a planned malicious act. One reason for this is clearly that the planned act involves many acts. Another reason is that when an agent purposes to do an act which he believes wrong over a considerable period of time, conscience starts to nag. The thoughts keep occurring to the agent, forcing themselves to the front of his awareness in a way hard to suppress, that this act ought not to be done. The agent is indeed wicked if he acts in the face of such intruding moral beliefs. When a man does a sudden wrong act, his conscience has sometimes not had time to get going, as it were; it is taken by surprise, half-asleep. For a reason similar to the first one given in connection with blameworthiness, an agent is also more praiseworthy in so far as his purpose to do good continues for longer.

---

[8] St Thomas Aquinas, *Summa Theologiae* 1a. 2ae. 19.5. The translation, and all translations of other passages of Aquinas quoted by me, are from the Blackfriars edn., Eyre & Spottiswoode, 1964, *et seq.*

[9] For Aquinas' views on the fallibility of *conscientia* and the infallibility of *synderesis*, see the extract from his *Quaestiones Disputatae. De Veritate*, as well as extracts from the discussions of the issue in other medieval writers and a most valuable introduction to them, in T. C. Potts, *Conscience in Medieval Philosophy*, CUP, 1980.

Recent centuries have seen a number of challenges from different directions to this traditional view. There is first the objection that no praise or blame is due to action in accord with a highly erroneous conscience. The Stalinist is not to be praised for conducting his purge even if he does think it morally good. The reason usually given for this is that we think the Stalinist's action on balance a bad thing. Yet the fact that it is bad in one respect and on balance does not mean that it is not good in some respect; and it is good in the respect that the agent is attempting to forward the good as he sees it, and it is to such intentional contributions to action that praise and blame belong.

Then there is Hume's objection in defence of his rival criterion that an agent is to praise or blame for his actions only in so far as those actions reflect a similar character. An agent is only to blame for a disloyal action in so far as he is naturally inclined to disloyalty, to praise for a generous action in so far as it proceeds from a generous character. Hume wrote: 'Actions are by their nature temporary and perishing; and where they proceed not from some cause in the character and disposition of the person who performed them, they can neither redound to his honour, if good; nor infamy, if evil.'[10] In so far as actions proceed from nothing in an agent 'that is durable and constant', an agent is not answerable for them. What he does out of character is, Hume claims, a casual accidental act, for which the agent is not to be held responsible.

Now as regards the actual moral assessments of such cases made by most of us, Hume seems entirely mistaken. Do we not think that the coward who does an heroic act out of character is greatly to be praised for it, praised for rising above his habitual reactions and natural inclinations? He is worthy of praise more than the man to whom the heroic act is almost second nature. And do we not also think that the man who, despite a naturally honest character and little temptation to do evil, suddenly cheats is more culpable for that act than the man to whom cheating is second nature?

If we are ever inclined to make moral assessments in the way that Hume suggests that we do, I think that we (and Hume) are being led astray by a number of things. The first is that of course a bad character, a natural inclination to do bad actions is itself a bad thing (and a good character itself a good thing); and, as we have noted, we

[10] D. Hume, *Enquiry Concerning Human Understanding* (first pub. 1748), (ed.) L. A. Selby-Bigge, 2nd edn., Clarendon Press, 1902, 98.

assess agents for their character as well as their conformity to conscience. But character, consisting of desires and beliefs, is at a given moment involuntary; an agent cannot help the character he has. He can only do actions in conformity with it—which is easy, or against it—which is hard. And if he does the latter in pursuit of the good as he sees it, surely he deserves praise. Secondly, an agent may be to praise or blame for his character, not for having it at a given time but for encouraging or allowing it to develop in a certain direction over time, and so he is to praise or blame for getting himself in a position where a certain action was easy or difficult. But an agent's responsibility in this respect is a responsibility for actions done or omitted earlier (in conformity to or against his then conscience) and does not alter his moral responsibility for how he acts when he does have a certain character. Thirdly, where the wrong act is contrary to the law of the land there may often be a lot less point in punishing the normally good man for his evil deed than there is in punishing the normally bad man for his evil deed. For a major purpose of punishment is the reform of the criminal so that he does not do such an act again; and the normally good man is unlikely to do such a bad act again. But we must not confuse the issue of whether there is point in punishing a man with the issue of whether he is blameworthy for his conduct. Even if there is something unsatisfactory in punishing a man for doing an act for which he is not blameworthy (e.g. because he did not believe it wrong), there are often reasons why a man who is fully blameworthy for a wrong act should not be punished for it; and one such reason is that he needs no reformation.

A third objection to the traditional account of moral responsibility made recently by both Bernard Williams and Thomas Nagel is that the true locus of moral assessment is not what the agent tries to do, but the finished action—what the agent succeeds in doing or fails to do (whether the failure is a failure of effort on his part, or simply bad luck). For them it is the objective goodness or wrongness of an act which deserves praise or blame. Their two papers formed a symposium entitled 'Moral Luck',[11] and they both agreed that luck can determine whether and to what extent a man is to praise or

[11] B. A. O. Williams and T. Nagel, 'Moral Luck', *Proceedings of the Aristotelian Society*, 1976, **50**, 115–35 and 137–51. Nagel's paper is reprinted in G. Watson (ed.), *Free Will*, OUP, 1982. The references to Nagel's paper are to pages in the reprint in Watson (ed.). Williams' paper is reprinted in his *Moral Luck*, CUP, 1981.

blame for his conduct. Williams considers the case of the artist, abandoning his wife and children to devote himself to his art. If the artist becomes a great artist, Williams suggests, his conduct is excusable; otherwise it is appalling. Our verdict is not based, Williams claims, on whether the artist reasonably believed that he would become a great artist, but on whether he did become one or not—and luck, perhaps in the shape of whether or not the environment in which he lived stimulated great ideas in him, could determine that. Nagel considers the driver who neglects to have his brakes checked. If that negligence leads him to run over and kill a child, Nagel writes, the driver 'will blame himself for the death'; but 'if no situation arose which required him to brake suddenly and violently to avoid hitting a child . . . he would have to blame himself only slightly'. Yet, as Nagel himself comments, 'the *negligence* is the same in both cases, and the driver has no control over whether a child will run into his path'.[12]

I can only suppose that Nagel and Williams take the view that they do because they are influenced by the practice of lawcourts and conversational gossips condemning or praising the public act rather than the purpose which lies behind it. Lawcourts have their reasons for punishing successful crime more severely than unsuccessful crime, which have nothing to do with its greater blameworthiness. To start with, what is called 'punishment' is often in part the exacting of compensation for harm done; and, as I shall argue more fully in a later chapter, we owe compensation for the harmful effects of our actions (e.g. compensation to the parents for the death of the child), even if the causing of harm was purely accidental. Hence intentional successful crime should get greater punishment than intentional unsuccessful crime for a reason which has nothing to do with its greater blameworthiness. A second reason for this is that if there is the sanction of a greater penalty for success, there remains an incentive to the criminal to draw back at the last moment when the crime is only half-executed. Unfortunately, as we saw earlier, the close connection between blameworthiness and what is punishable by the majesty of the law may lead to total confusion between them. Further there is the point that praising and blaming others is something in which humans have a natural propensity to indulge; yet we are not always in a position to know what a man had the

[12] Op. cit., p. 178.

purpose of doing, let alone whether he honestly believed that to be morally right. So the temptation to pass judgement on men for their actions performed or not performed (rather than intended), in respect of whether objectively or by our standards they were good or wrong actions, rather than whether they were thus by the agent's standards, is great.

But this is a primitive way of assessing people, used by prehistoric societies, insensitive to subtleties of human behaviour, of which more civilized men have become aware—a way of assessing, tempting to the censorious gossip—but a temptation to be avoided. For the kind of moral worth which deserves praise or blame is something intrinsic to the agent, belonging to him not in virtue of his circumstances but in virtue of what he intentionally does; and so it cannot depend on luck. As Nagel himself admits, the 'negligence' of the two drivers is exactly the same; and so he who assesses their inner responsibility for their acts must pass the same judgement on each.[13]

I conclude that these objections to our normal understanding of moral responsibility fail. They are indeed largely attempts to drag us back to more primitive standards of responsibility—in terms of whether the agent does good, not whether he does what he believes good; what he succeeds in doing, not what he tries to do. The progress of civilization has taught us that responsibility belongs to an agent for and only for what he tries to achieve, for whether it is what he believes (supererogatorily) good or what he believes wrong. For that is the sole contribution which an agent can make towards forwarding good or evil in himself and the Universe—everything else is indeed luck.

Weakness of Will

But how is it possible for an agent not to try to do what he believes to be the best action open to him? There is a long tradition in Western philosophy, deriving from both Plato and Aristotle,[14] that necessarily

---

[13] For another account of why our public allocation of praise and blame is influenced by our belief about the objective goodness or wrongness of the act, which, like my account, nevertheless maintains that the true ground of praiseworthiness and blameworthiness is whether the agent is trying to conform to his own moral beliefs, see Norvin Richards, 'Luck and Desert', *Mind*, 1986, **95**, 198–209.

[14] See Plato, *Protagoras* 351b–358d, and Aristotle *Nicomachaean Ethics* 1145a–1147b. Both these passages are contained in G. W. Mortimore (ed.), *Weakness of Will*, Macmillan, 1971.

a man will try to do what he believes to be the best act open to him, and so will try to do what he believes it morally good to do in our sense—at any rate if this is physically and psychologically possible for him. Aristotle is concerned to show that those who act contrary to what they say or others say that they believe, don't really believe it. Now certainly (for a reason which will become apparent shortly) performing an intentional action involves believing the action to be in some way a good thing—either because it involves bringing about a good state of affairs or because the bringing about which it involves is itself good. If you search for food, then you regard the having of food by you as a good thing; if you sing or dance, then you regard the production of noises or movements as a good thing. And if you go to see your aged aunt instead of watching the football, that too can only be because you regard it as in some way a good thing that you visit your aunt—either because being with her is good in itself, or for some further purpose which being with her serves. To believe that it is in some way a good thing to do some action is to believe that there is reason for doing it. But there are many possible actions open to an agent at any given time, and he has to choose between them. He may believe that one of the possible actions is overall the best, or that a number of actions are equal best. His ranking of possible actions may be purely selfish. He may believe the best action open to him to be that which will earn the highest standard of living in the long run. Or he may believe the best action open to him is that which derives its overriding importance from a universal property, such as being an action of keeping his promises or making others happy. In that case, in the terminology which I introduced in Chapter 1, his belief about which action is the best will be a moral belief. Moral beliefs are by their nature overriding—if we have a belief about what is morally best to do, that is a belief about what is overall best to do (but we may have a belief about what is overall best to do without it being a moral belief). To believe that some action is overall the best is to believe that there is overriding reason for doing it.

   Although men always act on reason, they do not always act on what they regard as overriding reason. When a man is idle, or lies, or steals, there is always a reason for doing so, i.e. what he does is in some way a good thing, and so he believes. For it is pleasant to idle, and there is profit in lying or stealing. But it is often better to work for your living, tell the truth, and abstain from depriving others of what is theirs. And those who idle, lie, or steal often believe thus, but still do not act for the best as they see it. Despite Aristotle, yielding to temptation is a genuine phenomenon evident in the personal experience of each of us and in what others say to us about their experience. We see the best and ignore it. This is because men are subject to desires, natural inclinations to do certain actions, causes which incline a man, make it easy for him, to do some action, even if it is not the best; and sometimes we yield to such desires.

'Desire' or 'want' are not always used in precise senses in ordinary language, but, as I am using the terms and as ordinary language most usually uses them, a desire to do action *A* is an inclination to try to do action *A*, when the agent believes the opportunity to be available to him. It is a readiness to act spontaneously which the agent finds in himself and cannot alter readily at will. There are short-term desires (to scratch or to eat) and long-term desires (to obtain a degree, get to the top of one's profession, or become president of the USA); and of both groups some are short-lasting and some are long-lasting. They are caused either directly by physiological factors (as is the desire to scratch or eat) or, to varying degrees, by cultural factors also. We will inevitably act on a desire unless (i) we have a stronger desire to do some incompatible action or simply to to nothing, or (ii) we have a belief that it would be overall not the best thing to do the action in question—the action may have bad long-term consequences for ourselves, or be morally bad. When the agent is subject to a balance of desire to act contrary to what he believes the best, including the morally best thing to do, an agent must choose whether to conform to reason or yield to desire. It needs effort, struggle, and self-persuasion, to resist desire, and if the agent does nothing the strongest desire will win.

Plato and Aristotle were right in that an agent will indeed do the action which he believes overall best—other things being equal, i.e. if he is subject to no contrary balance of desires. In general, of course, for an agent to have a belief about some action open to him, that it has this or that nature or effect, has no consequences for whether the agent does or does not do the action. Consequences only follow when combined with the agent's purposes. I may believe that saying to you, 'You are a fool' will cause you pain. Whether I say it will depend on my purposes—whether I seek to hurt you or to save you from hurt. If I seek to hurt you, then (other things being equal, i.e. given that with my other beliefs it won't impede any of my other purposes) I'll say it; but if I seek to save you from hurt I'll refrain.

But to have a belief that there is a reason, and especially an overriding reason, for doing some action, is different. To have the belief that there is a reason for doing an action is to acknowledge that, thus far, it would be sensible, appropriate, reasonable, rational, to do the action, that it is the thing to do. Really to believe that some action would be sensible, appropriate, etc., to do is to acknowledge, to put the point dramatically, the summons of the action to me to do it; and thereby to have an inclination to do the action—other things being equal. I couldn't recognize R as a reason for doing A unless I accepted pressure from how I see things to be in the direction of doing A. To admit that R was a 'reason' for doing A but to deny that I had any inclination at all in consequence to do A would be to say something apparently contradictory, and to suggest that, when I said that R was a 'reason', I was using the word in an 'inverted-comma sense' and meant something like 'what most people would consider a "reason"'. To recognize a reason for doing A is only to have an inclination to do A other things being equal. But other things may not be equal. There may be other and better reasons for not doing the action. To believe that there is an overriding reason for doing the action is to believe that, on the balance of reason, it would be sensible, appropriate, reasonable, rational, to do the action. I may still not do the action because I may be subject to non-rational forces, viz. desires, which influence the purposes I form. But to believe that there is overriding reason to do it entails being inclined to do it, and doing it in so far as unimpeded by irrational forces. 'Reasons', as I have been concerned with them, like more obviously moral terms such as 'good' and 'ought', are action-guiding terms. That is a lesson which the emotivist and prescriptivist moral philosophers taught us. While we have in my view rightly abandoned their view that moral judgements do not have objective truth-value, we must not abandon the insight that mistakenly led philosophers to that view—that to have a moral belief entails having an inclination to action. Moral beliefs are not as irrelevant to action as beliefs that things are square or yellow. There is a difference between moral and non-moral beliefs.[15]

[15] J. L. Mackie saw this connection of moral beliefs with inclination to act as grounds for supposing that things could not be as moral beliefs represented them. For it was 'queer' to suppose that there was a property, moral goodness, the recognition of which provided not merely a belief but an inclination to act. His argument from queerness does therefore assume the point that (however erroneously) moral beliefs do move to action. See J. L. Mackie, *Ethics*, Penguin, 1977, 40 f. For elaboration of

We humans are moved by reason—in part. Rational considerations affect our choices. But we are also subject to 'desires', inclinations which sometimes incline us to do actions which are not overall the best, which reason does not advocate, and to which we may yield or against which we may fight. Of course the satisfaction of desire is pleasure, and so there is always a reason to yield to desire. And since, if we do not act for the best as we see it (perhaps because there is no best among the choices open to us, as we see it) it will be because we yield to desire, we shall always have been guided by the minimum reason for acting as we do—that it is doing what we want to do. We shall have seen what we are doing as good in this minimal respect. Hence there are no totally irrational actions. But although there is always a reason to yield to desire, there is often more reason not to yield to desire, and then we must choose whether to yield to desire or whether to struggle to conform to (the balance of) reason.

In a situation where desire and moral belief are in conflict, mere knowledge of the relative strength of an agent's desires and of his moral beliefs will not allow us to predict what he will do. For, evidently, in similar situations of choice, agents with the same moral beliefs and the same relative strengths of desire do different actions. Thank goodness, there have always been men who resisted the worst torture which torturers could devise for them, while others with similar beliefs and desires have yielded to it. And similarly for situations of less agonizing choice. And more generally, mere knowledge of mental factors (understood as factors to which the agent has privileged access in consciousness) is often insufficient to allow us to predict what the agent will do. For this reason psychological determinism, in the sense of all actions being necessitated by mental factors alone, seems false. That does however leave open the question of whether men are predetermined by brain states in respect of whether they yield to the strongest desire or do the action which they believe to be the most worthwhile (or do some intermediate action which they believe to have some worth and also desire to do). But there does not seem to be any logical incoherence in supposing such determinism to be false. It does not seem to be

the point, while denying that our moral beliefs are delusory, see John McDowell, 'Are Moral Requirements Hypothetical Imperatives?', *Proceedings of the Aristotelian Society*, suppl. vol., 1978, **62**, 13–29. For the connection between reasons for action generally (not necessarily moral reasons) and desire, see also T. Nagel, *The Possibility of Altruism*, Clarendon Press, 1970, Part II.

logically necessary that when you fail to act for what you believe is the best, physical forces have stopped you from so doing.[16] But it does seem logically necessary that if you fail so to act, you must find it in some way difficult to do what you believe to be overall best; for it is hard to give any sense to the notion that an agent, subject to no contrary influences, could fail to do the action which he believed to be overall the best. For what could his belief amount to if in these completely favourable circumstances it had no consequences for action?

It follows from what has been said so far that an agent subject to no balance of contrary desires will inevitably do what he believes to be the best action, and so if the best is the morally best he will do that. If he believes that there is no best action, but a number of rival equally good actions, he will choose among them.[17] If an agent has no beliefs about what is best to do, he will simply be guided by his strongest desire; or, if a number of rival desires are equally strong, he will choose between them. And, above all, as we have seen, he will exercise choice in the face of a conflict between his desires and his evaluative beliefs. But in the absence of such a conflict his choices will be between alternatives which he believes to be equally worthwhile.

We saw earlier in the chapter that the basic intuition of the traditional account of moral responsibility was that praise and blame belong to an agent for his unowed intentional contribution to what happens. He deserves praise if he tries to make good things happen which would not otherwise happen, when doing good is not obligatory; he deserves blame if he fails to try even to perform his obligations. Given the understanding we have just developed of how reason and desire combine to influence action, it follows, as we

---

[16] For powerful advocacy of this position that an agent can fail to do what he believes to be most worth doing without being compelled not to, see D. Pears, *Motivated Irrationality*, Clarendon Press, 1984, chs. 9 and 10.

[17] An agent, such as God, to whose power there are no limits, may be faced with a choice of actions which can be arranged in an infinite series each member of which is (he believes) better than any earlier member and worse than any later member, and which has no last member. In that case there would be no believed best or equal best action open to him, and a more complex account is needed of the role of reason in the choices of such an agent. (I provide such an account in the course of a paper on another topic—'Could there be more than one God?', *Faith and Philosophy*, 1988, **5**, 225–41.) However, unless subject to extraordinary delusion, humans are never in that situation. There is an upper bound to the goodness they can try to achieve, set by their limited powers. (A human benefactor has only a finite amount of wealth to give away, for example.) Unless they are mad, humans will be aware of that.

normally suppose, that an agent is more worthy of praise for his good actions the stronger his desires not to do them. The harder he has to struggle with contrary desires, i.e. the worse the temptations to which he is subject and which he finally overcomes, the more worthy he is of praise. A man who has got in the habit of telling lies when it will do good to his reputation finds himself thereby subject to a natural inclination to lie. If he resists this inclination, and on a given occasion when it will harm his reputation he tells the truth, he is more worthy of praise for this than is the habitual truth-teller for telling the truth in such a situation. Conversely an agent is more blameworthy the weaker the desire to which he was subject to do what he believes to be wrong. Someone subject to almost irresistible desire gets little blame for wrongdoing.[18] If everyone around him steals and expects him to steal, if he has been taught since childhood to steal, it becomes very difficult for a man not to steal. If he then steals, he is worthy of relatively little blame. The most praise belongs to the action (or inaction) for which most effort was needed to overcome contrary desire; the most blame belongs to the action (or inaction) which could have been avoided with little effort.

It follows also that an agent is not praiseworthy for doing a supererogatory good action unless he was subject to some contrary desire (even a desire to do a less good but nevertheless supererogatory good action). For in the absence of contrary desire he will inevitably pursue the good as he sees it, and so the good will inevitably occur; there would be no scope for choice as to whether it should occur, nor, therefore, would it be appropriate to praise the agent for making such a choice. We normally and correctly assume that the supererogatory good act is done in the face of contrary desire; it doesn't often come naturally to humans, as I shall argue in Chapter 7. So in ignorance of the inner life of some agent of goodness, we give the benefit of the doubt and praise him for his act. We assume that generosity is costly. Spontaneous goodness is also good, but the arguments of this chapter suggest that it is not praiseworthy in the kind of way that moral effort is praiseworthy. And so the discovery that some supererogatory good act was done despite any temptation

---

[18] As so often, Aquinas captures our natural intuitions on these matters: 'Causes which weaken judgement, e.g. ignorance, or interfere with the free movement of the will, e.g. sickness, force, and fear, lessen sinfulness, just as they lessen voluntariness. If the act is entirely involuntary it is not sinful at all'—Aquinas, *Summa Theologiae* 1a. 2ae. 73.6.

to do otherwise ought to lead us to conclude that the sort of praise which we have been discussing is not appropriate to it.

Since he who does the good does it for reason and he who does the bad does it despite reason, badness of action and character are not always the opposites of goodness of action and character. In the last chapter I distinguished three kinds of goodness of action—objective goodness, spontaneous goodness, and subjective goodness—and three kinds of goodness of character—goodness of desires, of beliefs, and of will. What kinds of badness are there? There is objective badness and there is spontaneous badness; there are objectively bad acts, and among them objectively wrong acts, and acts of each kind may be done spontaneously and readily. There could not, however, be subjective badness in the sense of trying to do the bad, especially in the face of contrary desire. The nearest thing to an opposite for subjective goodness is simply yielding to temptation, to a desire to do what is believed to be bad (which is blameworthy when the action is believed to be wrong). It is this which I shall call subjective badness. Corresponding to goodness of desires there is indeed badness of desires; there are desires to do what is objectively bad, and among them desires to do what is objectively wrong. Corresponding to goodness of beliefs (the goodness of the agent whose moral beliefs are correct) will be badness of beliefs, in the sense of the badness of an agent whose moral beliefs are incorrect (viz. false). But there cannot be an exact opposite of goodness of will. Goodness of will is a matter of being naturally inclined to pursue the good as such. Again, if my arguments are correct, there could not be a natural inclination to pursue the bad as such. The nearest thing to an opposite for goodness of will is simply weakness of will, the weakness of any inclination to fight temptation in the interests of pursuing the good. The extreme form of weakness of will would be the lack of any motivation to pursue the good, which could only belong in a full form to an agent who didn't have any moral beliefs.

3

The Relevance of Free Will

On the assumption that agents are in general morally responsible for their intentional actions, I devoted the last chapter to considering for which of their actions they deserved praise and for which they deserved blame. My answer (with many qualifications) was that they deserved praise for doing what they believed was supererogatorily good and blame for doing what they believed was wrong. But I also concluded that an agent could be in a state of belief and desire such that it was inevitable that he would do what he did, or an action as good as the action he did do, and then neither praise nor blame would be deserved. It is a continuation of that thought to suggest that an agent would not be morally responsible at all (he would never be praiseworthy or blameworthy) if he was caused necessarily, predetermined, to try to do what he did, by his brain state, and that in turn by some prior state, until we come to causes outside the agent's body and ultimately to causes long before his birth. For in that case in a crucial sense the agent could not have done other than he did do (i.e. it was not physically possible in the circumstances for him to do otherwise). The whole argument of the last chapter implies that moral responsibility belongs to an agent only in so far as his contribution has its beginning in himself and is not made inevitable by other causes. That implication seems to me correct. Moral responsibility (and so openness to praise and blame) belong to an agent only if he has 'free will' in the traditional and obvious sense that his will is free from necessitating causes. The other necessary condition of an agent being morally responsible is that he have moral beliefs in accord with which he may choose to act or against which he may rebel. An agent with free will but no moral beliefs could not be held morally responsible for his actions. An agent is morally responsible if, and only if, he has free will and moral beliefs. I shall seek in this chapter to defend that view against 'compatibilists' who think that agents would still be morally responsible even if they were caused to act as they do, and against what I shall call 'incoherentists' who claim that, whether or not we are caused to act as we do, the idea that we are morally responsible for our actions is incoherent—it cannot be made comprehensible.

Compatibilism

The compatibilist holds that agents would be morally responsible (and so deserve praise or blame for their actions in accord with some such criteria as those set out in the last chapter), even if they were causally necessitated to act as they do in every detail. The view that we are causally necessitated so to act follows from determinism, the view that every event is caused to occur in all its detail by prior causes. The compatibilist holds that moral responsibility is compatible with determinism. However, he often expresses his view in a rather paradoxical way. He understands having 'free will' not in the traditional sense, but as definitionally equivalent to being 'morally responsible'; and then expresses his thesis as the paradoxical claim that there is no incompatibility between free will and determinism. I shall avoid the resulting paradox and confusion by keeping the traditional sense of 'free will' and expressing compatibilism as the claim that moral responsibility is compatible with determinism.

The most extreme form of compatibilism is exemplified by the advocate of what J. L. Mackie called 'the straight rule of responsibility'[1]—that an agent is responsible for *every* intentional act which he does or fails to do. The 'straight rule' leaves intact the kind of account of moral responsibility which I gave in the last chapter, and teaches that it holds quite independently of whether we have been caused to act as we do. The 'straight rule' does of course rule out holding an agent responsible for what someone else physically forces him to do. If I push your finger against the trigger of a gun so that it shoots John, you are not responsible for killing John—for killing John was not an intentional action of yours, something which you chose to do. But an agent is responsible for what he does intentionally (and in so far as he acts intentionally, he has 'free will' in the compatibilist's sense).

The straight rule can allow for the fact that we often excuse an agent when he is subject to threats—on the grounds, not that he is

---

[1] See J. L. Mackie, *Ethics*, Penguin, 1977, ch. 9, 208.

not then responsible for acting as he does, but on the grounds that the issuing of threats makes a difference to the situation and so to what an agent believes to be right or wrong to do in it.

Most of us believe that which action is a good action to do or an obligation sometimes depends on the alternatives which lie within an agent's power and the circumstances in which he finds himself. Some simple kinds of action *may* be obligatory whatever the circumstances, e.g. not telling a lie, or fulfilling a promise to do something which is not intrinsically wrong. But almost all moralists would allow that the circumstances and consequences of actions, and the range of alternatives, often play a role in determining what we ought to do. Among those circumstances and consequences are those constituted by threats and offers. Normally it is wrong for a bank clerk to hand over his cash to a stranger who has no legal claim to it. But if he is threatened with a gun most of us would hold that he is justified in yielding to the threat. Coercion of this sort does not abolish an agent's freedom. Bank clerks, when threatened, are free as they were before, not to hand over money. As before, they can refuse. It is in general rather that in the circumstances of the threat we and they do not think it wrong for them to hand over the money; it is because they are not doing what they believe wrong, that they are not culpable. The advocate of the straight rule can thus explain much of our excusing the conduct of someone subject to threats.

Note however that the situation is not always so simple. The bank clerk may think that, despite the threat, he has a duty not to hand over the money; and yet may hand it over all the same. In that case the advocate of the straight rule must hold the bank clerk culpable for his action; but, it is compatible with the straight rule to hold (as I urged myself in Chapter 2) that an agent is less to blame for not doing an action when subject to a very strong contrary desire, say a heroic action such as the action of a bank clerk not handing over the money and so allowing himself to be killed, which he believed to be his duty, than for not doing some less demanding action.

The straight rule states a simple compatibilist view for it claims that man is morally responsible in so far as he does what he chooses to do, while allowing that all his choices may have causes, which necessitate his choosing as he does. His genetic inheritance and his upbringing may make it inevitable that a man do the intentional actions which he does; but on this view, so long as an action is intentional a man is doing it 'freely'. Compatibilism was advocated by both Hobbes and Hume in the simple form of the straight rule. 'Liberty', wrote Hume, 'is simply a power of acting or not acting, according to the determination of the will.'[2] The view that not merely is compatibilism true, but determinism is also true, is known as soft determinism.

The difficulty with such a simple account of moral responsibility is evident. We feel that men are not morally responsible for their intentional actions on those occasions when (to all appearances) they are caused so to act by irresistible desires. The bank clerk (if startled by a gunman) may perhaps panic and be overwhelmed by an irresistible desire to hand over the money.[3] Such desires may be caused by drugs or hypnosis or brain-washing. A man is hypnotized and told that when he awakes from hypnosis, he will smash a cup. He awakes and does so. Shall we blame him for smashing the cup? Or he has got hooked on heroin, and has not had some for some time, heroin and the syringe lie within his grasp. Shall we blame him for taking it? True, in these cases we may blame the man a little; we may judge that there remains to him a small amount of responsibility for his actions. But if we do so judge, it is because we hold that the man's desires are to a small extent resistible; with a heroic effort he could have resisted them. If we really think the desires irresistible, we do not blame the agent for yielding to them. But if this reaction is right, it is surely equally unreasonable for us to hold an agent morally responsible for *any* action to do which he had an irresistible desire, whether that desire was caused by drugs or advertising, upbringing, or genetic inheritance. And the general justification of this stance must surely be that an agent is not responsible for actions resulting from his choices, when those choices are caused by factors over which he has no control. By the choices being caused, I mean not just that there were factors which made it likely that those choices would occur, but there were factors which together made it necessary, inevitable, that the choices would occur. But if that is the justification why we excuse a man from blame when he is subject to irresistible desires (and I can see no other), then surely it also follows (as I argued independently in the last chapter) by parity of reasoning that we must withdraw praise from a man who only acts as he does in

[2] D. Hume, *Enquiry Concerning Human Understanding* (first pub. 1748), (ed.) L. A. Selby-Bigge, 2nd edn., 1902, 95.

[3] On this see Michael A. Slote, 'Understanding Free Will', *Journal of Philosophy*, 1980, **77**, 136–51.

doing the supererogatory good act because he is subject to irresistible desires. The man who gives generously because of irresistible desire is no more to praise for his act than the habitual criminal subject to irresistible desire to steal is to blame. In both cases the agent acts as he does because he is causally necessitated so to do. It then follows also that we must withdraw praise from an agent causally necessitated to act by any factors, whether those factors operate by creating an initially irresistible desire or whether they operate by causing him to struggle against and finally overcome contrary desire.

For after all the reason why we excuse the agent whose finger is forced by another against the trigger is because causes over which he had no control made the gun go off. And surely the situation is in all essentials the same even if the chain of causes does go through the agent's will. Maybe I take the heroin because I choose to take the heroin, but if my choices are inevitable given my desires, and my desires are inevitable, given the structure of my brain, then my injecting myself is as inevitable as the killing produced by another pushing my finger. Is not that why I am not responsible for it? And if there is a chain of causes which goes through my will, what difference does it make that those causes cause me to resist initial desire rather than to yield to it?

We have reached incompatibilism, the doctrine that an agent being morally responsible for his choices is incompatible with those choices being caused and so with determinism. To be morally responsible for some choice an agent must have free will in my sense of the power to make that choice or decline to do so, given the state of the world at the time including the agent's brain state. The incompatibilist who believes also that every event does have a cause is known as a hard determinist. The incompatibilist who believes that a man does have free will (and so that determinism is false) is often called a libertarian.

In recent years compatibilism has waged a subtle rearguard action against the train of argument which leads to incompatibilism. Compatibilists have acknowledged that the simple straight rule will not do, and that there are some intentional actions for which the agent is not morally responsible. But they have sought to develop a form of compatibilism which acknowledges that the mad, the addict, the hypnotized, and the brain-washed are not responsible for their actions; while continuing to hold that the normal sane man is responsible for his actions, even if his choosing to do them is caused by his brain state, and his brain state is formed in ways beyond his control by his genes and environment.

These more subtle forms of compatibilism stem from an article by H. G. Frankfurt, published in 1971, 'Freedom of the Will, and the Concept of a Person'.[4] Frankfurt claimed that persons, unlike animals, have second-order wants or desires. They have various first-order desires (for food and sex, fame, and company); and then as well second-order desires, which are desires for one of these desires to be their will, i.e. to be the desire which affects action. A man has 'free will' according to Frankfurt, if his second-order desire is efficacious (if his desire that his desire to be generous defeat his desire for money is effective). But if his second-order desire does not win, then the agent feels mastered by an alien force. Frankfurt is thus in a position to distinguish between the heroin addict who wishes that he was not addicted—on Frankfurt's account he desires that his desire not to take heroin defeat his desire for heroin—and the heroin addict who is glad to be addicted. Only the latter, according to Frankfurt, has 'free will' and is thus culpable.

Second-order desires certainly exist; and we must be grateful to Frankfurt for calling our attention to them. But Frankfurt's exposition of what I take to be his main point does suffer from the deficiency of so much modern philosophy of mind, of confusing purposes and desires. Desires are passive things; they happen to a man. But which desire wins is a matter of which the agent allows to win, i.e. a matter of purpose (alias trying or intention). Frankfurt's account does not bring this out.

An account less open to this objection is one given by Gary Watson.[5] He draws our attention to the fact that some of our desires are for things we think worth doing and some not. The conflict, according to Watson, is between what one values and what one merely desires. Although Watson does not give a formal definition of 'free will', he does seem to think it at least necessary if an agent is to be acting freely that he should be pursuing what he values; and he

---

[4] *Journal of Philosophy*, 1971, **68**, 5–20. Repr. in G. Watson (ed.), *Free Will*, OUP, 1982.

[5] 'Free Agency', *Journal of Philosophy* 1975, **72**, 205–20. Repr. in G. Watson (ed.), op. cit. Watson is now dissatisfied with the view developed in this article. See pp. 149 ff. of his very good survey of the present state of the debate on the conditions necessary for moral responsibility—'Free Action and Free Will', *Mind*, 1987, **96**, 145–72.

cites the kleptomaniac as unfree because pursuing an activity which he does not value.[6]

A somewhat similar view is put forward by Wright Neely.[7] He has a number of necessary conditions for free will; among them is the condition that an agent acts freely only if, were he to be 'given what he took to be good and sufficient reason for not doing what he did, he would not have done it'.[8] His freedom consists in his readiness to act otherwise if he sees good reason for doing so. Thus again the unwilling addict comes out as unfree; for he still takes the drug, despite having what he takes to be good and sufficient reason for not taking the drug.

All of these are basically definitions which define 'free will' in terms of rationality, and then go on to claim that one is only morally responsible for one's free acts. The free man is the rational man, the man who pursues what he values and does what he sees reason for doing. But now we must ask—are the desires which act on a man inducing him to act irrationally resistible or irresistible? If they are resistible, and still the agent caves in to them, surely he is to be held responsible for his resulting actions. A man who yields to desires which he could have resisted is morally responsible for his actions[9] just as much as is one who overcomes those desires (even if we grant that the degree of moral responsibility varies with the strength of the desires). If on the other hand the desires are irresistible, it may indeed be granted that a man is not morally responsible for acting on them. But then, one may ask, if a man is caused (necessarily and inevitably) to overcome his initial desires and do the morally best action, why should he be held responsible any more for his action than if he cannot help yielding to desire and does a morally wrong action?

Whether an agent has freedom cannot depend on how he chooses (which is what in effect rationality theories are claiming that it does), but on whether he can help making the choice he does. It is very odd to suppose that you are free if you choose to go one way, but unfree if

[6] 'It is because [the kleptomaniac's] desires express themselves independently of his evaluational judgements that we tend to think of his actions as unfree', op. cit., p. 220.
[7] 'Freedom and Desire', *Philosophical Review*, 1974, **83**, 32–54.
[8] Op. cit., p. 48.
[9] This point is made in the detailed assessment of the theories of Frankfurt, Watson, and Neely, in Michael A. Slote, op. cit., pp. 147 ff.

you choose to go the other way; free if you follow your conscience, unfree if you don't.

So we are back with the natural definition of free will that an agent has free will if his intentional actions do not have necessitating causes; and the claim of the incompatibilist that we are morally responsible for our actions if and only if we have free will and moral beliefs. If every event has a cause, then our actions will be caused by our brain states and those by previous brain states or environmental circumstances and those ultimately by the genes which we inherited from our parents and the state of the society into which we were born; and so ultimately they will be caused in all their detail by states of affairs long before we were born. Why should a man be praised or blamed for actions which were totally determined to occur by circumstances holding long before the man was born? Determinism, if true, rules out moral responsibility. In a deterministic universe actions will still be good and bad, right and wrong. Whether or not our actions are caused, it is still good to feed the starving on our doorstep, and bad not to do so. But men would not be blameworthy for not feeding the starving. There might indeed still be a point in punishing the evildoer, for punishment may still have the effect of reforming the criminal and deterring him and others from committing similar acts in future. But a man would not be punished because he *deserved* to be punished. The punishment of a criminal would be deserved no more than would be the punishment of a man for a crime which he had not performed, as an example to others to deter them from committing similar crimes in future. There might even be still a point in blaming people, in heaping moral censure upon them when they committed bad acts—for such condemnation might have the deterrent effect of leading them not to commit similar acts in future. But the point of blaming them would no longer be that they were blame*worthy*. It would be false to say that an agent was culpable—though saying it might have some desirable effect[10] (though I would not myself condone such dishonest censure).

---

[10] Some writers write as though the only consideration on whether we should praise or blame a man is what effect it will have on his conduct; that whether or not such praise and blame is merited is not relevant. Parfit for example suggests with respect to rich nations giving to poor nations, that 'the best pattern of blame and remorse is the pattern that would cause the rich to give most' (D. Parfit, *Reasons and Persons*, Clarendon Press, 1984, 114).

Writers generally agree that an agent is morally responsible for some intentional action if he 'could have done other than he did'.[11] But in what sense of 'could have done otherwise' is this to be understood? The compatibilist interprets 'could have done otherwise' as 'would have done otherwise if . . .' he had so chosen, or wished, or if circumstances had been different. Just as I may say that my car could have done 100 m.p.h. yesterday (although it didn't), and mean by that that it would have done 100 m.p.h. if I had pressed the accelerator hard enough on an open road with enough petrol in the tank, etc., so according to the compatibilist, to say that an agent could have done other than he did do is only to say that he would have done otherwise if things had been different. But according to the incompatibilist when we say (in this context) that an agent could have done other than he did do, we should mean that, given all the circumstances, all the causes operating on the agent at the time of his action, he had uncaused freedom to act one way or to act the other way. The preferability of the incompatibilist understanding of 'could have done otherwise' follows from the general defence which I have given of the incompatibilist account of responsibility.[12]

Incoherentism

Compatibilism is, I believe, beginning to lose its popularity among philosophers. They are beginning to accept the force of arguments such as I have just given that determinism rules out moral responsibility. Instead it is now becoming popular to suggest that, while determinism rules out moral responsibility, so does indeterminism (i.e. the falsity of determinism). Moral responsibility, it is suggested, is an incoherent notion and it is illusory to suppose that

[11] Dennett has claimed that some agents are morally responsible for actions which they could not help doing. See his 'Freedom and Determinism', *Journal of Philosophy*, 1984, **81**, 553–65. (See also his *Elbow Room*, Clarendon Press, 1984, ch. 6.) He claims, for example, that Luther's 'I could do no other' does not have the consequence that Luther's conduct is unfree. My argument has the consequence that if indeed Luther could not do other than he did, given all the circumstances, then praise and blame for his conduct are not in place and it is misleading to speak of him as 'free'; we may still think his action good and admire his character, but moral praise and blame are out of place. Of course, Luther may have been mistaken about the extent of his freedom.

[12] See Additional Note 1. (Additional Notes are to be found at the end of the book.)

any agent could be morally responsible for his actions in such a way as really to *deserve* praise or blame.

The opening move of such an attack is to point out that if we were to allow that no causes determined whether a tossed penny landed heads or tails, we would not hold that it was morally responsible for landing as it does. No doubt there are causes which determine how pennies land, but, I believe, genuine physical indeterminism operates on the subatomic level—there are no causes which determine the exact moment at which an individual atom of radium decays; it is a random event.[13] Yet we do not hold the atom responsible for decaying. If human actions are as much a matter of chance and accident as atomic decay, holding humans responsible for their actions would seem as inappropriate as holding atoms responsible—claims an opponent.

However, the use in such an argument of words like 'chance', 'accident', and 'random' makes an unfair comparison between not fully caused human action and not fully caused atomic decay. Of course both are not fully caused, but there is otherwise the all-important difference that atoms do not mean to decay; decaying is not an intentional action of atoms. Calling an event 'random' or 'chance' suggests not merely that it is uncaused but that it is unintentional. Of course, uncaused unintentional events are not the proper subject of praise and blame, but it does not follow from that that uncaused intentional events, i.e. actions which agents mean to perform, are not the proper subject of praise and blame.

The next stage of the attack is to point out that, caused or not, there seem to be some intentional actions which are not the proper subject of praise and blame. Animals other than humans perform intentional actions. Watson raises the question of whether we can properly praise or blame a spider for trying to capture a fly.[14] Fairly obviously, no. But my account had already taken this point into consideration. An agent has to have both free will and moral beliefs in order to be morally responsible; and, as animals other than humans do not have moral beliefs,[15] they are not morally responsible. However, in an important recent book, *Freedom and Belief*[16] Galen

[13] On this, see my *The Evolution of the Soul*, Clarendon Press, 1986, ch. 13.
[14] See his 'Free Action and Free Will', p. 168.
[15] See my *The Evolution of the Soul*, ch. 12.
[16] Galen Strawson, *Freedom and Belief*, Clarendon Press, 1986. The whole discussion in the main part of Strawson's book of the kinds of attitude to one's actions

Strawson has argued that rather more is necessary for moral responsibility—an agent needs to have a certain attitude towards himself. He must view himself as one who chooses between alternatives in the light of reasons. Strawson describes a race of 'spectators' who view their reasons as influencing their bodily movements while remaining detached from this whole process. They just watch themselves having reasons and those reasons influencing conduct without their choosing to act for those reasons; 'the Spectator never has the experience of participatory involvement in the mental stages of action-production that we can have.'[17] That Spectators are not morally responsible seems right, but it provides no further qualification to the view that agents are responsible for their intentional actions. For an intentional action is one which the agent means to do; and so without participatory involvement there would be no intentional action. Strawson goes on to describe[18] a race of 'Epictetans' who never hesitate about what to do, who have desires which they automatically pursue and which they always succeed in fulfilling. Because they do not ever experience choice between alternatives, they do not, claims Strawson, have free will of the kind which involves moral responsibility. Strawson's basic point here seems correct though I have described it somewhat differently from the way he does. Certainly Epictetans would never be praiseworthy or blameworthy for their actions; and that follows from my account, for on that account agents are praiseworthy or blameworthy only when they make a choice between yielding to their desires and conforming to their moral beliefs. But, as I described the situation, they are morally responsible agents in virtue of having free will in my sense and also moral beliefs, from which it follows that if they were to be subject to desires to act contrary to their moral beliefs, praise and blame would be appropriate to them. My way of putting the point is, I suggest, more satisfactory for a reason which will appear in the next two chapters—that intentional agents with moral beliefs acquire a kind of moral guilt or merit which does not arise from their conformity to, or rebellion against their own moral beliefs. Epictetans would still acquire that sort of moral guilt and merit; and

that one needs if one is to have free will is deep and original. My brief comments, both favourable and unfavourable, do inadequate justice to the many subtleties and qualifications involved in Strawson's position.

[17] Ibid., 239.
[18] Ibid., ch. 13.

for that reason I wish to say that they are morally responsible agents and so describe the fact that they never deserve praise or blame in my way rather than Strawson's.

However, Strawson now goes on yet further[19] to suggest that even with participatory involvement and choice between alternatives, agents would still not have enough. To have the sort of freedom pertaining to moral responsibility an agent would have to believe that his choice was free; he would have to see himself as the ultimate locus of responsibility. But this further restriction seems to me quite uncalled for. So long as agents choose between alternatives in the light of reasons and are not caused so to choose, and thus are the ultimate loci of responsibility, it seems to me irrelevant whether they have the philosophical conviction that they are. They are individuals who are choosing how the world is to go, and are trying to make it good or letting it be bad, aware of the moral nature of their action and of alternatives to it, and of themselves as so contributing; their philosophical beliefs which lie in the background do not affect what they do and why they do it, and it is for the latter that they are to be held to account.

The whole argument about moral responsibility begins with a natural moral intuition that humans are morally responsible for their intentional actions. This natural intuition, which I have spelled out carefully, is rightly challenged by the suggestion that really they are causally necessitated to act as they do. If that was so, they would indeed not be morally responsible. But if it is not so, we are back with the original natural moral intuition. Those who are the ultimate sources of the way things go and have knowingly chosen that they go the way they do are morally responsible for that choice—to blame if they are trying to do what they believe wrong and to praise if they are trying to do what they believe is supererogatorily good. Galen Strawson asks challengingly, in presenting what he regards as the strongest argument against the coherence of the idea that we are self-determiners in a sense that makes us morally responsible—surely we do not really think that 'the cases in which reasons *are* determinative of the action are *less* likely to be cases of free action than the cases in which the reasons are *not* fully determinative of the action:'[20] The answer to that challenge must surely be—'Yes, indeed, some of us

---

[19] Strawson, *Freedom and Belief*, ch. 14. As Strawson admits (p. 301), my position, contrary to this final position of his, 'cannot be simply disproved'.

[20] Ibid., 41.

do and all of us ought to think this, for the free agent is one who *chooses* whether to be rational and is not necessitated to be determined by reason.'

I conclude that men having moral beliefs, are morally responsible for their actions if and only if they have free will in the traditional sense that their intentional actions are not causally necessitated in all their detail by prior causes.[21] I believe that men do have free will in this sense and I have argued for it elsewhere;[22] I shall assume that men do have free will in this sense in subsequent chapters

---

[21] A different objection to the view that men are morally responsible for some actions is the objection that there is no continuing subject of experience and action from moment to moment, only a somewhat similar bundle of bodily matter and character. From that it would follow that there is in reality no later person identical with the earlier person, able to bear responsibility for the past deed. Thus Nietzsche wrote: 'Popular morality also separates strength from expressions of strength, as if there was a neutral substratum behind the strong man, which was *free* to express strength or not to do so. But there is no such substratum. There is no "being" behind doing, effecting, becoming: the doer is merely a fiction added to the deed—the deed is everything.' (*The Genealogy of Morals*, 1. s.13, trans. W. Kaufmann in *Basic Writings of Nietzsche*, Random House, 1966.) This was part of Nietzsche's reason for recommending that 'bad consciences . . . should be abolished' (*Thus Spake Zarathustra*, trans. R. J. Hollingdale, Penguin, 1969, 113). I have argued elsewhere that, as common sense supposes, there is indeed a continuing subject of experience and action. See my contribution to S. Shoemaker and R. Swinburne, *Personal Identity*, Blackwell, 1984; and my *The Evolution of the Soul*, chs. 8 and 9.

[22] See my 'The Indeterminism of Human Actions', *Midwest Studies in Philosophy*, 1985, **10**, 431–49; and my *The Evolution of the Soul*, ch. 13.

4
Merit and Reward

In the next three chapters I shall concern myself with the consequences of intentional actions for the moral standing of the agent. I begin with the good side, while warning my readers that what I have to say about the good side may convince more when we have dealt with the bad side as well.

My fulfilling my obligations simply clears a debt; it does not in general create a situation which makes positive action from anyone else appropriate. Works of supererogation however do create such a situation. I distinguished in Chapter 1 between two kinds of supererogatory act—favours and creative acts. Favours are acts of directly benefiting other individuals; creative acts are good acts which confer no direct benefit on anyone except the agent. What are the consequences of favours for appropriate action? In general, favours need not be accepted—I can send your present back, or refuse to allow you to help me to clean my house when you have offered to do so. There is normally no obligation whatever to accept favours. But it is often (though not always) good that one should do so. It is courteous, gracious, to allow others to do one favours; for it involves allowing them to become part of one's web of personal relations and thus brings them into one's friendship and love. To refuse a favour often implies that the would-be donor does not have anything worth offering, that one is superior to him and what he can do. There are indeed occasions when it is good (and sometimes even occasions when it is obligatory) to refuse favours. There are friendships among imperfect and emotion-dominated humans, which can lead to trouble. To accept a present may sometimes encourage a friendship which the intended recipient knows will disappoint the donor—it is often good that a lady should send back the presents of a suitor, friendship with whom will lead only to an unhappy love affair. Again, it is often good and sometimes obligatory to refuse a present, the acceptance of which may be seriously misunderstood by others—which is why government ministers ought not to accept large presents from foreign businessmen.

If it is accepted, however, the favour creates a new situation. It is now appropriate that the beneficiary should respond—in word and deed. The word is 'Thank you' or similar words or gestures which express gratitude. Thanking is giving public recognition and appreciation of the benefit—either of the object given or of the agent's benevolent intention in giving, or preferably of both. It is saying that these things are good, and/or that the beneficiary is glad that he has the gift and/or that it was given. If the beneficiary neither thinks good nor desires either the gift or the giving, it is dishonest of him to express gratitude; and to avoid causing hurt by not doing so, he ought not to accept the gift. For it is not merely good to express gratitude, it is an obligation, an obligation which the beneficiary takes upon himself by accepting the gift. I owe it to you to make this small return for what I allow you to do for me, of giving you the pleasure of knowing that you have given me something which I appreciate. There is an obligation to express gratitude for the reason that unreciprocated friendship is painful. By accepting a gift I encourage a friendship, which by not expressing gratitude I refuse to develop. I must not by accepting a gift make the donor more unhappy than he would be if I had refused it. That is cheating, using his gift in such a way as to make him unhappy.

Often it is good (though not obligatory) that someone who accepts a gift or a service should do more than show gratitude. It is good that I should give a present or do a service in return for what you have done for me (except in the case where your present or service was one given in return for mine.) If we are equally well or badly off, a present of similar worth is not inappropriate; but if the donor is rich, and the recipient poor, only the giving of a small gift in return would be good; and sometimes not even that. A poor man can sometimes, despite his poverty, do something for a rich man which the rich man cannot do for himself or get anyone else to do for him. For example, he may be able to defend the donor's reputation when he is being maligned. It is good that a beneficiary should go beyond obligation and give a present or service in return, for the reason that friendship is good. If you do a favour for me, you show that you want to be friends with me. If I say thank you, that means that you are not unhappy in having your generosity spurned. But if I give you something in return, that develops the friendship, makes you more happy than you would otherwise be. For doing what the other desires is part of what friendship involves.

For certain very large favours doing more than show gratitude in return is not merely good but obligatory. This is because in the case of very large favours the obligation not to make the donor less happy by accepting the gift than he would otherwise be, and the consequent obligation on the recipient to show that he was glad that the gift was given often involves more than saying 'Thank you'. For just to say 'Thank you' would suggest that I regarded the gift as an ordinary one; it would not show that I appreciated its worth. I can do that by making my expression of gratitude costly; I can show that my words are meant by joining them to a present or act which makes the expression of gratitude costly.[1] If you save my life or give me a million dollars, and although I say 'Thanks very much', I fail to do some small service for you when appropriate, that is tantamount to not saying 'Thank you' in return for a smaller gift. In effect I use but spurn your gift.

Note that the giving of a present or doing a small service for someone may sometimes be a good act if done in return for a present or service given, when it would not be otherwise. If my rich uncle gives me a large present, it is good that I should give him a small present in return (if I suddenly see something which I know that he would like). Yet if the rich uncle had not given me a present, there would have been nothing especially good in my giving a present to the rich uncle. There are better uses for my money than in giving a present which might easily be misunderstood.,

Such is the web of obligation and supererogation which favours create. What about creative acts? Since they have no immediate beneficiary, one might suppose that they create no new obligations, and make no acts supererogatorily good which were not so anyway. But I suggest that supposition is mistaken. They do make acts supererogatorily good which are not otherwise so. For two reasons

---

[1] R. A. Duff, in the course of his extensive discussion of punishment in *Trials and Punishments*, CUP, 1986, makes what is to my mind a useful comparison between punishments and rewards. He writes (pp. 237 f.): 'Rewards, like punishments, serve an expressive purpose . . . The primary purpose of such expressive actions is not (unless they are corrupt) instrumental: it is to express to [someone] the thanks or admiration which are due to her for what she has done.' He goes on (p. 242) to comment on the danger that rewards may lose their expressive purpose, and come to function solely as bribes.

they make it good that others should show their acknowledgement and appreciation of such acts, perhaps constituting such acknowledgement as serious by conjoining it with some service or present.

The first reason is that it is good in itself that one person, whoever he is, should acknowledge the achievements of another. The artist who paints great pictures, the runner who runs a marathon in record time, the crippled man who looks after himself, deserve recognition. To acknowledge what they have done is to give public recognition to significant truth (that such creative acts have been done), to those who have done them (the recognition of goodness is good), and to confer a favour on those who have done the creative acts (they deserve recognition). It is of course only good that such recognition be given if the creative acts have in fact been done.

The second reason is that, although one who does creative acts is not directly conferring a benefit, he is doing so indirectly. He is conferring a benefit on the community which has educated him by making their educative efforts to make him a doer of good deeds, successful. The community includes the agent's parents who brought him into the world, nourished him, taught him much, and gave him an example; teachers who taught him items of factual knowledge, fellow children from whom he gained an understanding of people, and gurus who taught him what was most worth doing. Everyone has an obligation to those who educate them to fulfil their own obligations and not make a mess of their lives. For we let down those from whom we accept education voluntarily, if we then make a mess of our lives, for we make their efforts on our behalf of no avail. Certainly our initial acceptance of life and early nurture was involuntary. But in cases where we do not have the option to accept or refuse what is obviously beneficial, our utilization of it does also create an obligation. For in deciding whether to confer an obvious benefit (such as life or nurture) on someone, such as a baby, who lacks the ability to choose whether to accept or decline it, one gives him the benefit of the doubt by presuming that if he had the option, he would have accepted it: We deem the recipient to have accepted the benefit, and the fact that that presumption is reasonable has, I suggest, the consequence that the recipient has an obligation in return. But, as we grow older, receiving benefits becomes a less involuntary matter; acceptance of education becomes progressively more voluntary. In so far as it is up to us whether we accept a benefit or not, and we do so, again obligation results.

But the obligation is limited to not making a mess of our lives; it cannot be an obligation to perfection. We are *given* a life, nurture, and education, and so it is basically ours to use as we choose; we wrong no one if, having done the minimum, we choose what beyond that we shall do with our lives. But if we do what is beyond obligation, that is giving something back to those who have educated us. If we do a heroic deed, then we use abundantly well what has been given to us. And that, indirectly and often unintentionally, is to confer a benefit on those who gave it to us. For it is a benefit to an agent to bring it about that his labours are abundantly fruitful. One who does a creative act does not create an obligation to acknowledge his achievement on his educating community, for his creative act benefits whether or not the benefit is accepted, and (apart from the case of those such as babies unable to accept) only acceptance produces obligation. But he does make it good that his community should respect his achievements, that they should acknowledge by word and deed those achievements. One who does a creative act may benefit not merely those who educated him generally, but any who inspired him to that particular act—the man who makes a generous gift to a charity makes fruitful the effort of those who talked him into it.

Those who begat, nurtured, educated, and inspired a creative act may be dead. But they have heirs who have themselves benefited by the nurturing and education which they have received, the community of brothers and sisters and fellow-pupils of creative agents. This benefit makes it (supererogatorily) good that this community should do for their educators, on their behalf as their agents, what they cannot do themselves but which it would be good that they should do—honour those creative agents who have used the education given by their educators in a highly worthwhile way. It is good that the community from which an agent comes (whether his original educators, or their heirs) should show grateful acknowledgement of his creative acts. For those agents have made the community a richer place by great deeds being done by its members.

The notion of his nurturing community to whom a man has obligations and which is benefited by his supererogatory acts is an important one for me, and I shall use it a lot later. It is a shorthand way of talking of all the people to whom a man owes something in view of the benefits which he has received from them. The strength and nature of the obligations will vary with the kind of benefit received and the immediacy with which it is given.

Some of our strongest obligations of course arise from responsibilities undertaken explicitly. Through marriage we acquire a responsibility for the well-being of spouse and children, and that means not just a responsibility for ensuring that they have enough to eat, but a responsibility for ensuring that their lives have a worthwhile happiness, a happiness, for example, which is not derived from hurting others. And we acquire similar but lesser responsibilities in joining any organization, varying with the extent of the importance of the organization. Obviously the responsibilities incurred by one who joins a local chess club are far less than those incurred by one who joins a kibbutz or a monastic order. But other and sometimes equally strong obligations arise from receiving benefits, which, as we have seen, is sometimes involuntary. The obvious example is a person's responsibilities, especially in their old age, towards his parents. The child owes his life to his parents and normally his upbringing as well; and years of shared enjoyment of things bring their own responsibility towards those with whom we have shared the enjoyment. Again, it is not just a responsibility for material well-being, to be satisfied by an anonymous cheque by post. But neither is it a responsibility just for company. No one has a duty to educate his parents morally, but he does have a duty to try to prevent a parent of his going off the rails—damaging himself or doing gross harm to another; to ensure that the happiness he seeks for the parent is not a happiness obtained in a way hurtful to the parent himself or to others.

Among the responsibilities owed to parents is the responsibility of respect, of acknowledging their worth by word and gesture and deed. It is good, I have argued, that we all acknowledge each other's worth; but it is the least, and occasionally (while they retain their independence) the only thing beyond expressing gratitude we can do for our parents who have done so much for us. And it is because there is that obligation on the child to respect the parent that the parent wrongs the child so badly if he accepts from the child a respect which he does not deserve; if he allows the child to respect him as an honest businessman when really he is cheating. Such a parent has indeed let his child down.

As we incur responsibilities towards parents involuntarily, so we incur similar but lesser responsibilities towards others who have given us life and well being, and with whom we have been involved in lesser ways: towards grandparents, and brothers, and the friends of our youth, to the members of our old school or village or country, that is, to members of our nurturing community.

Such special obligations are none too far to the forefront of the contemporary moral consciousness, which thinks only of obligations voluntarily incurred (and that tends to mean, explicitly, on a signed document), or of general obligations, that is, obligations towards types of people (the old, the poor) which exist independently of their special relationship to ourselves. But such a way of thinking fails to recognize the deep need of people to 'belong'; people need other people who feel a special responsibility for them, not just for their material well-being but for all of them (who care about the kind of people they are and become—spiritually and mentally), a permanent responsibility (not just a 9 to 5, five days a week, responsibility), and a responsibility which does not arise out of their plight (being old or poor) but out of some morally neutral condition (e.g. blood relationship), and preferably one which gives rise to a natural affection (so that obligation to help is reinforced by desire—as ideally of parent for child, and child for parent, reinforced by years of shared life). Only a society oblivious to these needs is likely to fail to recognize the existence of special responsibilities.[2]

After this digression on the nature of some of the strong obligations which arise through explicit undertaking or through receiving benefits, which will be important for later argument, I return to the point that favours and creative acts, the two kinds of supererogatory act, both make appropriate beneficial acts towards the donor, of giving him some present or service. We may describe this situation by saying that works of supererogation give to the agent merit; and that his merit makes it appropriate that others should give him a reward. (I am thus using the word 'reward' in a wide sense to cover all the gifts of present or service and verbal expressions of praise or gratitude which supererogatory acts make appropriate.) The supererogatory agent stacks up merit for himself. Merit is of two kinds—objective and subjective; and, although

---

[2] MacIntyre commenting on 'The Virtues in Heroic Societies' (i.e. societies as depicted by Homer or the Icelandic Sagas) comments that for them: 'the given rules which assign men their place in the social order and with it their identity also prescribe what they are and what is owed to them and how they are to be treated and regarded if they fail and how they are to treat and regard others if those others fail' (Alisdair MacIntyre, *After Virtue*, Duckworth, 1981, p. 116). He sees the chaos of modern morality as arising in part from its repudiating the idea that a person's moral identity (his duties, obligations, etc.) depends on his place in society.

actions which confer one normally confer the other also, they may not do so. Objective merit belongs to an agent who has done an act of supererogation, even if he did not believe it to be supererogatory. This includes cases when I do not realize that I am doing the act which is in fact supererogatory—I work hard to get Latin taught in the local school in order that my children may learn it, not realizing that thereby I make available an opportunity for your children of which you and they will wish them to take advantage. And there are also cases when I realize that I am doing the act but do not believe it to be supererogatory. I may have an exaggerated view of what I owe to my parents, and think that I would be letting them down if I did not become a great artist. Even in these cases certain responses become good when they would not otherwise be. It is good that you who benefit by all my hard work in getting Latin taught should show appreciation, and good that men should honour the artist for his artistic achievements (whatever his motives). Subjective merit belongs to an agent in virtue of his trying to do an act which he believes to be supererogatory, whether or not it is. It belongs to him in virtue of the goal he is trying to achieve and his beliefs about the worth of trying to achieve that goal. (If an act is done as a step towards attaining a more distant goal, it is the act of attempting to achieve that further goal which may be assessed for subjective merit.) I may have forgotten a promise which I made to you that I would help you if ever you became poor. When you do become poor, I am sorry and still help you. I did what was obligatory, believing it to be merely supererogatory. Is it appropriate that you should show more gratitude than would be suitable to one who has merely kept his promise? Yes, indeed. 'In view of what you believed, you were very kind,' you say. Similarly, of course, gratitude is due to one who tries to help beyond obligation, even if circumstances frustrate his efforts. But of course the full response of gratitude and reward is appropriate only where there is both subjective and objective merit. It is due to the man who benefits me when he is indeed and knowingly going beyond his obligations.

It follows from the above that there is no subjective merit, but rather what I shall be calling subjective guilt, in doing some action in order to gain gratitude or other reward from others who thus honour me because I lead them to suppose that I am doing the action for a quite different reason. If I give a large donation to Oxfam, not out of concern for the starving, but that others may honour me for my generous concern for the starving, I am doing them a wrong by deceiving them as to my motives so that they give me something (e.g. honour) which they would not otherwise do. In saying this I am not claiming that there is anything wrong in acting openly in order to gain a reward in the normal sense of the term, e.g. to win a prize; only that there is something wrong in acting in order to deceive others as to your motives into rendering you gratitude or other reward. Recall the telling words of Christ about hypocrites who give alms, or fast, or pray, in order to get human approval— they have, he said, 'already received their reward';[3] and he meant by that that they have got the human approval for which they were seeking, and no merit belonged to them for which a reward in my sense would be appropriate.

The subjective merit which belongs to an agent would seem to belong to him in virtue of his intentionally intervening in the ongoing stream of events in order to do supererogatory good; and if so it can only arise from an action done in the face of a balance of contrary desire. Similar subjective merit would seem to belong to an agent who fails to wrong someone despite strong contrary temptation. Someone who owes me a small sum of money deserves some thanks from me if he goes to enormous trouble to pay his debt on time. If that is right, then subjective merit turns out to be what I called in Chapter 2 praiseworthiness.

But 'subjective merit' is a more satisfactory name for this. For 'subjective merit' suggests an inner feature in virtue of which (as we have now seen) various responses, various kinds of reward in my sense are appropriate; it does not pick it out only by one kind of response which is normally appropriate to it. Why an agent who has subjective merit is praiseworthy is because praising (of the kind with which I was concerned in Chapter 2) is ascribing inner worth, i.e. subjective merit; he is praiseworthy because he has that feature of which praising consists in the ascription. But it is not always good that the ascription should be made. Occasionally, for example, it is not good to praise people, and especially children, when praising them might 'turn their heads'; the goodness of ascribing praise is sometimes outweighed by other disadvantages. But normally the ascription of subjective merit to those with subjective merit is good, and I have been arguing in this chapter that it is especially good that beneficiaries should make the ascription.

[3] e.g. Matt. 6: 2.

5

Guilt, Atonement, and Forgiveness

I considered in Chapter 4 the merit which is acquired through acts of supererogation, and the responses appropriate to it which I called in a wide sense 'rewards'. I turn now to the consequences of wrongdoing.

Guilt

In virtue of doing wrong (or failing to fulfil his obligations) an agent acquires guilt. Like merit, guilt has objective and subjective forms; normally these go together but sometimes they exist independently of each other. An agent who fails to fulfil his obligations (or does what is obligatory not to do) is objectively guilty. I am objectively guilty for failing to educate my children properly, even if I believe that I have no duty to educate my children, or if I believe that sending them to a certain school, which, unknown to me, is totally incompetent, is educating my children properly. Objective guilt is the status acquired by one who does objective wrong. An agent who fails to try to fulfil his obligations is subjectively guilty. If I believe that I have a duty to educate my children and neglect to do anything about it, then I am subjectively guilty, even if by accident or through the agency of someone else they acquire a good education. Subjective guilt is the status acquired by one who intentionally does wrong. Talk of guilt has its paradigmatic application in connection with the law—you are legally guilty if you are found by a competent court to have broken the law of the land. But just as we talk of moral law, as a set of principles which imposes obligations, independently of their having been promulgated by some king or parliament, so it is appropriate to talk of moral guilt as belonging to a person who breaks the moral law, who fails to fulfil his obligations. This guilt belongs to a person before and independently of any court pronouncing him guilty.

To say that someone is morally guilty is not just to say that he has failed in the past. For if I fail in an obligation, I don't just do a wrong, I do a wrong to someone. If I promise you that I will give a lecture and then don't turn up, or if I kick you in a fit of anger, I have done a wrong to you. By hurting you, I put myself in a moral situation somewhat like the legal situation of a debtor who owes money. The wrong needs righting. There is an obligation to do something like repaying. But the morally guilty man is not merely one who has acquired certain obligations. He has also acquired a present status something like being unclean. By borrowing money and giving a promise to repay it an agent puts himself under certain obligations, but his status is in no way unclean in consequence; the guilty one is unclean[1]—in a way, as we shall see in a moment, even if his guilt is merely objective. Breaking the moral law is like incurring a debt (when not allowed to do so by your creditor—e.g. when you do not repay your loan at the promised time). But clearly the kind of debt owed by failure to perform one's moral obligations is often no mere financial one, or anything similar. In so far as the victim is a person, that person is known personally to the wrongdoer, and the failure is a failure of personal trust, and above all if there is ill will (deliberate malice or negligence) on the part of the wrongdoer then there is a totally new kind of harm involved—the harm done to personal relations by a wrong attitude by the wrongdoer. A philosopher who does not like to talk of moral guilt deprives himself of an obvious expression for making the point that a person who fails in his obligations has got something wrong with him which needs dealing with.

There is something wrong with a person even if his guilt is purely objective. If I unintentionally break your best vase, or light the fire with the only copy of your book, I acquire the status of a wrongdoer even if my actions were done in total ignorance of their nature or consequences (and even if I had taken all reasonable precautions to ensure that they had no such nature or consequences). It is, I suggest, the virtually unanimous moral intuition of men that this is so, that in such circumstances I acquire a status which needs purging by reparation if possible, and certainly by an apology. This is because in interacting with my fellows, I undertake responsibility for seeing

---

[1] For this analogy, see St Anselm, *Cur Deus Homo* 1.19. See also Gabriele Taylor, *Pride, Shame, and Guilt*, Clarendon Press, 1985. She writes (p. 98) of one who believes himself guilty as regarding himself as 'disfigured'.

that certain things are done and certain things are not done (e.g. in holding your vase, I take responsibility for its not getting broken); and bad luck (my actions having bad consequences despite my taking reasonable precautions) no more removes the responsibility, than it excuses me from repaying you £10 which I have borrowed from you, if I have £10 stolen.

But of course the guilt is of a different kind if I knowingly fail in my obligations towards you—if my guilt is subjective as well as objective. Here again I suggest that the virtually unanimous moral intuition of men suggests that far more is wrong, and far more needs doing to put it right. If I deliberately break your best vase it's no good my saying 'I really am very sorry'. I have got to make several speeches distancing myself totally from the act and I've got to make reparation very quickly. I have wronged you so much the worse that my guilt is of a qualitatively different kind. The reason for the vast difference is that when I deliberately break your best vase, I have failed not merely in my outward obligation towards you, but also in the attitude of purpose towards you, which I owe you, the attitude of seeking no harm for you. I owe you this attitude whoever you are, but the obligation is greater if you are related in certain ways to me—e.g. you have been my friend. To put the point in another way—when my guilt is subjective as well as objective, I am guilty for the act of harming you as well as for the consequences of the act. Even without objective guilt being attached to it, subjective guilt is a very serious matter. I wrong you by trying to break your best vase, even if by accident I break my own instead. We can see that that is so by considering more serious cases. I try to kill you but the shot misfires. From the obvious need for reparation of rather more than a short apology, we can see that wrong has been done and guilt acquired. Both subjective and objective guilt are stains on a soul requiring expunging; but subjective guilt is embedded in the soul while objective guilt lies on the surface.[2]

I argued in Chapter 2 that there are circumstances in which failing to fulfil what one believes to be one's obligations is not merely excusable but what a good agent should be doing. It seems right, therefore, to say that under those circumstances an agent does not acquire subjective guilt. In that case subjective guilt turns out to be

---

[2] 'For a sin knowingly committed and a sin done in ignorance are so different that an evil which men could never do, were its full extent known, may be pardonable when done in ignorance'—St Anselm, op. cit. 2.15.

identical with the blameworthiness of Chapter 2. An agent is blameworthy, we saw there, in so far as he does not try to fulfil his moral obligations (or tries to do what he believes it obligatory not to do), whether or not there was such an obligation, given that he was not trying instead to do an act which he believed to be at least equally obligatory or otherwise better (i.e. of such supererogatory goodness as to outweigh obligation). 'Subjectively guilty' is, however, a better description than 'blameworthy' for the status of such an agent (as 'subjectively meritorious' is a better description than 'praiseworthy'), for it suggests an inner feature in virtue of which, as we shall see shortly, various responses are appropriate; it does not pick it out only by one kind of response which is normally appropriate to it. Why an agent who acquires subjective guilt is blameworthy is because blaming is ascribing inner guilt. But it is not always good that the ascription should be made; it is sometimes better not to comment on the faults of others.

We saw in the last chapter that all favours which confer a direct benefit on some recipient also confer an indirect benefit on the nurturing community. Analogously, when a man neglects his obligations, he wrongs not only the obvious victim—the one he cheated or to whom he lied—but also those who taught him what is morally obligatory, showed him by their example how to live, and encouraged him to do what is right. He makes their efforts on his behalf of no avail.

Favours benefit both the recipient and the nurturing community; creative acts benefit only the community. Analogously, as I suggested earlier, there are failures of obligation which wrong only the nurturing community or those who have given us particular gifts which we abuse. I suggested earlier that the obligation to use gifts we are given is a limited one. It is not an obligation to perfection, but it is an obligation not totally to abuse the gifts which we are given and which we accept or may reasonably be presumed to have accepted. If a rich man's uncle gives him a lot of money to set himself up in business, but he makes no effort to make a success of the business, then, even if he does not do wrong to his customers or any trading partner, he still wrongs the rich uncle. Similarly we wrong those who begin to develop abilities in us if we do nothing to develop those abilities further—if I allow someone to teach me the violin without payment, I owe it to him to make some effort to practise playing between lessons.

The fact that supererogatory acts will always benefit someone other than the agent, at least a nurturing community, arises from the fact that humans are so dependent on others for their existence and upbringing. God, however, can do a supererogatory act which benefits at most himself. The fact that failures of obligation always harm someone other than the agent is however a necessary truth. There is no guilt unless wrong is done to someone else. It is true that many people feel that a failure to develop talents or an act of self-deception is an act for which they bear guilt. But that, I suggest, is because they think of themselves as harming those who brought them into being and educated them for higher things—and that may include, above all, God or some less personal supernatural power. Some people do talk in such cases as if they acquire a guilt through wronging themselves—'I let myself down,' they say. Certainly some people think of themselves as having obligations to themselves—see the phrases 'I owe it to myself' or 'I can never forgive myself for that'. But there is, I suggest, a confusion in such thought. For obligation is basically owing, and how can one owe anything to oneself ? If an agent fails to develop his talents, thinks this bad and yet does not think of this failure as wronging those who nurtured him, he ought, I suggest, to think of himself as having done something bad but not wrong (in the terminology I introduced in Chapter 1, something infravetatory) and therefore something which confers no guilt.

Shame and Pride

We must distinguish subjective guilt from shame, and subjective merit from pride. A person is ashamed of an action if he regrets having acted for the kind of reason that he did, quite apart from the consequences of the action. The soldier who fled in battle in order to save his own life is ashamed of his action if he regrets having allowed the desire to save his life to influence his conduct. Whereas if a person regrets having done some action because it had some unforeseen consequence—say, I regret having bought a car because I then did not have enough money for a holiday—shame is not involved. Analogously a person is proud of an action if he is glad to have acted for the kind of reason that he did, quite apart from the consequences of the action. The soldier who resisted the desire to flee, in order to carry out his orders, is proud of his action if he is glad to have chosen to carry out orders despite a desire to flee.

I regret having done an action if I desire not to have done it, and am glad at having done an action if I desire to have done it. This desire not to have done an action is a natural inclination to make myself (if it were possible—which it is now not) not have done that action. Such a desire can go with a belief that there was nothing wrong in having done the action; and conversely I can believe that I did a wrong action, without having any natural inclination to undo it. Hence subjective guilt may exist without shame, and conversely; I may believe that I have done wrong without having any natural inclination to make myself not have done the action (if that were possible). I may know that I did wrong in knocking down the man who insulted me, while really being rather pleased about it. Conversely I may be ashamed at having fallen short of a particular ideal of myself (e.g. as a man of courage) without believing that I did anything morally wrong. The soldier may believe that he did nothing wrong in fleeing from the battlefield (he may have been given permission to flee), but he may wish deeply all the same that he had not yielded to fear. Likewise, the soldier may be proud of his courage, desiring to have been courageous (in that he is naturally inclined to make himself have acted courageously, if that were now in his power) without thinking it morally good that he should.

If we are subjectively guilty, it is good that we should believe ourselves thus guilty—for it is good that we should understand the consequences of our actions, which includes our guilt, for we are responsible for such consequences. It is good too, that if we are subjectively guilty, we should be ashamed of our actions. For it is good that our desires be aligned with our moral beliefs—that we should have a natural inclination to do what we believe right and avoid what we believe wrong. Hence it is good that a moral belief that we have done an action we believed wrong be aligned with a desire not to have done that action. But, alas, with the best will in the world, sometimes we do not desire the good, and shame does not accompany subjective guilt. Shame in appropriate circumstances requires cultivation. It is good too that if we are subjectively meritorious we should be proud of our actions. But while 'proper pride' is good, the trouble with pride is that we are often proud of actions when they are not subjectively meritorious. We are proud of actions other than ones done in pursuit of the good, we deceive ourselves about our motives, and are proud of aspects of an action for which we are not responsible, believing ourselves to have acted as we did without the inspiration of others, or to have been totally responsible for the success of our endeavours, so much of which was due to luck. The trouble with pride is that so much pride is not proper pride, and even a little proper pride can so easily lead to a lot of improper pride.

One may be ashamed or proud not merely of one's actions (in virtue of which alone one acquires merit or guilt), but, more wide-rangingly, of things that happen to one unavoidably or unavoidable facets of oneself which concern (in a broad sense) the sort of person one is. One may be proud of one's inherited possessions, or ashamed of being (by accident) found naked. Such pride or shame is desire to be or not to be the sort of person to whom certain things happen or who has certain characteristics.

Pride and shame of this kind can, of course, so easily become excessive or misdirected. We so easily invest in the more extraneous features of ourselves (e.g. the extent of our possessions) the kind of pride appropriate to more intrinsic features (e.g. intelligence and, much more importantly, the features of character described in Chapter 1); and we invest in unavoidable features of ourselves the kind of pride appropriate to ourselves as the performers of intentional actions (i.e. our subjective merit). Similarly with shame. Pride and shame, I suggest, ought to be greater in respect of the actions which we do than of the things which unavoidably happen to us, although some of the latter are important.[3] I have written of people *being* subjectively guilty or ashamed. We often talk of people 'feeling' guilty or ashamed. What's the difference? It may be much or

[3] What I have just written about shame and guilt and pride to some extent coincides with and to some extent diverges from ideas developed in Gabriele Taylor's interesting book (see n. 1, above). She brings out, as I do, that pride and shame are concerned with one's state as a person; pride is a matter of self-esteem, shame a loss of self-respect. (Self-respect, she holds, involves believing that one has reached some minimum standard, whereas self-esteem involves believing that one has reached quite a high standard. On the other hand, self-respect concerns matters more akin to the moral than self-esteem needs to.) I am grateful to her for drawing to my attention the fact that pride and shame may be concerned not merely with one's status as the performer of intentional actions, but may be focused on quite unavoidable aspects of oneself. Anthony O'Hear ('Guilt and Shame as Moral Concepts', *Proceedings of the Aristotelian Society*, 1976–7, **77**, 73–86) also makes this point with respect to shame. The examples of pride at one's possessions or shame at being found naked are Taylor's. She also usefully discusses (p. 132) the shame which a daughter feels at the wrongdoing of her father; she loses her value as her father's daughter.

none at all, because the concepts of 'feeling' guilt or shame are very vague. The only point which might be made by talking of someone 'feeling' ashamed rather than 'being' ashamed that I can see is that the regret of the man who 'feels' ashamed is accompanied by sensations such as palpitations of the heart which are not necessarily present in the man who merely 'is' ashamed. There are, however, various differences which might be being made by talking of someone 'feeling' guilty rather than of his 'being' guilty. First, there is the contrast between subjective and objective guilt—doing what a man believed wrong as opposed to doing what was wrong. To say that a man felt guilty might be just to say that he did what he believed wrong. Then there is the contrast between subjective guilt and belief that you are subjectively guilty. To say that a man felt guilty might be to say that he believed that the taint of guilt belonged to him in virtue of his wrong actions. Then, there is the contrast between subjective guilt and shame. To say that a man felt guilty might be to say that he was ashamed of his action. And finally to say that a man felt guilty may be simply to say that his belief that he was subjectively guilty was accompanied by various sensations. Freud tried to cure us of some of our guilt feelings; but, as surely Freud must have recognized, some guilt feelings are a good thing. It is good that we believe ourselves objectively guilty when we are; it is good that we believe ourselves subjectively guilty when we are; it is good that guilt be accompanied by shame. And it is also good, I suggest, in the case of our more serious failures, that our beliefs about guilt be not too cold, that bodily sensations chime in, as it were. We are embodied beings and there are appropriate bodily reactions to the events of life. We feel that there is something wrong with the 'cold fish' who lacks 'natural feelings', and that includes the appropriate bodily reactions. That our body be numb and our eyes ache are reactions as appropriate to our failures as are palpitations of the heart at our unexpected successes. But the guilt feelings of which Freud might reasonably try to cure us are beliefs that we are guilty (objectively or subjectively) when we are not, the exaggerated involvement of our sensations in such beliefs (e.g. overwhelming numbness at a minor crime), and shame for doing morally right acts.

Sometimes when we change our moral views and come to believe some action right which previously we believed wrong, we nevertheless feel uneasy and ashamed when we do it and have similar pangs. One example of such feelings is the desires and pangs which nag us to conform to a moral code overstrict in detail, and which moral theologians have called 'scruples'. 'Scruples' are a nuisance; they are unpleasant and they make it difficult for a person to act on his real moral views. Freud's view that therapy is needed to undermine the power of an over-powerful conscience may most reasonably be seen as an attack on feelings of this kind or on false moral beliefs rather than an attack on the attempt to conform one's behaviour to one's moral views.[4]

Atonement and Forgiveness

A wrongdoer is under an obligation to deal with his guilt, subjective and objective; and this 'dealing with' the guilt is not unnaturally seen as removing it. In so far as guilt is analogous to a debt, it can be removed either by the action of the wrongdoer in (in some way) paying it off; or by the action of the victim in (in some way) taking compensation. But, I shall argue, for total removal of the guilt, the wrongdoer must make a small contribution; and it is better that he do all he can to remove the guilt and his victim forgive him for his action. A meritorious agent, by contrast, unlike a guilty agent, has no obligation to do anything about his status, nor is it good that he should. And unless in some way he disowns his past and spoils his status, his merit remains. Merit is like a credit balance, but one which cannot be taken away by others. On the other hand, mere objective merit seems a less deep thing than objective guilt. As we saw earlier, objective guilt makes its bearer in a way unclean; mere objective, or accidental, merit does not seem to give its bearer an equally deep positive status.

For perfect removal of guilt, then, the wrongdoer must make atonement for his wrong act, and the victim must forgive him. Atonement involves four components—repentance, apology, reparation, and what, for want of a better word, I shall call penance (though not all of these are always required). They are all contributions to removing as much of the consequences of the past act as logically can be removed by the wrongdoer. The consequences are, first, the harm caused by and distinguishable from the act of causing it and, secondly, the purposive attitude of the wrongdoer

[4] For discussion of Freud's account of this matter, see David H. Jones, 'Freud's Theory of Moral Conscience', *Philosophy*, 1966, **41**, 34–57.

towards the victim manifested in the causing of the harm. By removing the former harm the wrongdoer makes reparation. Sometimes he can literally restore the status quo. If I steal your watch and have not sold it, I can return it to you. Sometimes I can only make things rather similar to the way they were, so that the victim is almost equally happy with the new state. I can compensate him adequately, that is. If I steal and sell your watch I can buy you another one. If I smash up your car, I can pay for the repairs. The harm done by stealing, injuring, and similar acts is not only the physical damage, but the inconvenience of temporary loss and the trauma and anxiety resulting from it, and for these too compensation is needed. Sometimes, alas, full compensation is not possible. If I run you over with my car, and paralyse you for life, nothing I can do can compensate you fully for that. But some things which I can do can compensate you in part. I can pay for wheelchairs, and machines to life you out of bed in the morning. But clearly reparation, as far as lies within the wrongdoer's power, is essential for removal of the taint of guilt. I remain guilty for hurting you if I do not do what I can to remove the harm I have done you.

But the consequences of the act are not merely such harm but the fact that the wrongdoer has by doing the act made himself someone who has harmed the victim. He cannot change that past fact, but he can distance himself from it by privately and publicly disowning the act. The victim has been hurt, and so it is to the victim that the disowning is owed and must be shown. But the disowning which is owed must be sincere and so must reflect the attitude which the wrongdoer now has, and naturally expresses to himself. The natural expression to oneself is repentance, the public expression to the victim is apology. Repentance involves, first, acknowledgement by the wrongdoer that he did the act and that it was a wrong act to do. Thereby the wrongdoer distances the act from his present ideals. Repentance also involves a resolve to amend—you cannot repent of a past act if you intend to do a similar act at the next available opportunity. Preachers often draw our attention to the etymology of the Greek word translated 'repent', μετανοεῖν, which means literally 'to change one's mind'. By resolving to amend, the wrongdoer distances the past act from his present purposes. In acknowledging his initiation of the past act, but distancing it both from his present ideals and from his present purposes, the wrongdoer makes the sharp contrast between the attitude behind the past act and his present attitude. He disowns the past act publicly by expressing to the victim the repentance which he expresses to himself privately, assuring the victim that he recognizes its wrongness and that he purposes to amend. There are conventional ways of doing this; one may say 'I'm very sorry' or 'I really do apologize'. An agent cannot alter the fact that he did the past act, but what he can do is make the present 'he' in his attitude as different as possible from the past 'he' who did the act; that is the most he can do towards undoing the act.

The above account of repentance and apology applies in so far as there is an element of subjectivity in the guilt, in so far as deliberately or through negligence the wrongdoer has some moral responsibility for doing the harm. If the guilt is purely objective, arising from the performance of an unintentional act in performing which there was not even the slightest negligence involved (for instance, dropping your best vase, when startled by a loud noise), an apology of a sort is still owed, for the reason that in interacting with others we accept responsibility in advance for not causing them certain kinds of harm (e.g. in handling your vase, I accept responsibility for not damaging it). If unintentionally we are the agents of harm, we must distance ourselves from that agency. But in so far as we never intended it in the first place (and had every intention of preventing it), what we must do is to emphasize that our present benevolent ideals and purposes were our past ones also. An apology (but one which brings out the unintentional character of the action) is needed; but it needs behind it no repentance in the form of change of mind, only sincerity in the re-emphasis of ideals and purposes.

Apology can often be very difficult, it costs many a person a lot to say 'I'm sorry'. But sometimes for some people, apology can be very easy. We all know the smooth amiable people who say 'I'm frightfully sorry' with such a charming smile that our reaction is 'Yes, but do you really mean it?' And what else can show 'meaning it', what else can show the sincerity of the apology? You lend your friend £1,000. He forgets to return it, until you remind him five times; in consequence of which you have to borrow money yourself and disappoint your own creditors. He then acknowledges his wrongdoing and resolves not to do it again (publicly, and, let us suppose, also privately). He pays you the money back and compensates you for any interest payment and loss of time, and says that he's sorry. And yet that's still not quite good enough, is it? We feel something else is required. The 'something else' would be some token of his sorrow—a favour which you didn't expect, interest on the money additional to that needed to compensate you for your own borrowing, perhaps a bunch of flowers—something more than mere compensation.[5] The giving of the costly gift does not have the function of making clear something which was true whether or not the agent made it clear, that he meant the apology. Rather, it is a performative[6] act whereby he disowns his wrong act (in a way which mere words do not do, where the wrong is a serious one). By doing his act of disowning, by doing something which costs him time, effort, and money, he constitutes that act as a meant and serious act. To give what we cannot too easily afford is always a serious act. The penitent constitutes his apology as serious by making it costly. Similar considerations apply to conjoining a present to a 'thank you' in expression of gratitude for a very large favour (see p. 66). The recipient constitutes his expression of gratitude for such a favour as meant by making it costly.

With reparation, repentance, apology, and penance, the wrong-doer has done what he can towards removing his guilt, towards atonement for the past (towards making him and the victim at one again). Not all such are needed in every case. For some wrongs reparation is inappropriate—there is no reparation for an insult; for the less serious wrongs penance is not needed; but sincere apology is always needed. In the case of subjective guilt, apology must be accompanied by repentance of the kind described.

The final act belongs to the victim—to forgive. In making apology, reparation, and penance, I am giving you something. All gifts have to be accepted (explicitly or implicitly) or else they remain with the giver. Gifts are accepted by the recipient completing the

---

[5] 'When anyone pays what he has unjustly taken away, he ought to give something which could not have been demanded of him, had he not stolen what belonged to another'—St Anselm, op. cit. 1.11.

[6] J. L. Austin introduced the terminology of 'performative utterances' to describe such utterances as 'I promise', 'I solemnly swear', 'I name this ship', which do not report already existing states of affairs but themselves bring about states of affairs. (See e.g. his 'Performative Utterances' in his *Philosophical Papers*, OUP, 1961.) The man who promises does not report an interior mental act, but creates an obligation upon himself to do something, an obligation which did not previously exist. Actions other than utterances may create or abolish states of people or relations between them describable in such moral terms as responsibility and obligation. I convey money to you and thereby abolish my debt, and in the context of an auction a nod is enough to constitute a bid (i.e. a promise to pay).

process which the giver is trying to effect by presenting them to the recipient. You accept my box of chocolates by taking it from me, the elephant I give you by accepting responsibility for its upkeep. What I give you in making reparation, penance, and apology is my contribution towards destroying the consequences (physical and not so physical) of my act of hurting you. You accept my disowning by forwarding the purpose I had in showing you this disowning—to make it the case, as far as logically can be done, that I was not the originator of an act by which I wronged you. You do that by undertaking that in future you will not treat me as the originator of an act by which I wronged you. Your acceptance of my reparation, penance and, above all, apology, is forgiving. Forgiving is a performative act—achieved perhaps by saying solemnly 'I forgive you', or perhaps by saying 'That's all right', or maybe just by a smile.

An agent's guilt is removed when his repentance, reparation, apology, and penance find their response in the victim's forgiveness. Just as an agent's guilt is far more serious if it is subjective guilt than if it is objective guilt (and most serious of all if the guilt is both subjective and objective), so the kind of atonement will need to be correspondingly more serious—a longer apology, deep repentance, a larger penance, and the forgiveness less casual.

The wrongdoer has his guilt removed if he does his acts of atonement and the victim forgives him. Can the victim forgive him without any act of atonement on his part? The victim can indeed disown the act, in the sense that he explicitly says something like 'Let us regard this as not having happened' and then acts as though it had not happened. Such disowning could be done at any time, even if the wrongdoer made no atonement; but unless it was done in response to atonement it would not be an acceptance of that. And it will not then suffice to remove guilt, for the wrongdoer has not distanced himself from that act. We can see this by example. I borrow your car and damage the bodywork. I don't even apologize, but all the same you say 'That's quite all right'. But I remain one who has wronged you and I need to purge myself of my guilt, as I may well realize in later life. A mere financial debt can easily be removed by the creditor, but the unclean status of guilt requires some work by the debtor.

Indeed not merely is it ineffective but it is bad, in the case of serious acts, for victim to treat the acts as not having been done, in the absence of some atonement at least in the form of apology from

the wrongdoer. In the case of the acts done to hurt us which are not
done with much deliberation and where the hurt is not great, this
may indeed be the best course of action. (It would be inappropriate
to treat very seriously acts which were not in their intentions or
consequences very serious.) But this would not be the best course in
the case of a serious hurt, and above all one done deliberately.
Suppose that I have murdered your dearly loved wife; you know
this, but for some reason I am beyond the power of the law. Being a
modern and charitable man, you decide to overlook my offence (in
so far as it hurt you). 'The past is the past', you say; 'what is the
point of nursing a grievance? The party we are both going to attend
will go with more of a swing if we forget about this little incident.'
But of course that attitude of yours trivializes human life, your love
for your wife, and the importance of right action. And it involves
your failing to treat me seriously, to take seriously my attitude
towards you expressed in my action. Thereby it trivializes human
relationships, for it supposes that good human relatons can exist
when we do not take each other seriously.[7]

It is both bad and ineffective for a victim of at any rate a serious
hurt to disown the hurt when no atonement at all has been made.
What, however, is within the victim's power is to determine, within
limits, just how much atonement is necessary before he is prepared to
give the forgiveness which will eliminate guilt. The wrongdoer must
offer some atonement—certainly repentance and apology and some
attempt at reparation in so far as it lies within his power. But the
victim may if he chooses let the wrongdoer off more; his forgiveness
without insisting on more would be efficacious. But if he chooses,
the victim can insist on substantial reparation, and sometimes it is
good that he should do so, that he should insist on the victim for his
sake making a serious atonement; for that allows him to take
seriously the harm that has been done.

Is the disowning of a hurtful act by the victim even forgiveness
when no atonement at all has been made? I do not think that
ordinary usage is very clear here, and a verbal decision is called for.
In view of the fact that forgiving is normally thought of as a good

---

[7] Gabriele Taylor writes that if a victim 're-establishes a relationship without there
being a change of heart on the [wrongdoer's] part then it seems it is not genuine
forgiveness he offers, but condonation. For in reaccepting the unrepentant agent
he would seem to think little of the wrong done and so compromise his own values'
(op. cit., p. 105).

thing, I suggest that a victim's disowning of a hurtful act is only to be called forgiveness when it is in response to at least some minimal attempt at atonement such as an apology.[8]

What now if the wrongdoer makes due amends, gives a serious apology with due reparation and penance, but the victim fails to forgive? Does the guilt remain? My answer is that it does remain initially; the victim has the power to retain it for a while. But if the apology is pressed, the penance increased, and still the victim refuses to forgive, the guilt disappears. Ideally both those involved—the wrongdoer and the victim—need to disown the act, but if the wrongdoer does all that he can both to disown the act and to get his victim to disown the act, he will have done all he can to remove his involvement in the act. All that is logically possible for the guilty one to do to remove his status has been done. If by my past act I have wronged you, that gives you a certain right against me—a right to accept or ignore my plea for pardon. If we were to say that the wrongdoer had, as it were, a fixed fine to pay in the way of atonement, that guilt did not disappear before the fine was paid but that it disappeared automatically when the fine was paid, that would have the consequence that I can wrong you and then remove my guilt at will. That would not take seriously the fact that the act is an act by which you are wronged, and in the wiping out of which you ought therefore to have a say. One consequence of my harming you is just that it is in part up to you whether my guilt is remitted. But although my act gives you a right against me, it does not give you an infinite right. The harm which I have done you and the guilt which in consequence I acquire is limited. Hence your power to keep me

---

[8] One of very few recent philosophical discussions of the issues of this chapter is one by William Neblett—'The Ethics of Guilt', *Journal of Philosophy*, 1974, **71**, 652–63. As I do, he claims that men become guilty through performing wrong actions, and that this guilt needs atonement; but he claims that a man can be forgiven even when he has not made atonement. One recent article which in my view fails to see what forgiveness is about is Anne C. Minas, 'God and Forgiveness', *Philosophical Quarterly*, 1975, **25**, 138–50. She claims that God cannot forgive because forgiveness is either changing one's moral judgement, or remitting deserved punishment, or abandoning a feeling of resentment; and she has arguments to show that a good God will not do any of these. However, forgiveness does not involve changing any moral judgement, and feelings need not be involved (I can easily forgive that which I do not resent). It is true that if I forgive you for some act, I ought not subsequently to punish you for that act. Yet forgiveness still has application in contexts where there is no question of punishment; and, as we shall see in the next chapter, there is often no obligation anyway to impose deserved punishment.

guilty is limited. The victim has the right, within limits, to judge when the wrongdoer's atonement suffices. He can take an apology which sounds sincere and so indicates repentance as sufficient, or refuse forgiveness until the apology is renewed with reparation and penance. He cannot forgive when the apology is totally casual and so shows no repentance, and if he refuses forgiveness after a serious repeated genuine apology with reparation and penance, the guilt vanishes despite the lack of forgiveness. But, within those limits, the final remission of guilt depends on the victim. There is of course no obligation on the victim to forgive. How can my hurting you and then trying to undo the harm, actions all of my choice and not yours, put you under an obligation to do something, which did not exist before? So long as you have the power of choice, your obligations to me arise from your choices, including your acceptance of my favours, not from my choices. However, forgiving the serious penitent is clearly good—a work of supererogation.

There is, however, an obligation to forgive others on anyone who has solemnly undertaken to do so. For this reason Christians have an obligation to forgive all who seek their forgiveness. For it is a central theme of the Gospel, embedded in the Lord's Prayer, that God's forgiveness can only be had by those prepared to forgive others; Christians who accept God's forgiveness thereby undertake the obligation to forgive others.

It may well be that there are wrongs for which the wrongdoer cannot make adequate atonement. One possible such case is where the victim is dead. If I kill someone, how can I make atonement to him? I can repent, and I can also do quite a bit for the dead man by way of reparation and penance. A dead person can be benefited or harmed by the fulfilment or frustration of his most recent desires, even if he cannot enjoy that fulfilment. Our desires may most usually be for future states of our conscious selves. But they are not always that. We desire the well-being of our children, even if we shall not know of it; and we may take steps to secure that well-being. I may seek to do you a good turn by forwarding the fulfilment of your desires, including those of whose fulfilment you will not know. If I help your children while you are alive, but unknown to you, I am benefiting you. So too after your death. Your desires may be very specific (for your daughter to pass her examination), or very general (for your daughter's future happiness). Hence a killer can by way of reparation and penance seek to fulfil the dead man's desires by providing for his children, promoting his memory, and giving to his favourite good cause.

Sometimes, of course, none of these things is possible—the dead man may have no children, no favourite good cause, and no past life worthy of recall; and more generally he may have no desires for states of affairs other than ones which involve his own conscious experiences. And in any case, of course, the two things the wrongdoer cannot do by way of atonement are to apologize and make full reparation (viz. restore to life). And the victim cannot forgive. If the wrongdoer does what he can by way of repentance, reparation, and penance, will that suffice to obtain remission of guilt, even in the absence of forgiveness? Perhaps, perhaps not. Maybe too there are some crimes which are too horrific for guilt to be removed by anything which the wrongdoer can do during a few years of earthly life. Could the Nazi butchers really make adequate atonement in a few years?

If there is an endless life after death, in which the wrongdoer can meet his victim, then I am inclined to think that a wrongdoer will always have adequate opportunity to make atonement for any wrong, however bad. Analogy and, I suspect, the intuitions of most of us educated in a semi-Christian society, suggest that no wrong is so great that no atonement will suffice. However large your debt, some cheque would pay it off. So surely whatever evil a man has done in a few years of life on Earth would be remittable if he had the time and resources to make proper apology, due reparation and generous penance. However, maybe sometimes wrongdoers do so much wrong on Earth that they cannot make adequate atonement during the remainder of their earthly life. But if there is an afterlife where they can confront their victims, surely they can make there adequate atonement to them.[9]

---

[9] Kant, to my mind mistakenly, claims that in a way we are always in this situation of being unable to make adequate atonement. (See his *Religion Within the Limits of Reason Alone*, trans. T. M. Greene and H. H. Hudson, Harper and Row, 1960.) He claims this because he holds that we have duties enough to fill each moment anyway: the wrongdoer cannot 'through future good conduct, produce a surplus over and above what he is under obligation to perform at every instant, for it is always his duty to do all the good that lies in his power' (p. 66). But since atonement involves doing more than otherwise would be one's duty (i.e. what would, but for the past, be a work of supererogation), no one can ever atone for any of his sins. My arguments in Chapter 1 that obligations form only a limited set have the consequence that there is scope for doing more than would otherwise be one's duty. If cogent, those arguments defeat Kant's implausible conclusion. Kant's way of avoiding his own conclusion is to

Responsibility for the Guilt of Others

So far I have assumed that an agent acquires merit or guilt (and so the need to do something about it by way of atonement) only in respect of those actions which he has done *himself*. But it is implicit in what I have written that we have some responsibility, and so merit or guilt, for the acts of others, in respect of the influence for good or ill which we have had or ought to have tried to have upon them. Thus we acquire guilt for the bad influence we have exercised and for the failure to exert good influence when we ought to have done. The nurturing community has a duty to influence its members for good. Within the community parents and others such as teachers in positions of parental responsibility have a duty to educate their children morally to have and pursue true values. Of course a parent can't make his children be good; there are other influences on the child, and also, I am assuming, the child has some indeterministic freedom of choice. Still, the parent has a responsibility to influence, and if bad behaviour results when he has failed to do so, the parent has some responsibility for this. If my child's thieving is the consequence of my bad example, my lack of moral instruction, or my lack of loving care, then I have some responsibility for it. But within the community, all members have some obligation to each other, in virtue of the mutual benefits conferred within the community and our debt to the fathers of the community (our ancestors and benefactors) to care for those whom they would have desired us to care for (our brothers and the other beneficiaries of our benefactors). Hence there is a lesser responsibility on a member of a community to deter a fellow member from doing some particularly gross immoral act on which he is intent. A husband has a duty to try to deter his wife from shoplifting; a German a duty to protest against his country's extermination of Jews. Failure to protest involves a share in the resulting guilt.

claim that if a man adopts a new moral attitude, he is 'morally another person' (p. 67), and so presumably atonement is not appropriate. However, our whole talk about personal identity does presuppose that a person remains the same person over time while his character may change, and so the later person bears the responsibility for the deeds of the earlier person. This presupposition of our ordinary talk may, of course, be challenged, but I believe that it is correct. See my *The Evolution of the Soul*, Clarendon Press, 1986, chs. 8 and 9. Oddly, Kant himself seems to go on to claim that it is appropriate that a man should allow himself to suffer for the deeds of his former self. But this suggestion does not seem consistent with the main drift of the argument.

These points having been made, a person is surely not responsible for, not guilty in respect of, the acts of others; above all, he is not guilty for the acts of others which he could not have influenced. And yet, there is a sense in which a person is 'involved' in the objective or subjective guilt of others of his community or others towards whom he has accepted voluntary responsibility—although he bears no guilt for it himself. This sense is that belonging to the community involves a duty to help others in the community with their burdens, and especially those others who are closest to us and to whom we owe most. But burdens are not only lack of food or housing. One of anyone's heaviest burdens is his past—his guilt, objective and subjective. I cannot share my friend's guilt, but I can treat it as my burden and help him to cope with it in the ways in which he needs to cope with it; and they include centrally the need to make atonement. If I have an obligation to my friend in his need, as I have been urging, then, since that includes the obligation to help with this need, the need for atonement, necessarily I am involved in his guilt. To take the strongest example—if my wife commits a horrible crime (which I had no notion that she was intending to commit, and for which I bear no responsibility and guilt myself), then, in so far as I can, I must help her to bear her burden (if she will let me) and treat it as mine. I must acknowledge that she has done the crime, and help her to atone for it. My involvement in the guilt of those less close to me is obviously less; but some involvement there will be.

I can help my friend to make atonement by encouraging him to repent and apologize, and providing the means for him to make reparation and penance if he does not have them himself.[10] But the word is 'help'; unless the wrongdoer participates in the process of 'atonement', his guilt is not removed. If my child damages your property, and I tell you that he apologizes profusely, I pay the damage and I give you a bottle of whisky at Christmas, my child's guilt remains. But I can help my child carry out the process of atonement—by encouraging him to set about it, by giving him the money to pay for the repairs and a penitential present, by helping him to repent, and by accompanying him to your door and providing him with the words of apology to utter. But it is he who must use what I

---

[10] Aquinas urges that, although confession has to be made and contrition shown by the sinner himself, 'satisfaction has to do with the exterior act, and here one can make use of instruments' (*Summa Theologiae* 3a. 48.2 ad 1), i.e. one can use reparation provided by others.

provide if he is to make the atonement. More I cannot do, if the atonement is to be his.

Since in doing wrong a wrongdoer brings upon others the obligation to help him cope with his guilt, it follows that he wrongs those of his community who were in no way able to save him from his actions—e.g. his children—but on whom he has brought involvement in his failure. He rightly apologizes to his children, that he 'let them down', that he brought on them the involvement in his failure.

6

Punishment

If the wrongdoer does not seek to remove his own guilt, it can in large part be removed by others. Others can take the reparation by force. As when there is voluntary atonement, reparation will need to include reparation for the inconvenience of temporary loss and the trauma and anxiety resulting from it. It will also need to include reparation for the hard work required to discover the wrongdoer's identity and the anxiety and danger involved in getting reparation. Also, since the wrongdoer does not at this stage offer a sincere apology with penance (for the apology would only be sincere if the sincerity was manifested in an attempt to make reparation), the penalty should include compensation for the harmful attitude or malevolent purpose of the wrongdoer towards the victim which he has made no attempt to disown; and thus it should include an element corresponding to the penance which the wrongdoer ought to have offered. Compensation beyond the reparation owed by one who makes voluntary atonement we may call the penalty; and the exacting of reparation, including the penalty, we may call the exacting of retribution.

The penalty, including compensation for the wrongdoer's hostile attitude, must include a reprimand expressing the victim's or (where, in a way we shall see shortly, the state acts as the victim's representative) the state's adverse moral judgement on the wrong-doer. Such public reprimand conjoined to the infliction of harm is a performative act which makes the infliction of harm an exacting of retribution, and not an act without justification which would legitimize further infliction of harm in return. By constituting the infliction of harm as meant and serious, it takes seriously the wrongdoer's hostility. By, for example, fining him purportedly because he has wronged the victim, and not simply to deter others from committing a similar crime, it treats the wrongdoer as a free agent, not as an object to be used for communal benefit. By attaching stigma to the wrongdoing, it may help the wrongdoer to see the evil of his ways; although that is only a by-product of something integral to punishment.[1] The act of retribution is often called revenge if it is carried out by the victim or someone close to him, punishment if it is carried out by an official in virtue of a more general authority than simply authority to make retribution of some sort when hurt personally. The victim of injury is said to take revenge when he injures his assailant in return, whereas if the state takes action to hurt the assailant in consequence of his act (whether by imprisonment, beating, or whatever), this is often termed punishment.[2]

If the distinction between punishment and revenge is made in these terms, revenge is rightly seen as a bad thing and (when rightly applied) punishment as a good thing in Western societies in the 1980s. That, however, I shall urge, obscures the fact that the primary justification for punishment is as a substitute for revenge in circumstances where it is better that some authority act as the agent of the victim in exacting his revenge. The fact that those circumstances hold in Western societies in the 1980s must not blind us to the fact that they do not always hold.

In future I shall call any infliction of harm as retribution for wrongdoing, whether by the victim or by some authority, punishment; and I shall argue that the only justification for an authority punishing is when it acts as an agent for the victim. Punishment in my sense will, I emphasize, include exacting the reparation which would be owed by one who made voluntary atonement but will go beyond it.

If you suppose that the state has a right to punish which has nothing to do with its acting as an agent for the victim, it becomes impossible to provide any satisfactory retributionist justification of punishment (i.e. punishment being justified because it constitutes retribution for harm done). For what else can justify the state effecting retribution? What gives *it* that right? What gives the state the right to effect retribution on one man for stealing from another? The only other available answer to that question is the answer of Kant and

---

[1] See Additional Note 2.

[2] J. R. Lucas claims wrongly that punishment differs from revenge, among other ways, 'in admitting of rational debate. If a man insults me, and I kill him, nobody can say that my revenge is excessive' (op. cit., pp. 130 f.). It certainly sounds a little odd to say that my 'revenge was excessive', but not at all odd to say that the retribution which I exacted in taking my revenge was excessive. Since the natural meaning of the former is the latter, I conclude that the oddness of the former is merely a matter of English style, rather than of any inherent conceptual oddity.

Hegel that there is good in hurt being attached to wrongdoing. The state has the right to attach the hurt, because it has the power to apply universal principles impartially.[3] But this answer seems implausible—there doesn't seem to be any natural good in hurt being attached to wrongdoing; and so we begin to look for justifications of punishment which have nothing to do with retribution, utilitarian answers which justify the imposition of harm involved in punishing the criminal in terms of the harm done promoting 'the greatest happiness of the greatest number'. Utilitarians argue that punishment is justified in so far as it prevents the criminal from committing more crimes (e.g. because he is imprisoned for a period), it reforms the criminal (and so he commits no more crimes even when released from imprisonment), and it deters others from committing such crimes in future (through fear of similar punishment). However, if the state's right to inflict harm derives from the utilitarian benefits of doing so, it should follow that it has such a right independently of whether he on whom the harm is inflicted committed a crime and independently of whether the harm inflicted is in any way proportional to the crime. Utilitarian answers justify judges in punishing someone as an example to the neighbourhood, allegedly for committing a crime, even if the man in question didn't commit the crime and the judge believes that he didn't commit the crime. They justify exemplary sentences on persons believed guilty, quite out of proportion to the severity of the crime, in order to deter others, when the crime is becoming prevalent. And they justify sending any adult to a school for moral education, just because he has supposedly criminal tendencies even though he has committed no crime. That utilitarian justifications of punishment have such morally implausible consequences must, I suggest, count decisively against them. It would be wrong to use people in these ways as tools for improving the general well-being. And yet, the feeling will remain, its efficacy in deterring, preventing, and reforming is relevant to the imposition of punishment; I hope to show in due course how a satisfactory retributionist justification of punishment can show the relevance.

A satisfactory retributionist justification must begin by insisting that the right to effect retribution belongs in the first instance to the victim.[4] Consider a 'state of nature', as depicted by Locke, such as

[3] See Additional Note 3.
[4] The view advocated here is very much that of John Locke, *Second Treatise on*

the Mid-West of the early nineteenth century, where there is no government and no police to impose laws, and men live in uneasy tension with their neighbours. *A* takes something material from *B*, or otherwise hurts him, intruding into his privacy, damaging his reputation, bruising him or maiming him. In that situation surely in general *B* has the right to take back from *A* the items stolen or something equivalent in value to the harm incurred, and also to take compensation for the trauma involved, the inconvenience of the temporary loss, the difficulty, anxiety and danger of getting reparation, and *A*'s malevolent purpose. Exacting retribution is a right, not a duty; there is nothing wrong in *B* not effecting adequate retribution on *A*—barring special circumstances—but there is nothing wrong in *B* effecting that retribution, if he so chooses. *A* in hurting *B* gives *B* that right against him.

In simple paradigm cases where some material thing is stolen, all this will, I hope, seem obviously correct. *A* steals *B*'s cow. *B* has the right to take the cow back, and more besides. But if so, then surely the same ought to hold when the harm done to *B* by *A* is of a different kind—injury, rape, slander, or whatever—and when it cannot be repaired. *A* must still owe *B* something in this situation, and it must be some equivalent of the harm caused and a penalty beyond. *A* in infringing *B*'s rights gives to *B* certain rights against him; since *B* has to exact the retribution from *A*, it is *B* who must choose (up to a limit of equivalent reparation including proper penalty) how the retribution is to be paid. If *A* has things which *B*

Civil Government, and his modern advocate, R. Nozick, *Anarchy, State, and Utopia*, Basic Books, 1974. Locke holds (sect. 4) that in a state of nature individuals may dispose of their possessions and persons as they see fit; and if others injure an individual or steal his property, the injured party and his agents may recover from the offender 'so much as may make satisfaction for the harm he has suffered' (sect. 10). But he goes on to distinguish 'satisfaction' (alias reparation or compensation) from 'punishment', which (sect. 11) he holds to be a right which belongs to everyone in a state of nature to impose on a criminal a penalty sufficient to deter the criminal and others from committing a similar crime in future. Nozick (op. cit., pp. 137–42) also makes this distinction, but is uncertain whether to follow Locke in his view about 'punishment'. Locke and Nozick both use 'punishment' to cover only some of the total retaliatory penalty which I am calling punishment. For myself I cannot see that one individual has the right to hurt another in order to deter third parties. But I think that the exaction of retribution (including a penalty for trauma, difficulty of getting reparation, and intentional malevolence) will often in fact deter. Both Locke and Nozick then see the rights to exact 'punishment' and 'satisfaction' as I do, in different ways, ceded to a state or something approximating thereto (Nozick's 'dominant protective agency').

desires, *B* can choose them, be they money, goods, or service. But if *A* does not have things which *B* can use, *B* nevertheless has a right to take things from *A*, even if he cannot use them. That gives *B* the right to subject *A* to imprisonment or unpleasant experiences of various kinds. For a debt is a debt; and even if the creditor cannot use the only things the debtor has, such as his liberty and freedom from pain, he still has the right to take them.

No penalty is owed additional to reparation sufficient to restore the status quo and compensate for temporary loss (and, if appropriate, for difficulty in catching the criminal) if the harm done is unintentional. In such a case the guilt is merely objective, and the punishment must not include any reparation for malevolent purpose. If by mistake I kill your cow and you see me do it, you have the right to take mine; but, unless I try to stop you, you have no right to take additional compensation. If I do some act which hurts you and seek to avoid being caught, but honestly believe that I had the right to do that act, you do not, I suggest, have the right to take any compensation for malevolent purpose. Courts often take it into account that a wrongdoer was acting in accordance with his own moral beliefs. A court may deem someone who refuses to pay taxes which will be used for making nuclear weapons not to be intending harm to the state but simply refusing to give to it that to which he believes it not to be entitled; hence it may give him a punishment closer to that appropriate to objective guilt rather than that appropriate to subjective guilt on top of objective guilt.

I have no general rule as to how reparation 'equivalent' to the harm done is to be calculated except in simple cases where something is stolen with a clear monetary value, let alone how the penalty for malevolent purpose, etc., is to be calculated. But consideration of many cases reveals ones where reparation is clearly too high or too low; calculating a monetary equivalent for injury is the regular and thankless task of assessors in injury cases before law courts.

A good clue as to whether the total retribution is too low is often provided by its deterrent effect. If, with fairly high rates of detection, retribution *R* does not in general suffice to deter criminals from committing crime *C*, even when apparently they are reasonably calculating in their criminality, that shows that they judge *C* worth doing despite (probable) *R*. In that case *R* cannot be much more of a loss that *C* is a gain. It cannot include much by way of penalty. If rates of detection are lower, then (because criminals gamble against getting caught) R may fail to deter even if it does constitute adequate retribution. Although I wish only to suggest that deterrent effect provides no more than a valuable clue as to when the amount of retribution is correct, my account does have the great advantage (for this as well as for other reasons which will shortly emerge) of showing how deterrence is relevant to punishment, without needing to say that punishment is simply a deterrent device, with all the horrors of injustice to which that leads.

There is, however, one natural equivalent in non-monetary terms to the harm done by bodily injury and death. If A deprives B of a certain power, does he not lose the right to his own power of that kind?—'an eye for an eye, and a tooth for a tooth' and (given that agents can act on behalf of the victim) 'a life for a life'. And if my account of punishment as reparation has this consequence, does that not suggest that something is wrong with it? Note, however, that any abhorrence we may feel at such reparation arises only for one special reason—that the reparation taken is unusable. If eyes become transplantable, and A puts out B's eye, then, I suggest, most of us (however liberally-minded) would agree that B has a right to A's eye. But taking an eye when you can't use it does seem barbaric. This, I suggest, indicates that the right to take reparation is subject to a qualification, that there is another obligation at work limiting the right to take reparation. And I suggest that the limiting obligation is as follows: it is wrong to cause to anyone a harm which serves no good purpose, and it is wrong to cause anyone a great harm unless it serves a very good purpose. The good purpose may be the inflicter of harm using what he takes from person harmed—be it property or a bodily organ. Or it may be one of utilitarian purposes of prevention, deterrence, and reform. But enjoying watching someone suffer does not count as a good purpose. So if a wrongdoer puts out a victim's eye, the victim has the right to take the wrongdoer's eye—but only if he can use it or if taking it serves some purpose of deterring others from committing such crimes in future (and the harm is such that it would have *clearly* to deter *very* many others); but the victim does not have the right to take it just for the pleasure of watching the wrongdoer suffer. If there are limits to retribution, I suggest that my qualification captures them. But the fact that there may be a qualification such as mine, or some further qualification as well, on the right to take reparation, does not, I suggest, call into question the basic rationale for punishment as retribution. Subject to possible qualifications—if you hurt me I have a right to exact reparation for harm, inconvenience, and trauma, and a penalty for the difficulty of getting reparation and for your malevolent purpose; I am entitled to retribution. But unless you hurt me I have no right to hurt you. That they provide considerations which limit the permissible use of punishment is a second way in which utilitarian considerations enter into issues of proper punishment without providing the rationale of punishment.

Another consideration which may help the reader to see that retribution is the basic rationale of punishment is one which, at first sight, may seem to count against that view. That is that mercy is a virtue. It is often (though not always) objectively meritorious if I do not exact retribution from an enemy who has hurt me—any retribution at all, that is, even within the suggested permissible limits. But there is no merit in not hurting someone who has done you no harm. For that is your duty anyway, and there is no merit in mere fulfilment of duty. Whereas to refrain from hurting someone who has hurt you is a work of supererogation; it goes beyond duty. And that can only be if, when another has hurt you, you *no longer* have a duty not to hurt him. Mercy can only be meritorious if retribution is a right. Mercy goes beyond justice.[5] And no one can understand what it is to show mercy who does not understand what it is to be just.[6]

The State's Right to Punish

One person may cede to another his right to take revenge either before or after he has become the victim of a particular injustice. I who am too weak to catch the thief or assailant may allow you to do it for me and exact my revenge. If I have a right to take something from another, surely I have the right to allow someone else to do the taking for me. Plainly too, some others, such as my children who owe me much, have a duty to defend my rights, if I cannot do so myself and ask them to do it for me. They owe me much. But there is, no doubt, a limit to what I can require of them in this respect. I can perhaps require them to take my watch back from a known thief

---

[5] See Additional Note 4.   [6] See Additional Note 5.

in the next village, but hardly require them to spend years tracking him down. Still, if they wish to seek retribution for me in this way and I allow them to do so, they have the right to get it on my behalf.

I can hand over my rights to exact retribution from those who wrong me, in advance of suffering wrong, to an impartial state. I can make a bargain with my fellow inhabitants of the Wild West to allow the police and the judge to make our retribution for us. There are obvious reasons why this is a good thing to do—reasons both of self-interest and of benefit to others. A *system* of justice with a police and judge is more likely to ensure that whoever is hurt for the crime really did the crime. That is to my advantage. It helps to ensure that my retribution finds the right target. Police are more likely than I am to catch a criminal, and judge (and jury) on the whole more likely than I am to check efficiently that someone caught by the police really committed the crime. It helps too to ensure that I am not hurt in case someone else falsely thinks that I have wronged them. Further, since wrongdoing only gives the victim (and thus his agent, the state) the right and not the duty to punish, there then arises the opportunity of using the exaction or remission of punishment for other good purposes, such as again the utilitarian ones of prevention of further crime by the criminal, deterring others, and reforming the criminal. The state's systematic use of punishment (up to the maximum allowed by retributive principles) makes the use of punishment for such purposes more efficacious than it would be by a lone individual. But since the state acts only as an agent for others, it must accept its instructions from those others as to the terms on which it is to administer justice. Those founding the state may agree that it should accept individual instructions from victims on each occasion as to the punishment to be exacted from wrongdoers; or that it should operate its right to punish only in accordance with a uniform policy.

However, whatever might have been the case with the first states of the Wild West, the right to punish was not handed over to police, and judge and jury by the explicit consent of inhabitants in Britain today. So how did the state get this right, if it was not given it by its inhabitants? The answer is that, as we saw in the last chapter, those who had no initial option whether to accept an obvious benefit must be presumed to have chosen to accept it and so to continue by choice to accept it until they explicitly reject it. They must be presumed to consent to a rational arrangement under which they live and into which they were born (having no choice about it) until they explicitly deny such consent. It is so obviously to the advantage of an individual to hand over to the state his right to revenge that only a madman would voluntarily 'put himself outside the law'. But if someone does insist on making himself an outlaw by refusing the state the right to punish on his behalf, my arguments suggest that he has this right. I do have the right to say that the state has no right to punish those who steal from me, injure me, blackmail me, and threaten my life. (And to some extent our own legal system recognizes this right, even when the victim has not made himself an outlaw. For many crimes, if the victim refuses to 'bring a charge' there is nothing which the police can do about it.) But the outlaw has no right to defend himself against the state justly punishing him. For the victims of his crimes have ceded their right to punish to the state. Does the outlaw then have the right to punish those who hurt him? Yes, but since the state is acting to defend the rights of those whom the outlaw would punish, it surely has the right derived from others who have ceded their rights to it, to ensure both that the right person is punished and that the punishment is no more than is due. If the outlaw refuses to the state the right to punish on his behalf, the state nevertheless retains the right, in the interests of those to be punished, to ensure that the outlaw does not get his hands on them until it can be seen that the outlaw will punish only the guilty and inflict no more than due punishment on them—and it will be seldom that it can be reasonably sure of all that.

Not that all punishment has been entrusted to the state. Most people would admit that parents have the right to punish their children (although they might disagree about its limits), a right which does not derive from the state. It can only derive from the fact that parents are responsible for the existence and flourishing of their children, and, in return for what they give to children, have a right to obedience (within limits), and hence a right to punish disobedience.

The state punishes not only those who wrong individual citizens (e.g. those who kill, rape, or steal from individual citizens) but also those who wrong the state itself and only wrong citizens *qua* members of the state. It punishes for treason, tax evasion, theft of state property, etc. The state acquires such right to punish through laws passed by some formal legislative process. A developed political philosophy must set out and justify what are the limits to the right to punish which it can acquire in this way—e.g. what legislative processes have to be gone through (do they have to be democratic?) and what are the limits to the rights it can acquire by such processes from individual citizens (e.g. by way of right to taxes and service) and so the violation of which it can punish. But however such a philosophy is developed, when the state does have the right to punish, it does so in virtue of being itself the victim or, to put it another way, as acting on behalf of all its citizens (other than the wrongdoer) who have indirectly been wronged by the 'crime against the state'. Either way, the state's right to punish derives from it being the victim or acting on behalf of the victim.[7]

Duty to Punish

In general, as I have stressed, the individual victim has no duty either to punish or not to punish. There are, however, exceptions. The victim may have duties to the wrongdoer or someone else which impose on him an obligation in this respect. A parent who is responsible for the education of his child may have a duty on occasion not to punish him for some offence—e.g. in a case when punishment would badly damage the child's character. Conversely, the parent has a duty to punish when punishment would have a significant beneficial effect on the child's character. Also, as with any other permissible act, the agent has a duty to punish or not to punish if he has promised some third party that he will do so. One parent may have promised the other that next time their child disobeys, he will punish it. However, when the individual has handed over his right to punish to the state, the state's officials have a duty to execute the state's general policy—which may (as I said) sometimes be simply to do as the victim wishes in this regard. Alternatively the policy could be that the official concerned should use his own

---

[7] The retributive theory of punishment which I have been developing has considerable similarities with the theory expounded by Herbert Morris ('Persons and Punishment' in J. G. Murphy (ed.), *Punishment and Rehabilitation*, Belmont, 1973). On this theory, wrongdoers take unfair advantage of law-abiding citizens and punishment restores the just equilibrium of benefits and burdens which was disturbed by the wrongdoer's act. For a useful exposition and defence of this theory, see C. L. Ten, *Crime, Guilt and Punishment*, Clarendon Press, 1987, 52–65. Ten's book generally is a useful elementary account of the various theories of punishment.

judgement of which punishment would be best on utilitarian grounds.

A number of recent writers in the retributionist tradition have seen that there is no duty to equate desert and well-being, but that there is a right to punish and that this right arises because the wrongdoer has infringed the rights of others. But they usually write as though the primary right belonged to the state.[8] One writer who gives an account along these lines is Alan Goldman,[9] who goes on to claim that there is a 'paradox' because the retributionist account will only justify a degree of punishment which is inadequate for utilitarian purposes. If you make the thief give back what he steals plus some compensation for the trouble caused, such a penalty won't deter people from stealing. You will only do that if you impose a hefty sentence, which goes beyond retribution. Retributionism is charged with excessive leniency. But even if we consider theft to be punished by a fine alone, this charge does not seem to me to be justified. Here, as with other crimes, we must add to the compensation for loss a penalty for the trouble and anxiety caused by the crime, a penalty for the harmful purpose of causing the loss, a charge for the cost of catching the criminal, proving his guilt, and exacting compensation. All this could add up to a considerable fine and one generally sufficient for deterrence. For if it is difficult to catch criminals, you will need a large established police force if you are to have a reasonable chance of doing so, and that is expensive. The resulting large fine may well suffice to deter. On the other hand, if catching the criminal is easy, and so the cost of doing so is smaller, a smaller fine will probably deter. Despite this, however, it may well be that the resulting punishments are inadequate for purposes of deterrence. My conclusion in that case is that justice must take precedence—individuals must not be punished more severely than their crime allows in order that honest citizens may sleep more peacefully at night. That simply is not just.

I wrote that showing mercy is often a supererogatory good. It will

---

[8] One writer near the mark was W. D. Ross, (*The Right and the Good*, Clarendon Press, 1930, 56–64) who claimed that the state has a prima-facie right to punish the guilty (i.e. a right which may be overridden by some other duty), and also a prima-facie duty to punish arising from its having in effect promised the victims and society that it will do so; and Ross also thought that the state had some prima-facie right to inflict injury in the public interest (whether or not the person injured had committed a crime). But he does not answer the question from where the state got these rights.

[9] 'The Paradox of Punishment', *Philosophy and Public Affairs*, 1979–80, **9**, 42–58.

not be so when for one of the reasons mentioned on the previous page the victim has a duty to punish; nor will it be so if there are good utilitarian benefits to be gained (e.g. by way of deterrence) from exacting proper punishment. Nor, I will now urge, will it be so when the victim (or his agent, e.g. the state) has previously given to the future wrongdoer a solemn undertaking that under certain circumstances he will punish. An undertaking to punish may, of course, be a promise to a third party, who then has the right to let the promiser off the obligation to punish, should he so choose. But a solemn undertaking may be made in such a way that it is not the giving of a right to require something to someone else who need not require it, but an undertaking to someone (who has probably not requested it) to do (or not do) something to him under certain circumstances, whatever he or anyone else requests when those circumstances occur. Such an undertaking, intended to be such that its force cannot later be undone, I will call a vow. A vow to do something wrong cannot make the doing of it good, let alone obligatory. If I vow to kill you when you have done no harm to me or anyone else, my vow cannot make it good that I should kill. But sometimes, where what I vow is morally indifferent (and perhaps even otherwise bad, though not wrong), my vowing to do it under certain circumstances can, I wish to suggest, make it good that I do it under those circumstances. I suggest that this happens when I make a vow to exact from you the punishment which I have a right to exact, if you do me some wrong; and where I make this vow in order to deter you from doing that wrong.

Consider the case of the utilitarian parent who wishes to deter his child from doing a non-repeatable wrong act. The child has stolen from the parent in the past and the parent has left only one valuable item—a picture, say, worth £1,000—and no prospect of acquiring any more valuables nor any income apart from that needed for immediate expenses. The parent wishes to deter the child from stealing the picture, selling it and spending the money on drink and drugs. So the parent threatens, 'If you steal the picture I will punish you.' But the child knows that the parent is a utilitarian and that if the child does steal the picture the parent will then consider whether he should punish or not according to whether there will be subsequent beneficial effects of punishing, e.g. whether punishment will deter from future crime. But if the child has stolen the parent's only valuable item, sold it, and wasted the proceeds, there will be no possibility of future crime from which to deter. And there may be no other good utilitarian reasons for punishing. In such a circumstance a utilitarian parent cannot deter.

More generally, a threat by an authority to punish will only deter a potential wrongdoer from committing a crime in a case where there will be no utilitarian benefits of punishing, should the crime actually be committed, if the potential wrongdoer believes that the authority will punish just because he has threatened and not for utilitarian reasons. The absence of any utilitarian benefit in punishing will, in the absence of other considerations, make it indifferent or bad to punish. So a good authority can only deter in such a situation if it is the case that the issuing of a threat, in the form of a vow, makes it good to punish when it would not otherwise be. This consideration that an important good purpose can only be served if (in the above sense) vows bind for the future, may convince the doubting reader that vows do bind for the future in such circumstances.

It may be urged that mine is a very artificial example which hardly ought to lead us to accept a very general moral principle. In general, surely, the fulfilment of threats will have an effect on other potential wrongdoers. Laws contain threats to punish, and if the punishment is administered when the laws are broken, others will be deterred from breaking them. However, my kind of problem could arise frequently in family or small community situations when crimes of certain kinds are infrequent and so there is no general reliable record of whether punishments threatened for them are carried out. A small country has a law that all those who use heroin must be punished by corporal punishment. Foreign visitors are rare, and no one in recent years has been caught using heroin. A potential wrongdoer from abroad, who is visiting the country for only a short visit, is considering whether to use heroin. He will be deterred if he thinks that the community have committed themselves by a vow to execute punishment which will make it good that they punish; but he will not be deterred if he thinks that the community believe that only utilitarian considerations should govern the execution of punishment; for they will know that the wrongdoer will shortly leave the country and it will be a long time before there are any more visitors; and when there are they will again doubt whether old-fashioned procedures of punishment should still be applied. Further, even if there are utilitarian considerations which make it good to punish when the crime is committed and there are known to be such, there may also be and be known to be utilitarian considerations which make it bad to punish. Here again the threat will only deter if it is regarded as a binding vow.

Note that I am not claiming that breaking a vow is as such wrong, for, on the account which I have defended, a wrong is a wrong to someone, and no person is wronged when the vow is broken. But I am claiming that breaking a vow of this kind is bad; in the terminology of Chapter 1, infravetatory. A good person will not break his vows, though there is wrong done only if the vow is also a promise.

Vows, other than vows to punish, may have similar beneficial effects when it is believed that the vower intends to keep them, even when there are no utilitarian benefits in doing so. Consider some difficult task in which two persons co-operate, which will only be completed if both work hard at it. They therefore undertake to each other that they will both work hard at it. Now the undertaking may be regarded as a mere promise to the other party, such that the promisee can remit the promiser's obligation to keep it; or it may be regarded as a vow which cannot be remitted. If the undertaking is a promise, then when the task proves difficult there would be nothing bad in one party trying to persuade the other that they should both give up, and it might then be kind and so good for the latter to agree to the former's request. The task would then not be completed. But if the undertaking is regarded as a binding vow, then it would never be good to give up and so it would never be good to try to persuade the other party to give up. Since the question of giving up would therefore never arise for good co-workers, they will complete their task. The application to the way in which the marriage 'vow' to be 'faithful till death us do part' is understood should be apparent.

Completing the Theory

Just as atonement can be made even if the victim is dead, so too can punishment be exacted when the victim is dead. The victim's representatives may collect his debts on behalf of his heirs, and punishment, as I have represented it, is a debt. The representatives have no obligation to punish, unless they have promised to do so. (The state in effect gives such a promise if it makes the death penalty mandatory for murder.) But there is an obvious good in ensuring that murder is punished in so far as the punishment deters would-be murderers.

So, I have been arguing, punishment is the forcible taking of the due reparation which is offered voluntarily in atonement. The taking of punishment removes all the effects of wrongdoing which someone other than the wrongdoer can remove. But there is more that can be done to undo the act; and that is that the wrongdoer himself repent and apologize, and until that is done his moral guilt remains.

When the wrongdoer makes atonement, the victim has, as we saw, within limits, the power to keep him guilty by refusing forgiveness. But if the victim, or the state on his behalf, exacts retribution, it is entering into a process of attempting to restore the status quo. The victim has no right to refuse to restore the status quo on the grounds that the punishment taken constitutes insufficient reparation (including penalty), for it is a wrong to the wrongdoer to punish him and then treat him as though it had not done so. In announcing and then exacting a certain punishment, the state commits itself to that punishment constituting sufficient reparation. But, on the other hand, purported forgiveness where there is no apology involves refusing to take the wrongdoer's hostility seriously, and so is ineffective in removing guilt. Some, however half-hearted, repentance and apology is necessary for the removal of guilt, and, within limits, the victim can judge when that suffices and then forgive. Forgiveness involves the restoration of personal relationships, treating the wrongdoer as one who has not wronged you in those. The victim as a person can have personal relations with the wrongdoer. The state deals impersonally with people (gives them money or rights, but is not their friend). If punishment has been exacted, it seems to me the duty of the victim or the state to restore the status quo as regards formal relations, for that involves only external matters (restoring to the punished criminal his vote and right to social security). For otherwise the wrongdoer would have been penalized, both for the hurt caused and for his malevolent purpose in causing it, by punishment, and then treated as though he had not been punished. Yet the state cannot do more than restore formal relations, and talk of the state 'forgiving' seems inappropriate (except in the sense of giving a 'pardon' which is either a formal announcement that it will not punish for a crime committed or a formal recognition that, despite its having punished, no crime was committed). Forgiving must surely remain the prerogative of the victim, even if he has entrusted his right to exact reparation to the state.

Can someone else be punished instead of the wrongdoer? There are many cases in history of heroic men offering to take the punishment (corporal, capital, or whatever) instead of another. What happens is that the wrongdoer by his wrong act loses certain rights—e.g. the right to property or not to be injured or killed. If some saint then offers the state a bargain—that the state return to the wrongdoer his right to life or whatever in return for the right to the saint's life, which the saint has the right to cede to the state, then if the state accepts that bargain, the saint loses his right to life and the wrongdoer regains his. But here too the wrongdoer's guilt still remains unless he repents and apologizes—no one else can do that for him.

We saw in Chapter 3 that an agent is only praiseworthy or blameworthy if he has free will. It follows that he will only be subjectively guilty or meritorious if he has free will, and so the various responses which we have described in Chapters 4, 5, and 6 as appropriate to subjective merit or guilt will only be in place if he has free will. However, even without free will, there would still be objective merit and guilt, and in Chapter 4 I described the responses appropriate to objective merit, and in Chapter 5 the responses appropriate to objective guilt. In essence they are simply responses which compensate for the beneficial or harmful effects of actions, without taking into account any benevolent or malevolent purpose of the agent. If man did not have free will, punishment should also ignore malevolent purpose. Punishment would be merely the exacting of reparation for the harmful effects of actions.[10]

There might, I believe, also be a further effect on punishment of any serious acknowledgment that man does not have free will. From what do man's rights to life and liberty derive? Is it merely from his status as a conscious being capable of having sophisticated beliefs, including moral beliefs, and performing sophisticated actions? Or is it from such status together with his having the capacity to choose freely between good and evil and thereby determine how things will go in the world? If it is his having free will (actually, or in the case of babies, potentially) which gives him this status, then the discovery that he did not have free will would lead us to see that there would be

[10] See Additional Note 6.

nothing wrong in punishing someone for some crime he did not commit, or punishing him with a punishment which would normally be regarded as excessive, for the sake of utilitarian benefits to others. However, I shall not pursue this issue further, as I am in general making the assumption that man does have free will and working out the consequences of that.

7
Man's Moral Condition

In previous chapters I have been concerned very broadly with what makes for human goodness and badness. It is time now to use these results to comment on a feature of the actual human condition.

We saw in Chapter 1 that the goodness of a rational agent consists in goodness of action and goodness of character. He is good in so far as he does supererogatory good actions, and thus acquires merit, and in so far as he refrains from wrong actions; if he does wrong actions, he acquires a guilt from which he must purge himself in the way described in the last two chapters. Goodness of character has three aspects—goodness of desires, of beliefs, and of will. One who seeks goodness of character must aim at making himself naturally prone to pursue the good as he sees it, try to hold true beliefs about wherein the good consists, and try to make himself naturally prone to pursue the things which are good.

Objective, spontaneous, and subjective good acts are all as such good; but one who seeks to do good will seek the good character from which acts will flow which have all three kinds of goodness (and so acts which will not be maximally subjectively good). Conversely, the badness of an agent consists in badness of action and character. He is bad in so far as he does bad, and especially wrong, actions, and thus acquires guilt from which he must purge himself. Acts which are objectively, spontaneously, or subjectively bad are all as such bad. Badness of character involves badness of desires, badness of beliefs, and weakness of will; and in so far as he has a bad character, an agent will be naturally inclined to do bad acts of the various kinds.

As we saw in Chapter 2, human choices of action at any given time are made in the light of beliefs about what is morally good to do, and under the influence of desires which incline to actions of various kinds with strengths independent of the believed moral worth of the actions; desires being inclinations making it easy and natural to perform actions. Each of us can, however, act at a given time so as gradually to form our future character. But nature and nurture, our genes and our upbringing that is, begin to form our character before ever we can ourselves try to mould it; and as it forms it makes it harder or easier for us to act to change it according to the sort of character we acquire. Although humans are vastly different from each other in many aspects of their character, there is one central common feature of human character, which it is important for us now to note.

It is characteristic of human desire that many human desires and many of the strongest human desires, the ones with which we are born or to which physiological processes give rise as we grow older, that they are in each of us for our own believed future enjoyment. The bodily desires for food, drink, and comfort and the more sophisticated desires for power and admiration, love and company which evolve in us independently of language and culture (as we can see from the fact that the higher animals also have such desires) are self-centred desires, desires centred on oneself receiving bodily satisfaction and certain attitudes of respect and affection and obedience from others. There are also inborn altruistic desires, desires for the well-being of one's offspring, friends, fellow-workers, etc. (which find their ancestry in the desires of animals for the well-being of their offspring and social group). But these altruistic desires operate alongside the selfish desires and can often be quite weak.

In consequence human desires often conflict—in the sense that if my desire is satisfied, yours cannot be. Some desires, such as many desires for power and love, are such that conflict between them is logically necessary. My desire to be the sole ruler and your desire to be the sole ruler cannot both be satisfied; and your desire that Angela should love you and you alone cannot be satisfied at the same time as my desire that Angela love me and me alone. Some desires are such that whether or not they conflict depends on features of the world external to the desires. Whether your desire for a good meal and my desire for a good meal can both be satisfied depends on how much food there is. And my altruistic desire that my children should have a good education will be in conflict with your altruistic desire that your children should have a good education, when and only when there are only a limited number of places at good schools.

But clearly men are so made that some of their desires will always conflict, whatever the state of the earth; and the earth has always been such and maybe always will be such that many other human desires conflict. Humans and the earth are made that way. And although they can be modified by education, such conflicting desires are not the product of education—for they exist in babies and, as I have urged, in our own immediate animal ancestors, the apes and monkeys.

And yet it is no necessary truth about rational creatures that their desires be in conflict in some environment. It is easy enough to imagine a community of beings, all of whose desires were for the same things (e.g. the satisfaction of the bodily needs of all equally), and so not in conflict in any environment. The community would be like a community of ants, only much more intelligent. But it is a fundamental contingent truth about *humans* that they are not like this; and it is nature, not nurture—genes, not environment, which is responsible for it. It stems, I have suggested, from the very basic feature of human desire that (but for education and self-discipline) each of us desires in large part only that which he believes that he himself will enjoy.

But while two humans may desire each for himself the same thing, often only one of them will have a right to it; and even if it is not already owned, there are limits to the steps which it is morally permissible to take to stop the other getting it. We may both desire Angela, but if she is already married to you, I have no right to seek to get her to become my wife. And even if the small amount of food is not already owned and so we both have some right to try to get it, it would be wrong for me to break your leg in order to get to the food first. And yet our selfish desires are so strong that they influence us to satisfy them even when it would be wrong to do so. And so there is in man a proneness to objective wrongdoing, whether or not man realizes it. The strongest desire of all, which influences us to fail to fulfil our obligations (as also to fail to do acts of supererogatory goodness) is the desire to rest, sloth. Fulfilling obligations requires effort, and effort is often hard. But again it is no necessary truth that all agents should have a desire to rest; men could easily have been made so that they continued to work without a desire to stop until, needing rest, they suddenly fell asleep.

There could be creatures without desires at all, who simply chose what to do on the basis of reason alone. There could be creatures who had desires but whose desires were only operative in situations where they did not conflict with reason, when they gave rise to no temptation to act for less than the best. There could be creatures whose desires were always for the best, including the well-being of

others. Human desires are not like that. They are often selfish, and
they operate in situations where selfishness is objectively wrong.
Humans are subject to wrong desires, in consequence of which they
often do objectively wrong actions spontaneously. When a desire is
combined with a belief that the action desired is wrong, we get an
inclination to do what is believed wrong. Agents are subject to
weakness of will, in consequence of which they often do intentionally
wrong actions. Man's first moral insights were, no doubt, confused
and often erroneous. But at least part of their original content must
have been to lay down limits to the indulgence of desires in conflict
with those of others. Desire being desire, a man would then be in a
situation of temptation, under pressure to fulfil a desire which he
believed wrong. Man would then have a proneness to subjective
wrongdoing. Man's first morality might also have been concerned
with duties to worship. Although man might desire to worship, as
well as believe that he ought, such a desire would be in inevitable
conflict with other desires, above all the desire to rest; and so again
produce a proneness to subjective wrongdoing.

The proneness to subjective wrongdoing is reinforced by men
refusing to acknowledge to themselves their moral beliefs, refusing
to discover the consequences of their actions and hiding from
themselves the fact that they have so refused. This is the process
which produces the wickedness of the obedient official who
organizes the Holocaust. He hides from himself the consequences of
his actions (he doesn't know, he says, what happens to the Jews
whose transport he has been arranging), and he pretends to himself
that he does not have obligations to any wider community,
acknowledging only his duty to his superiors. The temptation to
conceal from ourselves the moral obligations we begin to recognize is
present in all of us, even if the luck of our circumstances prevents
our actions from having so evil a nature. This self-deceit is the
process which turns mere moral weakness (failing to act on the moral
obligations we acknowledge) into what looks like deliberate wickedness (and would be that but for the agent's success in blinding
himself to the nature of his action).[1]

When did objective wrongdoing appear on the evolutionary scene?
We do not consider that there is any wrongdoing in the tiger killing

[1] I am much indebted to Mary Midgley, *Wickedness*, Routledge and Kegan Paul,
1984, ch. 6, for bringing out the importance of self-deceit in generating wickedness.

his fellow creatures, including man. Yet we do consider that there is wrong in man killing man. Why do we make this difference? Surely it is because man is capable of making moral distinctions, of coming to believe that certain acts are morally right and others morally wrong (even if he does not see that a particular killing is morally wrong), that he is subject to objective moral obligations. So the arrival on the scene of moral beliefs (true or false) turned their possessors into moral agents, and thus made certain acts obligatory to do, and others obligatory not to do. Hence objective and subjective wrongdoing arrived on the evolutionary scene together. The first stirring of man's conscience which showed a capacity to understand what duty is, made some actions of his which he had a desire to do objectively wrong when they were not that before, and thus made him prone to objective wrongdoing; and also in giving him the inclination to act contrary to that conscience, made him prone to subjective wrongdoing. (I assume here that when man acquired moral beliefs he already had the capacity to act or not to act on his evaluative beliefs, i.e. free will. If free will came later than moral awareness, subjective wrongdoing arrived later than objective wrongdoing.)

For the propensity to wrongdoing then there is necessary both moral belief and desire centred on self or on one's own. But the fact of moral belief is good; it simply serves as the trigger which turns desires of certain sorts into a proneness to wrongdoing. While the transmission of moral belief is a cultural phenomenon, the transmission of the bad part, as it were, of the proneness to wrongdoing is biological, through our genes. Although the core of original wrongdoing is something transmitted genetically, environment plays a large role in determining whether its effects are magnified or not. To start with, as we have just noted, there is the paradox that only when moral belief is added to human desires are some human actions constituted as objectively wrong, and humans exhibit a proneness to subjective wrongdoing. And the transmission of moral belief, which is a social process, continues that proneness. Yet the fact that a man believes some act to be morally good will provide a counter-influence to desire, and may lead to actions which through habit develop good desires—so long as the morality taught is a true one.

The third aspect of bad character, additional to badness of desire and weakness of will, is badness of belief, i.e., false moral belief; and which moral beliefs a man acquires is considerably influenced by which ones are transmitted in his society. As I claimed in Chapter 1, the very fact of false moral beliefs, whatever their effect on conduct, is itself a corruption of character. Bad beliefs, as well as bad desires, are a disease of the soul. As I argued in Chapter 1, in order to be a morality at all a system of conduct must appeal to some of the distinctions which we recognize as moral distinctions—for example, it must recognize a duty to repay debts and keep promises, *or* a duty to respect property, *or* a duty to feed your starving neighbour, *or* something which we recognize as morally obligatory. But while taking off from distinctions which we recognize, it may fail to commend courses of conduct which we recognize as natural extrapolations therefrom (e.g. while recognizing a duty to help a starving Jew it may not recognize a duty to help a starving Gentile); or, it may commend distinctions which we see as incorrect extrapolations (e.g. while seeing that certain crimes ought to be punished it may devise a barbarous method of punishment). Or, through simple factual ignorance, society may not recognize that its moral principles have applications to certain cases—for example, through failing to realize that there is a God, it may fail to teach the duty of gratitude towards him.

By teaching an inadequate morality, society will fail to give men reason for pursuing the good. And by teaching a false morality it will give them reason for pursuing the bad. Morality will thus fail to put a brake on wrong desires. False moral beliefs will strengthen wrong desires, and so increase objective wrongdoing. Also, false moral teaching may conflict with a man's own true moral intuitions (perhaps ones very tentative and not even put into words). This may lead to the man having a general disregard for the moral teaching of the society which under normal circumstances would reinforce in him a desire for the good, and that, combined with his own doubts about his own moral intuitions, may lead to a general weakening of resolve to pursue the good. In this way false moral teaching may make for weakness of will and so increase subjective wrongdoing also.

Weakness of will, proneness to subjective wrongdoing, may have its power strengthened or weakened, not merely by false teaching, but by bad example. Even if the society's moral teaching is correct and so regarded by some man, it may be treated with such casualness and levity that the desire to imitate other men which would otherwise reinforce pursuit of the good now acts in a contrary direction, making it easier to yield to temptation. Conversely the power of good example is of course enormous.

So the genetically transmitted proneness to objective wrongdoing is wakened by morality to become a proneness to subjective wrongdoing. But this original proneness may be reinforced by a socially transmitted process; as it also may be weakened by such a process. An ideal education system would work by teaching and example to weaken bad desires and reinforce good ones. But systems of education approaching such an ideal system are rare, and there is an explanation for this rarity in the genetically transmitted proneness to wrongdoing itself. Men being, as a result of their genetic inheritance, prone to yield to bad desires, they are prone in particular to yield to the desires which lead to their failing to take seriously ideas which would lead to their developing a less selfish morality, and to yield to the desires which lead to their treating morality with levity and so to their becoming a bad example and a bad instructor of others. The genetically transmitted proneness to wrongdoing gives rise to and encourages a socially transmitted proneness. Badness of desire and weakness of will is the human condition, liable to be reinforced by false moral belief; it began when men first acquired moral beliefs, and is the lot of each subsequent man. The same factors which produce a proneness to wrongdoing obviously produce also a proneness not to do supererogatory good acts. Men have little natural desire to be saints and heroes, and in the beliefs and examples which it transmits society may often fail to encourage sanctity and heroism.

That there is in humans this proneness to wrongdoing is something which has been recognized in some form or other by all religions and by most poets and artists who have given any thought to the human condition. Note that it is not a proneness to do what is wrong because it is wrong, it is a proneness to do what is wrong *despite* the fact that it is wrong.

In virtue of their bad character, humans have, of course, often done great wrong (objective and subjective) to other men and other animals and humans have acquired a load of guilt, much of it unatoned and unpunished.

I do not wish to deny, of course, the good deeds which men have done and the merit acquired; and the good aspects of character which they have acquired partly through nature and nurture and partly through the hard work of self-reformation; and I shall have more to say about that in a later chapter. But I have drawn attention here to the conflict in men between some of their strongest genetically inherited desires and their culturally inherited moral beliefs; and to the partial corruption of character to which this conflict almost inevitably leads.

PART II

Its Theological Consequences

8

Morality Under God

Theological Assumption

The first six chapters of Part I were devoted to analysing what makes for the moral goodness or badness of agents, and what are the moral consequences which flow from their doing good or harm to others, by way of merit and guilt and the need for reward, punishment, atonement, and forgiveness. The final chapter of Part I drew attention to an important contingent feature of the human moral condition—our proneness to wrongdoing.

In Part II I now move to apply these results to assessing Christian theological doctrines concerned with man's present moral status and his future destiny. A Christian theological system is, of course, an integrated web of doctrine; and the ground for believing some doctrines to be true is often that they follow from others which in turn have their justification in considerations outside the theological system. Justification for the doctrines of man's status and future with which I am concerned lies partly in other theological doctrines and partly in considerations of moral theory. As I wrote in the Introduction, however, it is misleading to speak of 'the' Christian doctrine on any of the theological issues with which we shall be concerned. On each of these theological issues there are two or more rival positions within the Christian tradition, and each position has been defended partly by adducing other doctrinal claims and partly by adducing moral claims.

My way of attempting to sort things out will be to take the crucial elements of other doctrines common to various theological positions, and see what follows from them and from the moral theory for which I have argued in Part I, for the issues of man's status and future. These crucial elements I will call my 'theological assumption'. Adopting it does not beg any of the questions at stake between the different theological positions in any obvious way.

My theological assumption is this: that there is a God, that is, a being necessarily omnipotent, omniscient, perfectly free, and perfectly good, the creator who made and keeps in being the world and the natural laws which govern its operation—and hence (indirectly) made and keeps in being us men and the framework within which we operate; that he became incarnate in Christ who was both God and man, lived a saintly human life, allowed himself to be crucified (that life and death being openly intended by him as an offering to God to make expiation in some way for the sins of men), that he rose from the dead, founded a Church to carry on his work, and seeks man's eternal well-being in friendship with himself. (By Christ's living a saintly human life I mean that, both objectively and subjectively, he fulfilled all his obligations, and was ever, both subjectively and objectively, doing works of supererogatory goodness.)

This is, of course, a detailed theological assumption, but it is concerned with matters other than man's status and future. (In claiming that Christ 'openly intended' his death to make expiation, it is making a purely historical claim about the publicly expressed intentions of the historical Jesus Christ. It does not state whether or how that intention was fulfilled. In claiming that God 'seeks' man's eternal well-being, I make no assumptions about how far he will pursue his goal despite man's unwillingness to co-operate.) The arguments for some parts of my theological assumption will be arguments of natural theology, and the arguments for other parts will be both philosophical (e.g. showing that the concept of an incarnation is coherent) and historical. In calling my assumption an 'assumption' I do not in the least imply that it cannot be given adequate justification. It is simply that that is what I take for granted for the purposes of Part II of this book. Philosophy and theology are such integrated subjects that one's views on one issue are affected crucially by one's views on other issues, and we have to start somewhere. (I myself have provided arguments of natural theology for the earlier parts of the assumption in my book *The Existence of God*.)[1] Those who do not accept my theological assumption may nevertheless be interested in what consequences flow from it, whether the assumption has the consequences about human redemption, the availability of the means of grace and the hope of glory

[1] Clarendon Press, 1979.

which Christian theology has claimed. In other words, what difference would it all make? I shall argue that if there is a God who has acted as I have described, the moral worth of man is very much lower than it would otherwise be, for he fails to perform obligations which he would not otherwise have; but his prospects for the future are infinitely brighter.

Consequences for obligation and supererogation

Some Christians have maintained that, if there were no God, nothing would be obligatory or wrong, or even morally good or bad. I would, however, judge that this has not been a very common position among sophisticated theologians (if only because Christian theologians have not very often considered the question of what would be the moral situation if there were no God), and I have assumed the contrary position in Part I. There are certain minimal duties to one's fellow men which are duties whether or not there is a God—both positive duties (to tell the truth and to keep promises—possibly subject to certain qualifications) and negative duties (to refrain from murder and torture, rape, and theft). And other acts are good, even if not obligatory, and remain good, whether or not there is a God—to feed the starving in distant lands, to found a school, or die to save a brother's life.

Among duties are obligations to benefactors. There is the duty of children (within limits) to do what their parents tell them, or what will please their parents—and far more so if the parents are not simply biological parents but parents who at much cost have fed and educated their children and brought them to maturity. We owe a debt of gratitude to those who have given to us and conserved in us that gift which is the precondition of all other good things—the gift of life itself (to the extent, perhaps, to which that gift was the deliberate bringing to life and sustaining and forming of a person, rather than an unintentional accident which cost nothing). As we saw in Chapter 5, there is a duty to parents to make something worthwhile of our lives; and clearly it is good that we should do so, even if there is no duty to do so. *A fortiori*, if there is a God, men have a greater duty by far to obey his commands and to do what will please him. For our existence at each moment and all that we have depends on him—while our dependence on our parents is very limited in time (limited to occasional periods in the first years of our life), and in degree (other humans—our teachers and neighbours—help to educate us—and it is only by God's sustaining power that parents or anyone else can form and educate us). Man's dependence on God is so total that he owes it to him to live a good life. Hence when a man fails in any objective or subjective duty to his fellows, he also fails in his duty towards God, his creator. I shall follow common usage in calling failure in a duty to God sin. If a man does what is wrong (whether or not he realizes it), he sins objectively. If he does what he believes to be wrong, acts against his conception of the good, he sins subjectively. He may sin subjectively without believing that he wrongs God his creator (for he may not believe that there is such a God); if he sins, believing that he wrongs God, his subjective sin is of course much worse. Because a man's dependence on God is so much greater than a child's dependence on his parents, so there is a duty on a man to make much more of his life pleasing to God than there is a duty on the child to make his life pleasing to his parents.

If, further, as I have assumed, God seeks man's eternal well-being in friendship with himself, then there is a pattern of life and a goal of fulfilment open to man, which would not otherwise be available. The greatest human well-being is to be found in friendship with good and interesting people in the pursuit of worthy aims. God is a better friend with more interesting aspects of himself to reveal than human friends (an infinitely better friend with infinitely more aspects) and he has worthwhile tasks which men can share with him in bringing themselves and others to reconciliation with each other and God, and to growth in the contemplation of God and the Universe which he made, and to beautifying that Universe. If there is a God, such tasks will necessarily be vastly more worthwhile than secular tasks—for there will be a depth of contemplation of the richness of life of a person, God, open to man which would not be open to him if there is no omnipotent and omniscient being; and there will be the infinite time of an after-life which God, seeking his well-being, is able to make available to man to help in the beautifying of the world and the spiritual healing of his fellow men. And God, unlike any human, is a necessary being, a being who is the ultimate source of being and therefore of a kind quite other than finite things; the entering into contact with him has a richness and mystery and meaning which Otto so vividly described as the 'numinous', which cults and ceremonies vainly try to bring home to the worshipper and on which at the theoretical level Kant commented as follows:

Unconditioned necessity which we so indispensably require as the last bearer of all things, is for human reason the veritable abyss. Eternity itself, in all its terrible sublimity, as depicted by a Haller, is far from making the same overwhelming impression on the mind; for it only *measures* the duration of things, it does not *support* them.[2]

God offers us the prospect of eternal well-being of such a character. Because if there is a God there is so much more to be made of our lives than there would be otherwise; we let down those who give us life, above all God, if we fail to take any steps to make something of that life.

Just as a child lets his parents down so much more if he fails to take advantage of big opportunities which they have provided for him than if he fails to take advantage of small opportunities, so if God has made available to man the opportunities which I have described, man's failure to avail himself of them is a great wrong to God.

Because of man's total dependence on God, if there is a God, and because the possibilities for man are of a vastly different kind in quality and quantity, if there is a God, it follows that acts which otherwise would be supererogatorily good or not good at all become obligations; and failure to perform them is sin. If there is no God, man has no obligations to use his talents of reason and imagination to understand the nature of the Universe and to help others to do so, good though it is that these things be done. But if all talents depend totally on God, and if by using our talents in part in these ways we can begin to fit ourselves and others over a few years of earthly life to recognize God and so enjoy his beatific vision in the hereafter, then to use our lives in part thus passes into the realm of the obligatory. And some acts become obligatory which would not even be good otherwise—e.g. worship. If God made us, we have a duty to express our gratitude; and if God is as holy and wonderful a necessary being as I have posited, it is good that we should express our reverence; but, if there is no God, all worship is a pointless activity. So while the existence of God makes what is wrong anyway more wrong (because it becomes also a wrong against God), and what is obligatory anyway more so, it also shifts the boundaries between the

[2] I. Kant, *Critique of Pure Reason* B461.

obligatory and the supererogatory good, and the good, the indifferent, and the bad. Christian theologians have, however, differed as to just where the new boundaries lie; as to what proportion of our life we owe to God. I shall shortly be arguing that, while our obligations are much greater if there is a God, they do not cover the whole of our lives. Failure to lead a perfect life is not a failure of duty. I do not *owe* God my smallest thought or my lightest word.

I referred earlier to the view that if there is no God, nothing is good or bad. A slightly more sophisticated theological position is that *if* there is a God, he has the authority to command or forbid any action, and his commands alone make acts obligatory and his prohibitions alone make acts wrong. What he neither commands nor prohibits is morally indifferent; there is no scope for supererogatory goodness. Compatibly with his perfect goodness, God could command or forbid anything, and any such command or prohibition would impose an obligation to fulfil it. God could command us to steal or commit adultery, to torture—or even to hate God; and if he were so to command, his commands would impose on us the corresponding obligation. (Unlike the earlier, slightly cruder view, this view formally allows that if there were no God, acts might still be obligatory or wrong, good or bad, for other reasons.)[3]

In Plato's dialogue *Euthyphro*, Socrates asked the question: 'Is that which is holy loved by the gods because it is holy, or is it holy because it is loved by the gods?'[4] Put in Christian terms (and, for simplicity's sake, phrased simply in terms of command and obligation), the Euthyphro dilemma becomes: Does God command what is obligatory for other reasons, or is what is obligatory obligatory because God commands it? The view cited in the previous paragraph takes the second horn of this dilemma. Few Christian theologians have taken the first horn and claimed that God's command makes no difference to what is obligatory. Surely if we owe to God our life from moment to moment, that gives him some rights over us in respect of how we use that life. The whole

---

[3] One or other position is to be attributed to William of Ockham. See the exposition of Ockham's views on the status of morality in F. Copleston, *A History of Philosophy*, iii, Burns and Oates, 1953, 103–10. See too the Ockhamist Gabriel Biel— 'The reason why the divine will accepts things as thus or thus, is not a goodness found independently in objects by God but the reason lies only in the divine will, which accepts things as having such and such a degree of goodness; that is why they are good to that degree, and not vice versa'—*Canonis missae expositio*, 23E.

[4] *Euthyphro* 9e.

Christian tradition has had it as a fairly central tenet that it does. However, a few liberal Protestants have taken the contrary view, and held that duties are confined to this-world duties; Kant is the best-known example of a thinker who has held that position.[5]

More common in Christian thought than either of these extreme positions is the view that some actions are obligatory (wrong, good, or bad) apart from God's will; and some actions depend on God's will for their moral status. There are limits to what God, compatibly with his perfect goodness, can command or forbid; and hence, since he is necessarily perfectly good, to what he will command or forbid. There exist necessary moral truths which do not depend for their truth on the will of God and to which, in virtue of his necessary goodness, he will conform. Theologians have differed as to just how extensive these necessary truths are. Duns Scotus held that the only necessary moral obligations from which God could not dispense us were the duties to love and reverence God himself[6] (viz. the first three of the Ten Commandments). God could dispense us from the obligation not to have sexual intercourse with other than a spouse, or the obligation not to kill. Although Aquinas seems to claim that the unalterable 'first principles of natural law'[7] are more extensive than does Scotus, he does not state clearly where the line is to be drawn between unalterable 'first principles' and alterable 'secondary precepts'; and his examples do not suggest that his position is very different from that of Scotus.[8]

I suggest, however, that the limits to the commands to men which God can issue and which thereby impose obligations on us are narrower than the limits drawn by Scotus. They are limits both to the areas over which God has absolute authority and to the amount of service men are obliged to render. One powerful consideration in support of the former claim is that any duty to obey God must arise from certain properties which he has—e.g. being our creator. And

---

[5] See e.g. his *Religion Within the Limits of Reason Alone*, trans. T. M. Greene and H. H. Hudson, Harper and Row, 1960, 142—'There are no special duties to God in a universal religion'; and his *Lectures on Philosophical Theology*, trans. A. W. Wood and G. M. Clark, Cornell University Press, 1978, 159—'The knowledge of God . . . must not determine whether something is morally good or a duty for me. This I have to judge from the nature of things.'

[6] Ordinatio III, suppl. dist. 37, text and translation on pp. 268–87 and commentary on pp. 60–4 of Allan B. Wolter (ed.), *Duns Scotus on the Will and Morality*, Catholic University of America Press, 1986.

[7] *Summa Theologiae* 1a. 2ae. 94 4 and 5.

[8] See the spelling out in *Summa Theologiae* 1a. 2ae. 100.8.

why these properties give rise to an obligation will be because of some general principle, for example, that one ought to show gratitude to benefactors. But then it will follow that we also have a duty to show gratitude to our human benefactors (even if they only benefit us because God permits them to do so). Our theological assumption can only refine and deepen our views about what is obligatory and what is good, it cannot lead to their total replacement. No doubt God as our creator may command us to do what we ought to do anyway (e.g. fulfil our promises to our fellow humans), just as a human parent may command his children to do what they ought to do anyway; and in that case it becomes doubly a duty to do the act in question, and failure to do it becomes doubly wrong. No doubt, too, God may commend us to do what he does not command, for example, what will promote our eternal well-being. But a commendation imposes no obligation.

Some of the examples by which Scotus illustrates his thesis that God can dispense from any obligations except those of love and reverence to himself are more convincing than others which he might have discussed. Certainly (at any rate, within limits) God can allow a man to take a possession from another—for God it is who gives to men from moment to moment their possessions and he can transfer the right to a possession from one man to another without violating any man's rights. He could thus allow the latter to take the possession by force; forcible taking only becomes theft when not permitted by God. And likewise God, who gives to men from moment to moment their lives, can take away a life when he chooses; and he could therefore allow another man to act as his agent in this respect. Hence he could permit one man to kill another.

It would, however, surely be wrong of any 'benefactor' to give something to someone the very possession of which was nothing but an evil. Hence God could not give to someone a life containing pain which served no good purpose. Any pain would have to be a benefit to the sufferer or to someone else. In the latter case God, who gives a benefit of life, has the right to conjoin it up to a limit with an evil which serves a good purpose—just as a parent may give to a child the benefit of education while conjoining it with the harm of having to be educated with scholars of a different community who would despise him, so long as the parent does this for the sake of a good—for example, social harmony. It follows that God cannot command or even give permission to a man to impose an evil which serves no good purpose on another; he cannot make it morally permissible to torture another man for no good purpose. Similarly he cannot make it permissible for me to deceive (e.g. tell a lie to) another man for no good purpose.

Further, it seems to be incompatible with the perfect goodness of God that he should 'give' us life subject to very tight moral restrictions on its use. No giver can give a present with full instructions for its use; I cannot 'give' you five dollars and tell you what I want you to buy for me with it. It would not then be a gift. Something is only a gift if, maybe within limits, the recipient can choose what to do with it. And a gift is not a generous one if any instructions for its use, though not totally precise, are too detailed. Life is something special, the condition of being able to do or receive anything else. To my mind, a perfectly good God who 'gave' us life would indeed give it us as a gift, not subject to too tight moral restrictions on its use. That our life is a 'gift' from God is a normal Christian view. It follows that, within limits, it is up to us how we choose to use our lives, and if our choices are within whatever limits our benefactor has put to the use of his gift, we do no wrong whichever way we choose.

If we can choose within limits what to do with our lives, it follows that we can choose whether to make promises to others as to how, within those limits, we will use our lives; and that God cannot dispense us from those promises. If, however, life is not a gift, if God only keeps us in being subject to an obligation to do exactly as he wishes every moment of every day, we surely have the right to decline life on that condition; we have the right to commit suicide, and God cannot make it obligatory for us not to do so. No one rational being has the right to force on another the conditions of his existence in all their full detail.

So there are limits both of content (e.g. he cannot oblige us to hurt others for no further good purpose) and of quantity to the obligations which God can impose on us; and so, since he is perfectly good, to the obligations he will seek to impose on us. It follows that there is a range of activity open to man, not covered by obligation to God (or to any human) within which it is up to man how he may act. The introduction of our theological assumption does not alter the fact that there is scope for good works beyond the call of duty, works of supererogation; although it does, by increasing our obligations, narrow the scope for such works.

The doctrine of supererogation (that there is scope for humans to do good acts beyond the call of duty) is a traditional Catholic position, and one generally accepted in medieval thought from Augustine onwards. It would be said there, for example, that there is a duty to keep the Ten Commandments, but it is supererogatorily good if we take vows of poverty, chastity, and obedience.[9] Protestantism firmly rejected the doctrine of supererogation, partly, I suppose, because of an understandable but mistaken view that God would be less great (and so not God) if we were not bound to do his will every moment of the day. However, God is not diminished if he creates free agents who are not obliged to serve him every second of the day; it is his decision to create them. But I think that a major and perhaps *the* major reason why many Christians have rejected the doctrine of supererogation is that they have believed—mistakenly, I shall urge—that it clashes with a very central Christian doctrine, the doctrine of sanctity.

This is the doctrine that only those with wills firmly dedicated to the good will finally be saved. Heaven is not for those who have kept the Ten Commandments and have done and intend to do no more. Some more ultimate and total dedication is necessary, not necessarily in the form of achieved results but at least of intention, of readiness to act should the occasion arise. This doctrine has, I believe, been held in theory by all Christians, Catholic and Protestant alike. Protestants have urged that salvation is by 'faith alone'; but, as I have argued elsewhere,[10] when one looks at what faith is supposed to mean in that formula, it does not mean merely 'belief'. It involves a total trust in God and a readiness to do what he requires; in other words, it includes a crucial element of firm dedication—whether or not there was time and opportunity for the dedication to manifest itself in good works. No doubt, as we shall see in a later chapter and as Catholics and Protestants have urged, such firm dedication is only possible by God's grace. But sanctity (normally manifested in works) is necessary for salvation. No doubt, as both Catholic and Protestant have also affirmed, the works required to manifest such firm dedication will be different for each individual. All must fulfil

[9] See David Heyd, *Supererogation*, CUP, 1982, for a history of the development of the Catholic position and other reasons for Protestant opposition to it. The Catholic position is far from uniform or always clear. For one statement of it, see Aquinas, *Summa contra Gentiles* 3. 130.1.

[10] For analysis of what is required for salvation on different Catholic and Protestant views, see my *Faith and Reason*, Clarendon Press, 1981, ch. 4.

their obligations—such as telling the truth and feeding their children—but beyond that, the way to sanctity differs for each. God will help each to see which way or choice of ways God wants each to take.

I have no desire to deny the doctrine of sanctity; and I shall provide some positive argument in Chapter 12 for supposing that a good God would not admit to Heaven others than saints. Any attempt to whittle that doctrine down would make the Christian religion a trivial thing. But that doctrine is only in conflict with the doctrine of supererogation if one believes also a third doctrine—that each of us has an obligation to do those acts which most directly forward his salvation. For such an obligation would, by the doctrine of sanctity, be an obligation to take the most direct route to acquiring sanctity, and taking such steps would leave little, if any, scope for works of supererogation. That we do have an obligation to do those acts which most directly forward our salvation seems to me not to be a doctrine entailed by central Christian doctrines, good though it is that we do those acts.

It is a very important contingent truth about men, I argued earlier, that we form our characters by our actions—good acts lead to good character, bad acts to bad character. The way to forming a saintly character worthy of Heaven is by doing good acts. If this life is all the life we have in which to form a saintly character, the most direct route will be the only one with any prospect of success. For to form that character is likely to require all our earthly life and our utmost effort. If, on the other hand, there is a possibility of further years after this life in which we can continue the process of sanctification (viz. in Purgatory), then perhaps we can do enough in this life for God to give us those further years in which to complete the process. I argued earlier that, since God has given us a life which can be used in such a worthwhile way here and hereafter, that does impose on us some duty to use it well here, and to take some steps to use it to form a saintly character capable of enjoying Heaven. Yet I also argued that there are limits to any such obligation. It follows that if our earthly life is all we have for the purpose of such character formation, there can be an obligation only to live a moderately worthwhile earthly life (including the worship of God), but not to form a character worthy of Heaven. Alternatively, if there is the prospect of years beyond this life in which we can continue the process of character formation, there is some obligation to do acts which make some progress in that direction. Either way there is no obligation to do those acts which most directly forward our salvation.

The normal medieval view from Augustine onwards, enshrined in subsequent Catholic thought, was that, although there is no obligation to do those acts which most directly forward one's salvation, there is an obligation to do acts which make some progress in that direction, and that means at least fulfilling the Ten Commandments and various precepts laid down by the Church (e.g. attending Mass on Sunday), and to take some small steps towards forming our character for good, so that the soul moves slowly and not too painfully in the right direction. This view of course went with the view that there is a Purgatory in which the process could be completed. The distinction was made between 'precepts' (commands which impose obligation) and 'counsels' (advice as to how best to progress towards the sanctity needed for salvation). 'Counsels of perfection', which were held applicable to many, advised the poverty, chastity, and obedience of the monastic life. However, there was no obligation on men to pursue salvation with such directness; following a less demanding way with less guarantee of attaining Heaven, at any rate so immediately, would involve no breach of obligation.[11] On this view there is still much scope for works of supererogation beyond obligation.

I urged in Chapter 4 that if A gives free violin lessons to B, that puts B under an obligation to spend some small amount of time practising the violin (putting what he has been taught to some good use), but it does not put B under an obligation to use all his spare time for this purpose. An analogous conclusion holds with respect to the gift of life which God gives to humans; the gift imposes some obligation to use the gift of life to make ourselves better livers, but not a total obligation to devote all our time to that task. However, there is no obligation on the violin teacher to continue giving lessons, but it will certainly be good that he do so if the pupil devotes all his spare time to his practising; and he may even promise the pupil in that case he will continue the lessons. A pupil who devotes only a minimum of time to his practising certainly cannot count on more

---

[11] 'Since that which falls under precept can be accomplished in various ways, one does not become a transgressor of the precept by not fulfilling it in the best possible way; it suffices that [man] fulfil it in some way'—Aquinas, *Summa Theologiae* 2a. 2ae. 184. 3 ad 2.

lessons. Analogously, we who perform for God our minimum obligations of character improvement cannot count on more time in which to continue the process.

The view which I have sketched seems to me the most natural interpretation of the biblical perspective. The God of Christian theism is generous; he gives to man life and health and opportunity. Although there are some conditions attached to the use of these gifts, these are not totally constraining; within limits he gives us our life to use as we choose. God also advises us, yet does not command us, how we may best use his gifts so as to secure an even better gift. The Old Testament records the giving of the gifts of life, health, and opportunity; and the commands which God issued to their Hebrew recipients. They are limited commands, restrictions on what men may say and do, commands to give a tithe of the harvest (not the whole harvest). The New Testament records an offer (of salvation), but a conditional offer, conditional on faith and/or works, i.e. on the earlier gifts being used by men in a more generous way than God had previously commanded.[12] Of course, man never has kept even the limited commands, and hence the vast problem of sin. But man is under no obligation to go further and seek his salvation. Yet unless he does seek it, God is under no obligation to provide it for him, and it is not necessarily even good that he should do so. So many books and passages in the New Testament make a strong contrast between the keeping of a narrow set of Judaic or other obligations and the living of the Christian life, and it seems very natural to interpret this contrast as one between the obligatory and the supererogatory. (Some biblical 'imperatives' are thus to be read as commands, imposing obligations; others are to be read as commendations.)

Many medievals did, however, tend to assume that the monastic life was the best way to sanctity not just for many but for all. In view of the diversity of human capacities and desires, that seems to me unlikely; and Aquinas firmly resisted this tendency.[13]

[12] See Matt. 19: 16–22 for the contrast between the previous requirement of keeping a limited set of not-too-demanding commands, and the more demanding life which is necessary if a man is to 'inherit eternal life'. For other New Testament and patristic sources of a doctrine of supererogation, see Heyd, op. cit., pp. 17 ff.

[13] For the history of the application to Christians of the distinction between 'precepts' and 'counsels', and the tendency to equate mere keeping of precepts with living the secular life and going beyond them to seek perfection as directly as possible with living the monastic life, see K. E. Kirk, *The Vision of God*, Longmans, 1931, 240–57 and appendices K, M, and N. For Aquinas's affirmation that the monastic life was not the best life for all, see *Summa Contra Gentiles* 3. 113. But even Aquinas held

The Variety of Kinds of Goodness

I claimed earlier that, while our theological assumption must alter our views about which kinds of action and character are good, it can only refine and deepen those views. It cannot totally replace them. Actions of many kinds are good or obligatory in themselves, quite apart from the fact that God commands or commends us to do them; and their goodness may derive from some intrinsic character of theirs (e.g. they are actions of truth-telling) or from their promoting some more distant good goal. But God's commandment imposes obligation; and God's commendation always adds to the goodness of an action; and no doubt (given our theological assumption that God seeks our eternal well-being) he commends all actions which are good for other reasons. As we saw in Chapter 1, it is good that men desire to do those actions which are good, and good that they desire to do them for the reason that they are good; and so it is good that men desire to do actions for all the reasons which make them good, for example, both because they are actions of feeding the hungry and because God so commands. It is good both to seek and to desire to please God, to be united with God, to attain the joys of Heaven, to be united with our friends, that our friends be happy, that we ourselves be happy. As all actions which are good for other reasons are also commended by God, in each case there are two reasons for doing the action, and two good desires which we could indulge by doing it, but both motives and both desires are good. A few theologians, more Buddhist than Christian, seem to have denied that any desires are good.[14] Many more theologians have claimed that the sole good is to please God; other aims and desires, such as the attainment of Heaven, or the happiness of one's friends or oneself, are not good. My arguments suggest that all of these things are good, and so it is good to seek them, and it is good to desire them, for their own sake; and even better to seek and desire them also because God so wills.

that there is a sense in which the monastic life is higher than the secular life, and better to follow than the secular life unless there are contrary reasons, for it brings man into more direct contact with God. See *Summa Contra Gentiles* 3. 130. The Council of Trent also affirmed the superiority of celibacy to marriage (Denzinger 1810), presumably also in this sense that, other things being equal, celibacy makes for perfection.

[14] See the quotation from Eckhardt in K. E. Kirk, op. cit., pp. 453 ff.: 'He alone has true spiritual poverty who wills nothing, knows nothing, desires nothing.'

The history of Christian theological thought on this matter is not always easy to interpret, because theologians have not always kept sharply clear in their writing the distinction between pursuing Heaven or worldly goods or whatever for their own sake and pursuing Heaven etc. because God so commands. But, although it is risky to impose too sharp distinctions of this kind on ancient writers, there do seem to me to be two traditions in Christian thought. Augustine and Luther seem fairly clear in their claim that all good things other than pleasing God are to be sought and desired solely because seeking and desiring them pleases God. Thus Augustine:

Scripture enjoins nothing except charity, and condemns nothing except lust . . . I mean by charity that affection of the mind which aims at the enjoyment of God for his own sake, and the enjoyment of one's self and one's neighbour for the sake of God [*propter Deum*]; by lust I mean that affection of the mind which aims at enjoying one's self and one's neighbour, and other corporeal things, without reference to God.[15]

And Luther opposes those who love God 'with a covetous love, for the sake of their own salvation . . . not for God's sake, but for their own sake . . . To be blessed means to seek in everything God's will and glory, and to want nothing for oneself, neither here nor in the life to come.' He opposes those who 'babble that . . . everyone must first of all wish his own salvation and then his neighbour's as his own'.[16]

The later medievals whom Luther was attacking seem to be saying that pursuit of temporal and spiritual goods is good in itself independently of God having commanded or commended it. I write 'seem' because sometimes all they say is that pursuit of such goods is good, and they do not explicitly add 'for reasons other than that they were commanded or commended by God'; but their context and Luther's hostility to such a position suggest that this interpretation is often correct. Eckhardt was condemned by John XXII for holding, among other things, that it is wrong to aim at 'property, honour, or utility'.[17] One of Luther's more immediate opponents was Gabriel Biel, who held that it is possible to love oneself or one's neighbour by seeking temporal or spiritual well-being ('health, riches or life').[18]

---

[15] *On Christian Doctrine* III. 10. 15 and 16.
[16] *Lectures on Romans*, trans. W. Pauck, SCM Press, 1951, 262.
[17] Denzinger 958.
[18] See his *Commentary on Sentences* III d29 q. un. a2. concl.4.

The Council of Trent declared that it is not wrong to wait and hope for one's own eternal salvation.[19] I am also inclined to regard Aquinas as belonging to this tradition. He teaches the goodness of loving things other than God, and, although he claims that we love other things 'because of what there is of God in them',[20] he seems to mean by this that we do and ought to love them because of the good that is in them and so, that good being in fact derived from God, because of what there is of God in them—'The object of love is the good, in proportion as it exists in things.'[21] He holds that it is proper to love God for the sake of a reward, in the sense of loving God for the sake of enjoying him, but not for the sake of some temporal reward (e.g. ecclesiastical office) distinct from God.[22]

It is, of course, towards the view of this latter tradition (as I have interpreted it) that my arguments unequivocally lead; and I am happy to ally myself with that tradition.[23]

---

[19] Denzinger 1576 and 1581.

[20] *Summa Theologiae* 2a. 2ae.25 and 26.

[21] *Commentary on Sentences* III d29. a2 ad 1.

[22] Ibid. d29. a4.

[23] An extreme position, beyond that of the Council of Trent, is taken by Bossuet, who claimed, surely falsely, that all love is really self-love; we only love and seek our own happiness, but enlightened seeking will seek it in union with God. Christian tradition has always emphasized against this that God can be and is to be loved for his own sake. My claim is rather that other things in small part are to be sought and loved for their own sake, as well as, more importantly, for God's. On the history of these matters, see K. E. Kirk, op. cit., pp. 451–66 (especially for the Bossuet–Fenelon controversy) and J. Passmore, *The Perfectibility of Man*, Duckworth, 1970, 88–92.

My view is also that of R. M. Adams, developed in a very able paper, 'The Problem of Total Devotion' (in R. Audi and W. J. Wainwright (eds.), *Rationality, Religious Belief and Moral Commitment*, Cornell University Press, 1986). The paper discusses the question of how total devotion to God is compatible with love of one's neighbour. Adams' answer (which he claims to have gleaned from Anders Nygren, *Agape and Eros*) is that love of God inspires one to do as God does and so love one's neighbour for his own sake (and not just for God's).

9
Sin and Original Sin

Original Sinfulness

Although failure to live a perfect life is not a failure of duty, my theological assumption does have the consequence that the range of our duties is far wider than it would otherwise be, and so man's failure to try to make anything worthwhile of his life is vastly much more of a failure. Human wrongdoing becomes the heavy burden of actual sin, objective and subjective. And human proneness to wrongdoing, objective and subjective, which I described in Chapter 7, becomes proneness to sin, in other words, original sinfulness—one of the three component parts of a full doctrine of original sin, to the other components of which I will turn shortly. What arose in man with his first hesitant moral beliefs was a proneness to objective sin (to fail to worship God, and to misuse his God-given talents, whether he realized he was failing in these respects or not) and a proneness to subjective sin (to do what he believed wrong, whether or not his views on which actions were wrong were correct).

Man has a disease, original sinfulness, the bad part of which is transmitted genetically. That the transmission was by 'propagation, not imitation'[1] was the firm teaching of the Council of Trent against those who would whittle down sinfulness to a mere effect of a

---

[1] 'generatione, non imitatione', Council of Trent, *Decretum super peccato originali* 3. The claim that the proneness to sin was transmitted solely by way of 'social' as contrasted with biological inheritance was a hallmark of Pelagianism. For the 5th-cent. British monk Pelagius, Augustine's arch-enemy, 'evil is transmitted from generation to generation by bad examples, unjust laws, profligate manners, and actions' (N. P. Williams, *The Ideas of the Fall and of Original Sin*, Longmans, 1927, 343. For almost all other theologians the trouble was deeper than that. N. P. Williams' history of the doctrine of original sin is a classic history , and I am much indebted to it for historical points. For philosophical discussion of the ideas of original sin in Anselm and Kant, see Philip L. Quinn, 'Original Sin, Radical Evil, and Moral Identity', *Faith and Philosophy*, 1984, 1, 188–202; and a forthcoming paper, 'Original Sin in Anselm and Kant'.

corrupt environment.[2] All that follows from my theological assumption and the human proneness to wrongdoing described in Chapter 7 is a proneness, an inclination to act. The bad desires in which it consists incline, they do not (as such) necessitate. All theologians have affirmed a proneness to sin, but some theologians have wanted to go further and say that it is a proneness which led necessarily to sin. Man without divine grace (i.e. God's help) sins necessarily. This seems to be the teaching of Augustine,[3] and of his classical Protestant successors. Augustine wrote that 'the entire mass of our nature was ruined beyond doubt'.[4] Emphasis on this inevitable corruption yields Calvin's doctrine of total depravity.[5] However, Augustine taught that divine grace enables us to avoid sin; and he seems to have taught that without sufficient grace we necessarily do evil, but with sufficient grace we necessarily do good. We have no free will in my sense, although Augustine certainly wished to affirm 'free will' in some sense. I write that Augustine 'seems' to have so taught, for, although he wrote many volumes on this matter, he seems thoroughly unclear in his own mind (even at any one period of his life), and different expositors have derived different doctrines from him.[6] Certainly he encouraged thinking of this kind in the Western Church. On this, as on all other matters, Augustine's thought was enormously influential in the thinking of the Western Church for the next eight hundred years. Aquinas (normally the

---

[2] I suggest that the transmission of original sinfulness is not direct, by the child receiving some share of the parent's soul (as the traducionist would maintain), but by the body formed for the reception of the soul (newly created for each body—as the creationist maintains) being such (through its genetic inheritance) as to corrupt any soul united with it (see Aquinas, *Summa Theologiae* 1a. 2ae. 81.1 ad 2 and ad 4). I have argued in favour of the new creation by God of each soul in my *The Evolution of the Soul* (Clarendon Press, 1986), ch. 10. Aristotle (*De Generatione Animalium* 738b) taught that in generation the male parent contributes the form or active principle, and the female parent the matter. The male principle gives form to the matter provided by the female. Aquinas gave this as his reason for claiming that it was Adam's, not Eve's, sin that was inherited (see *Summa Theologiae* 1a. 2ae. 81.5). However, it must be made clear that the doctrine of seminal transmission is not committed to this account of the method of transmission, and is equally compatible with the modern Mendelian account, which gives to male and female a similar role in the process.

[3] See e.g. *Enchiridion* 9—'The hard necessity of possessing sin pursued the sinner.'

[4] *On the Grace of Christ and on Original Sin* II, ch. 34.

[5] 'The soul . . . is utterly devoid of all good'—Calvin, *Institutes of the Christian Religion*, II. 3.2.

[6] See the discussion in J. Tixeront, *History of Dogmas*, ii, B. Herder, 1923, 484–91.

clearest of thinkers) shares Augustine's ambivalence on this issue.[7] Later medieval thought gradually put aside many of Augustine's views, and in this matter it affirmed more definitely the view that some free will (in my sense) remains for man after Adam. Augustine's views were often readopted with enthusiasm and in a more extreme form by the Protestant reformers—Luther and Calvin[8] were explicit in their denial of human free will in my sense. Augustine had, however, adopted his position in opposition to the general tenor of Christian thought prior to his day. So many of the Fathers before Augustine were very vigorous in affirming a libertarian free will (i.e. free will in my sense)—Justin,[9] Irenaeus,[10] Origen,[11] and even Tertullian,[12] to name but a few.[13] In Augustine's time there was not merely his extreme opponent Pelagius, but also his more moderate opponents such as John Cassian, whose views were expressed by the Synod of Arles.[14] On this, as on other matters, later Eastern Orthodoxy was not much influenced by Augustine. The medieval theologian who seems to me to have turned the tide of Western thought in favour of free will was Duns Scotus; and his views received the stamp of Catholic orthodoxy in the declaration of the Council of Trent.[15] The more liberal Protestants (e.g. Arminius), too, soon began to rebel against the hard Calvinist position, which must today be very much a minority Christian position.

I see every reason internal to Christian theology for resisting the Calvinist position for, if the arguments of Chapter 3 are correct, unavoidable sin is not culpable; and theology has wished vigorously to affirm that 'fallen' men (i.e. men after Adam) are culpable for their sins; I believe, for non-theological reasons which I have given

---

[7] Compare *Summa Theologiae* 1. 83.1, 1a.2ae.79.1 and 1a.2ae.113.3 with 1a.2ae.79.3 and 4.

[8] 'Free will is not sufficient to enable man to do good works, unless he be helped by grace, indeed by special grace, which only the elect receive through regeneration'— Calvin, op. cit. II. 2.6. In other words—without grace we sin; with grace we inevitably do such good works as to gain salvation.

[9] *Dialogue with Trypho*, ch. 141, *Second Apology*, ch. 7.

[10] *Adversus Haereses*, bk. 4, ch. 37.

[11] *De Principiis*, 1.5, 2.1, 3.1.

[12] *Against Marcion*, 2.6 and 2.25.

[13] For other references see Tixeront, op. cit., pp. 143 f. Calvin found Augustine distinctly ambivalent on what 'free will' amounted to—see Calvin, op. cit. II. 2.8.

[14] Denzinger 331.

[15] Denzinger 1555 and 1556

elsewhere,[16] that humans have the power to act independently of natural causes such as prior brain states which act on them; and so I see good theological reason for supposing that God does not act outside the web of natural causes in order to overrule human free will. What led Augustine and Calvin to take the position they did was, I suppose, mainly a theological belief that if man had the freedom to choose to do what God did not prefer, God would be less great. God's greatness is not, however, impaired if he generously allows creatures to determine their own destiny. He remains omnipotent, for it is only by his continuing choice that they have the power to go against his preferences. There was, however, also at work in the background of the thought of Augustine and Aquinas the philosophical tradition derived from Plato and Aristotle, to which I referred in Chapter 2; that agents always pursue the best as they see it, from which it would seem to follow that, given our beliefs (which are unavoidable), we cannot but do as we do. Duns Scotus denied that the intellect fully determined the will, and he gave an account of the respective roles of intellect and will which enabled him to break the grip of this philosophical tradition on Christian theology.

The will, he wrote, has two 'affections'—for 'justice' (i.e. in my terminology, the morally best) and for the 'advantageous' (i.e. our own prudential advantage).[17] It has to choose between these different goods. The good is the object of the will; but the will may not choose the morally best, or even the prudentially best, for sensory appetite may incline us not to choose either, and we may yield to it.[18] The will may choose the morally best, it may choose the prudentially best, and it may choose neither, but how it chooses is not determined. It is, he claimed, 'a contradiction for the will to be forced to will'.[19] 'The will, as a power to act freely . . . does not will necessarily what is advantageous any more than it necessarily wills what is just.'[20] The similarity between this account and that given in Chapter 2 will be apparent.

---

[16] See *The Evolution of the Soul*, ch. 13.

[17] *Ordinatio* III, suppl. dist. 26. Text and translation in A. B.Wolter, *Duns Scotus on the Will and Morality*, Catholic University of America Press, 1986, 179.

[18] *Ordinatio* III, suppl. dist. 33 (Wolter pp. 337 f.). See also *Ordinatio* III, dist. 6 q. 2 (Wolter, pp. 465 ff.).

[19] *Ordinatio* IV, dist. 29 (Wolter, p. 175).

[20] *Ordinatio* II, dist. 39 (Wolter, p. 203).

Adam

At some stage in the history of the world, there appeared the first creature with hominoid body who had some understanding of the difference between the morally obligatory, the morally permissible (i.e. right), and the morally wrong; and an ability freely to choose the morally right. So much is obvious; since on modern evolutionary views, as well as on all views held in Christian tradition, once upon a time there were no such creatures and now there are some, there must have been a first one. It seems reasonable to consider such a creature the first man; and we may follow biblical tradition and call him 'Adam'. (The Hebrew word means 'man'.)

Christian theology has had two very different views as to the kind of man he was. One view, common to all theologians before the fourth century AD, was that Adam was a feeble creature, with strong passions and a weak will with which to resist them. 'Man was a child, not yet having his understanding perfected,' wrote Irenaeus.[21] Beginning with Athanasius[22] in the fourth century, however, a quite different doctrine of Adam developed, as a perfect man without proneness to sin, a doctrine of Adam's 'original righteousness' which reached its extravagant fullness in Augustine. He held that Adam was 'exempted from all physical evils, and endowed with immortal youth and health which could not be touched by the taint of sickness or the creeping debility of old age'. Adam also had enormous mental prowess.[23] Augustine, and those who after him were highly dubious about whether men after Adam had free will, were more willing to attribute to Adam free will (in my sense).[24] On the Augustinian view of Adam, when Adam sinned there was indeed a 'Fall' from a very high state; on the earlier view the first sin was clearly less of a 'Fall'.

There seems no reason whatever to adopt the Augustinian view,[25] since the modern account of evolution suggests a very gradual

---

[21] See the quotation from *Demonstration* in Williams, p. 193 ff. and the discussion by Williams there. See also pp. 175 ff.

[22] Ibid. 258 f.   [23] Ibid. 361.

[24] Ibid. 362. But even here there is Augustine's hopeless ambivalence—see *De Correptione et Gratia* 32.

[25] The hypothesis of original righteousness seems in fact to be contrary to the biblical text of Genesis 3; since it was only in consequence of the Fall, according to that story, that man acquired knowledge of good and evil, through eating the fruit of the forbidden tree (Gen. 2: 17 and 3: 7); and by 'knowledge of good and evil' seems to be meant not moral knowledge, but scientific and technical knowledge.

evolution of man from more primitive creatures with a very gradual development of his various capacities. Given that view, it seems highly plausible to suppose (and not to need an extra hypothesis to be added for this purpose) that the first man was also the first subjective sinner—such would be the force of the desires inherited from his ape-like ancestors in one who alone dimly perceives moral obligations which run contrary to it. The acquisition of some moral beliefs about what is obligatory would also, by my argument in Chapter 7, constitute any actions of the first man contrary to obligation as objectively sinful (whether or not he believed them to be so). Adam was very probably also therefore the first sinner.[26]

The Cause of Original Sinfulness

The second component of a full doctrine of original sin claims that it was the sin of the first sinner which caused in other men original sinfulness, the proneness to do sin, through their descent from Adam.

The claim that all men were descended from this first man is, however, dubious. Although convergent evolution is none too common, there is the possibility that moral concepts were acquired independently by different hominids in different parts of the globe, who each then did wrong.[27] There is, too, the possibility that others of Adam's community who were not descended from him would nevertheless have acquired from him their first moral intuitions, which would then have given rise to a proneness to sin, when coupled with selfish desires inherited genetically (but not from Adam). Some of the Fathers and Scholastics tied themselves into some fine knots about how Eve acquired original sin, while not being descended from Adam.)

But whether or not any men who were not Adam's descendants acquired original sinfulness, the second component of the full doctrine must be mistaken about how Adam's descendants acquired their sinfulness. Proneness to sin is there in Adam's descendants

[26] See Additional Note 7.

[27] Pope Pius XII discussed this matter in his 1950 Encyclical *Humani Generis*. He advocated monogenism, the doctrine that the whole human race was descended from a single pair; declared the opposite position, polygenism, to be a 'conjectural opinion'; and noted that it was in no way apparent how polygenism could be reconciled with Rom. 5 or the decrees of the Council of Trent. Even he did not, however, declare the opinion heretical.

because of genes giving rise to desires (genetically inherited), in conflict with socially inherited moral beliefs. But, given modern evolutionary and genetic theory, what was genetically inherited was not caused by Adam, for two reasons. The first is that, neo-Darwinian orthodoxy assures us, changes in genes are quite unaffected by changes in other parts of the body and so (contrary to Lamarck's supposition) there is no inheritance of acquired characteristics. God could, it is true, have overruled normal genetic processes on this unique occasion. But against that supposition stands the second and stronger consideration that the desires which cause all the trouble are there in the monkeys and the apes as well. The desires are not caused in us by Adam's sin. Indeed, as we have noted, they must have been already there in Adam himself.

Adam's responsibility for our sinfulness is confined to a responsibility for beginning the social transmission of morality (as such a good thing) which made sin possible, but a morality which, as a result of his own sinful example and perhaps false moral beliefs, was no doubt a corrupt morality and so made it easier for our genetically inherited proneness to sin to work in Adam's successors. And when we consider the enormous effect of corrupt moralities—of nominal allegiance to systems frequently broken, of a teaching to hate when a man's initial judgement might be that hating is wrong, this responsibility is considerable. But Adam only started the process of the transmission of corrupt morality; so many others have helped it along the way. I conclude that the responsibility for the genetically inherited proneness to sin belongs neither to a first man nor to any other man. Responsibility for the socially transmitted proneness to sin does indeed belong to man, but to so many of us (to Adam, as representing us all); and yet it belongs to the first man Adam peculiarly in this sense, that he began the process to which so many of us have subsequently contributed.

I have argued that the first part of a full doctrine of original sin, that there is a proneness to sin in all men, is correct; but that the second part, that the proneness was caused by the sin of the first sinner, is (with the above substantial qualification) false. Most of the Fathers who thought about the matter seem to have taken for granted the second part of the doctrine, though a few who treated the Genesis 3 account allegorically did not.[28] However, without a

[28] See Williams, ch. 4, *passim*. The allegorizers included Origen and Gregory of Nyssa.

doctrine of original righteousness, the issue was not of such great importance. For the theologians before the fourth century who did not accept the doctrine of original righteousness regarded Adam's condition in respect of proneness to sin as not greatly different from ours. Hence if Adam's sin did not cause our sinfulness, God could have implanted it in us by the same route (and for the same reason—whatever that was) as he implanted it in Adam. It did not require a new mechanism.

Original Guilt

The third component of a full doctrine of original sin is the doctrine of original guilt, that all of Adam's descendants are guilty for Adam's original sin. Most of the Fathers showed no knowledge of this doctrine. Clement of Alexandria explicitly denied it,[29] and Gregory of Nyssa[30] did so by implication. So did Theodoret[31] and Cyril of Alexandria.[32] However, Augustine fastened that doctrine on the Western Church for many years,[33] until the later medievals greatly toned it down. Scotus treated our condition of guilt as one of indebtedness. We inherit from Adam a debt to God for losing the treasure of 'original righteousness'.[34] Classical Protestantism[35] temporarily reverted to something like the Augustinian doctrine.[36]

My sympathies on this issue, as on the other issues discussed in this chapter, are with the liberal Greek-speaking theologians of the early centuries who rejected or showed no knowledge of this doctrine. I argued in Chapter 5 that no one can be guilty in a literal sense for the sins of another, unless he had some obligation to deter that person and did not do so. Since none of us today could have had

---

[29] Williams, op. cit., p. 207.

[30] Gregory writes of the newly-baptized Christian as 'as free from accusations and penalties as a newly born baby'—*In baptism. Christi*, PG 46, 579D.

[31] 'Every one of us receives the sentence of death, not because of the sin of our first parents, but because of his own sin'—*In Ep. ad Rom.* 5.12.

[32] 'Since we have become imitators of the sin of Adam, we incur a penalty like his'—*In Ep. ad Rom.* 5.12.

[33] *Enchiridion* 26. Augustine thinks of Adam's descendants as already contained 'seminally' in him and for that reason guilty for his sin. The human nature of which we are part sinned. Aquinas develops this view in *Summa Theologiae* 1a. 2ae. 81.1.

[34] Williams, op. cit., p. 412.

[35] Calvin, op. cit. II. 1.6. See also Williams, op. cit., pp. 432 ff.

[36] See Additional Note 8.

the obligation to deter the first sinner from sinning, we cannot be guilty for his sins. This was a truth proclaimed in the sixth century BC by both Jeremiah and Ezekiel. They quote the proverb 'The fathers have eaten sour grapes, and the children's teeth are set on edge.'[37] They understand it as a claim about the justification of holding children to blame for their father's offences, and they claim that a just society will not hold children responsible in this way. Thus Ezekiel:

The soul that sinneth, it shall die. The son shall not bear the iniquity of the father, neither shall the father bear the iniquity of the son; the righteousness of the righteous shall be upon him, and the wickedness of the wicked shall be upon him.[38]

The simple view of Jeremiah and Ezekiel, though basically correct, is, however, a little too simple as it stands. There is, first, the point which I have just made, that we do have some guilt for the wrongdoings and so the sins of those close to us, whom by teaching and example we could have deterred. Further, I also argued in Chapter 5, we are all 'involved' in the wrongdoings and so the sins of others of our community; in the sense that we must accept that they are guilty and help them to bear their guilt and to make atonement for it.

And what is the community with which we are thus involved? It is, I suggest, the human race. We share with all other men a mental life of sensation, thought, purpose, desire and belief, language and moral awareness, and free will—and not just some desires, beliefs, etc., but special kinds of desires, beliefs, etc., and a limited set of powers, arising from our peculiar kind of embodiment. And what we are is the result of genetic inheritance—our ancestors bring us into being as the sort of being they were—and social inheritance. Their discoveries and behaviour help to mould ours. All the human race are the descendants of our remote ancestors and so our brothers. We owe so much to our fellow members of the human race, and especially our ancestors, that we must regard ourselves as involved in their failures, and, above all, that first failure, which is symbolic of all the others and started the process—the original sin—that first yielding to our animal nature instead of bringing it into line with reason.

[37] Jer. 31: 29 and Ezek. 18: 2.
[38] Ezek. 18: 20.

Further, given my theological assumption, all members of the human race are brought into being and kept in being by one loving creator God. We who owe so much to God may help fulfil our obligation to please him by forwarding his purposes, which, in virtue of his perfect goodness, must include the purpose that those who sinned against him should atone for their sin. We can accept involvement in the sins of our ancestors and other brethren, and in principle we can help them to make atonement for their sins; how that could be done I shall discuss in detail in the next chapter. We do not inherit guilt for the sins of others, but we do, as Duns Scotus wrote, inherit a debt.

My conclusion on this third part of the full doctrine of original sin, added to my conclusions on the other two parts, puts me in a position with respect to the full doctrine close to that of the liberal Greek-speaking theologians of early Christian centuries, and far away from Augustine and his Protestant successors.

Human wrongdoing, objective and subjective, is an evident fact of experience; and, given my theological assumption, sin, objective and subjective, is evidently pervasive. Objective sin is almost unavoidable; even with the best intentions, we are morally ignorant (do not know how we ought to treat other men and our God), careless and forgetful. And subjective sin is very hard to avoid—we are saddled with temptations to sloth and greed, lust and envy, desires whose full indulgence we recognize as wrong. The guilt of our own actual sin requires much atonement towards God; and also there is the obligation to help in the process of atonement for the sins of others.

The burden of sin, when we think of it, is great. And who was more conscious of it than St Paul? Awareness of the web of moral obligation under which we stand came to him in the form of awareness of the law. 'I had not known sin except through the law.'[39] Yet this knowledge led to his own sin—more precisely, I would suggest, to his subjective sin, the more important sin. The objective sin existed before. As he puts it himself: 'Until the law, sin was in the world; but sin is not imputed where there is no law.'[40] 'When the commandment came, sin revived, and I died.'[41] 'What I hate, that I do.'[42] He recognizes the goodness of the law, and there is no doubt of his ultimate dedication to its goals; so that the temptations to which he yields seem alien forces acting upon him. 'I

[39] Rom. 7: 7.   [40] Rom. 5: 13.
[41] Rom. 7: 9.   [42] Rom. 7: 15.

delight in the law of God, after the inward man. But I see a different law in my members, warring against the law of my mind, and bringing me into captivity under the law of sin which is in my members.'[43] Who shall deliver Paul from the body of this sin?

It is tempting for the modern man who accepts my theological assumptions, the believer under the influence of the secular world, to feel that Paul and others have exaggerated the weight of sin, the burden of guilt. But the inclination to underestimate the importance of sin has always been before the sinner; it did not need the modern world to give it force. And the inclination is a temptation, I suggest. Serious reflection on the content of my theological assumption, the majesty of God, man's total dependence on him for all the good things of life, the marvellous opportunities available for helping our brethren and for growing in the knowledge of God, our neglect of these things for the sake of self-indulgence for the few years of our earthly life; serious reflection on these things may bring the believer to a more correct perspective on the burden of guilt and so the need for atonement.

[43] Rom. 7: 22 f.

10

Redemption

A wrongdoer is under an obligation to make atonement for his wrongdoing. In so far as our wrongdoing involves doing hurt to our fellow humans, we must make atonement for that to those humans. But, as we saw in Chapter 8, the theological backcloth of God as our creator and our possible goal makes wrongdoing so much worse; wrongdoing becomes sin, and those who have so badly abused the opportunities which God their creator gave them owe him a serious atonement. Each human sinner owes atonement to God for the sins (objective and subjective) which he has committed himself; and help in making their atonement to God to his fellow humans (of whom Adam was the first) the debt of whose sin he inherits. We saw in Chapter 5 that atonement involves repentance, apology, reparation, and penance. If you take seriously the theological background to human wrongdoing, you realize both the extent of atonement needed and the difficulty which man suffering from original sinfulness will have in making it. We need help from outside.

But why in that situation would a good God not simply ignore our sins? I argued earlier that it is wrong for any victim to ignore serious harm done to him by another—for it involves not taking the other seriously in the attitudes expressed in his actions. But why would not God forgive us in return for repentance and apology without demanding reparation and penance? The arguments of Chapter 5 have the consequence that someone wronged has in general no duty to require reparation, although he has the right to do so. Many of the Fathers accepted that God could have forgiven our sins without there being any need for a Crucifixion.[1] More explicitly, and thinking in the terms which I have used, Aquinas held that God could have forgiven us without demanding reparation and penance,

---

[1] By contrast, Athanasius regards God as having promised (or, in my terminology—see pp. 104–6—having vowed) to punish men for their sins; and so as having made it bad for himself to forgive man without a man suffering punishment. See J. Tixeront, *History of Dogmas*, ii. 147.

if he had chosen; and it would not have been wrong of him so to choose.[2] But, although there would have been nothing wrong in God forgiving us without demanding reparation, nevertheless, since our actions and their consequences matter, it is good that if we do wrong, *we* should take *proper* steps to cancel our actions, to pay out debts, as far as logically can be done. We have freedom to do much good or ill, and it is good that we do have that freedom. Involved in the freedom to do ill is the responsibility, if we do ill, for clearing up the mess. Our having the freedom subsequently to clear up at a later time the mess we make at an earlier time allows us to affirm our identities as agents continuing over time. If we are in no position to make proper atonement for what we have done, it is good that someone else (even the victim) put us in that position and thereby allow us to make proper atonement. A good parent may put in the way of a child who has wronged him an opportunity for making amends (an opportunity which he would not otherwise have had) rather than immediately accept an apology. If the child has broken the parent's window and does not have the money to pay for a replacement, the parent may give him the money wherewith to pay a glazier to put in a new window, or he may give him a cheque made payable to the glazier which he can then use to pay the glazier to put in the window, and thereby make due reparation. The parent can refuse to accept the apology until the window is mended. Thereby he allows the child to take his action and its consequence seriously, or rather as seriously as he can in the circumstances of the child's initial inability to pay. That treats the child as a responsible agent, and it treats the harm done as a harm. It treats things as they are. A good God may put a similar opportunity for making amends in the way of those who wrong him.

'No man can atone for the sins of another.' Taken literally, that remains profoundly true. You cannot make my apologies, or even pay my debts. If I steal £10 from Jones and you give him an equivalent sum, he has not lost money; but it remains the case that I still owe £10 to Jones. You have not changed that. But one man can help another to make the necessary atonement—can persuade him to repent, help him to formulate the words of apology, and give him the means by which to make reparation and penance. Individual humans

[2] Aquinas, *Summa Theologiae* 3a. 46. 2 ad 3. For the point about the Fathers, see L. W. Grensted, *A Short History of the Doctrine of the Atonement*, Longmans, 1920, 142.

can be helped to make their atonement and so also to fulfil their
obligations to help others make their atonement.

My claim that a good God might provide for men the necessary
reparation and penance whereby to make their atonement will
shortly be backed up by an argument that (given my theological
assumption) the life and death of Christ—and especially the death,
the Crucifixion—is adequate for that purpose. But first I must
comment on other accounts of how Christ effected the annihilation
of human sin and the reconciliation of God and man, suggested by
other models deriving from the New Testament which Christians
have used to describe what was effected on the Cross.[3] Christian
theology has no formal definition of what was effected on the Cross
with the kind of stamp of orthodoxy upon it possessed by the
Chalcedonian definition of the Incarnation (Christ as having two
natures in one person), but it has used undefined and unrelated a
variety of models in order to attempt to show what was done. Each of
these models has some grounding in language used in the New
Testament; but I suggest that (with one exception) each model
taken by itself, seriously and literally, provides little illumination as
to how the death of Christ on the Cross helped to deal with the
problem of human sin. I shall, however, argue that, when
interpreted in the light of the primary model, two at any rate of these
other ways of talking can be seen to have their point.

First, the Crucifixion has been described as a battle victory. But
whether the victory is thought of as victory over impersonal evil or a
personal Devil, that picture gives no explanation of how a victory
can remove sin and why the victory needed so costly a struggle. Why
could not God simply annihilate evil or the Devil?[4] Then the
Crucifixion has been described as a redemption or the payment of a
ransom. The question then arises as to to whom the ransom was
paid? The only possible answer seems to be—the Devil. But then
why did the ransom need to be paid? Could not God just annihilate

[3] For the doctrine of the atonement in the New Testament and subsequent
Christian theology, see G. Aulen, *Christus Victor*, SPCK, 1931; L. W. Grensted, op.
cit.; and F. W. Dillistone, *The Christian Understanding of Atonement*, Nisbet, 1968.

[4] Among other places in the New Testament, the Crucifixion is represented as a
victory in Col. 2: 15, and in Revelation's metaphor of the conquering lion (e.g. Rev.
5: 5). Aulen's *Christus Victor* is intended by the author as an affirmation of this view,
which he claims to find in the teaching of Irenaeus and Luther. Aulen does not
distinguish the victory model from the ransom model, though he distances himself
from the cruder connotations of the latter.

the Devil? The reply normally given is that in some way God had promised the Devil that he could control the fate of those who sinned against God. But why should God have made so foolish a promise? And it can hardly be said that the New Testament contains any account of such a promise.[5] (The word 'Redemption' is, of course, often used nowadays to describe what was effected on Calvary without the implications which its etymology suggests, which is my excuse for using it as the title of this chapter.) Then the Crucifixion has been described as the payment of a penalty. The suggestion is that God himself in Christ paid the penalty, underwent the punishment which men themselves should have undergone. As we saw in Chapter 6, the imposer of a penalty (in this case, God) may accept the offer of someone else to undergo the penalty due to be paid by the wrongdoer, or a lesser penalty. (The 'penal substitution' theory claims that the penalty paid was the full penalty due.) However, sinful man's only role in this process would be to repent and apologize; the debt owed would be cancelled by the creditor (God) without any other participation in the process by the debtor (man). That being so, it seems desirable that God should 'let man off' without punishing himself in this way; only the implausible Hegelian theory of the need to equate the wrong done with further suffering could justify the substitute punishment. In so far as Christ is God the Son, a separate person from God the Father, though one with him in the unity of the divine substance, we get the picture of God the Son suffering in order to placate the anger of the Father. Again, it seems desirable that the Father should not make the Son suffer instead of letting us off without anyone suffering punishment. (Traditional theology does, of course, maintain that God is three persons in one substance, and it is one of them, the Son, who is

[5] There is much talk in the New Testament of Christ redeeming us and even paying a ransom—e.g. Mark 10: 45, 'The Son of Man came . . . to give his life as a ransom for many.' There is much talk, too, of his rescuing us from evil, and sometimes this is put personally in terms of his rescuing us from the Devil. But any idea of a prior bargain with the Devil, so that God was obliged to pay a ransom, is alien to the New Testament. So too is the even more abhorrent idea that the Devil let men go in return for being allowed to tempt and kill Christ, and that thereby God deceived the Devil because he led the Devil to suppose that he had some chance of success in keeping Christ. It was Origen who developed this full-blown ransom theory; and many others of the Fathers, such as Gregory of Nyssa, followed him to a large extent in this. The theory of a ransom paid to the Devil was explicitly rejected, among the Fathers, alone by Gregory Nazianzen. For references and discussion see Dillistone, op. cit., pp. 95–8, and Grensted, op. cit., ch. 4.

incarnate in Christ and lives a life of service and dies on the Cross. Although here and subsequently I do briefly allude to the difference which is made to an account of redemption if we stress the separateness of the persons of the Trinity, I do so only to bring out that the difference so made is not great. Hence it is possible to discuss redemption without needing to analyse what is meant by the doctrine that God is three persons in one substance.) The penal model's talk of lawcourts and punishment makes the whole process too 'mechanical' for a means of reconciliation which ought to be intimate and personal.[6]

To my mind, by far the most satisfactory biblical model for what was effected by the life and death of Christ is the model of sacrifice. It is, of course, the way in which the doctrine of the atonement is worked out in the Epistle to the Hebrews, and is, I think, the way of expressing the doctrine which has the widest base in the New Testament. In the most primitive way of thinking about sacrifice lying behind Old Testament thought, a sacrifice is the giving of something valuable to a God who consumes it whole (by inhaling the smoke) and often gives back some of it to be consumed by the worshippers (who eat the roasted flesh).[7] The Old Testament itself does not in general think of God as literally inhaling the smoke; but the idea is there that God takes something valuable as a gift of reconciliation whose benefits he will often share with the worshippers—like, to use a humble modern analogy, the box of chocolates which one gives to one's host, who then offers one in return a choice from the box. The sacrifice of Christ is then Christ giving the most valuable thing he has—his life; both a lived life of obedience to God, and a laid-down life on the Cross—as a present to God, whose benefits will flow to others, through the Resurrection, in a way which I will consider in due course. Or, at least, that is how it would be if Christ were a completely distinct being from God the

[6] The obvious New Testament base for the penal theory is St Paul's extended analogy of the lawcourt in the Epistle to the Romans. We are guilty, but God 'justifies' us (however that is to be interpreted) and acquits us. That, combined with the obvious Pauline view that Christ suffered on our behalf, yields the theory that Christ suffered the punishment which we ought to have suffered. But that theory is not explicitly there anywhere in the New Testament, even in the Epistle to the Romans. 'Before the Reformation, only a few hints of a Penal Theory can be found'— Grensted, op. cit., p. 191. It is to Luther and Calvin that we owe its vigorous affirmation and development—see Grensted, op. cit., chs. 9 and 10.

[7] See e.g. J. Pedersen, *Israel, Its Life and Culture*, OUP, rev. edn., 1959, 299–375 (see esp. p. 359).

Father. And in so far as he is, and is thought of in the New Testament as being a distinct being, that way of thinking is to some extent possible.

But in so far as Christ is God himself, he cannot offer a sacrifice to himself. The sacrifice model has then to be somewhat transformed. God makes available the sacrifice (of himself), but it is we who have to offer it. Christ's laid-down life is there made available for sacrifice, like a ram caught in a thicket. Any man who is humble and serious enough about his sin to recognize what is the proper reparation and penance for it may use the costly gift which another has made available for him to offer as his sacrifice. On this model Christ's death has no efficacy until men choose to plead it in atonement for their sins. In so far as Christ the Son is distinct from God the Father, the sacrifice takes place independently of us, but even here we can hardly gain the benefit of forgiveness from it until we associate ourselves with it. That is even more obvious if we stress the unity of Christ the Son with the Father. I believe that this caveat is implicit in the New Testament. It seems to me quite contrary to the spirit of the New Testament to suppose that men's sins are removed without their being involved in the process of removal—this would be overlooking sin rather than taking it seriously. For if, as some Reformers have claimed, God forgives men before men seek him, God would not be taking men seriously, he would be treating with contempt the chosen hostility to himself of free agents. He would be saying 'Forget it!'. Rather, the sinner has to use Christ's death to get forgiveness. For example, in Revelation, the blessed are said to have 'washed their robes and made them white in the blood of the lamb'.[8] Their robes are not white before the sinners have done the washing; and only those who have washed their robes 'have the right to come to the tree of life'. If the sinner could be forgiven as a result of Christ's death, without using it to secure forgiveness, we could be forgiven by God as a result of what had happened on Calvary independently of our knowing about it; and that seems a suggestion very distant from the New Testament. Forgiveness is available through 'repentance and baptism in the name of Jesus Christ'.[9] And,

---

[8] Rev. 7: 14.

[9] Acts 2: 38. Of course there are places in the New Testament where there is talk of God 'forgiving' men, without there being any explicit mention of the need for prior penitence. But the presuppositions of that need must be assumed from such passages as the one cited, where there is explicit mention of it. I did, however, suggest (p. 86) that someone wronged might be right to overlook a wrongdoing which was not

as I shall emphasize later, baptism is baptism into the death of Christ; it is using that death.

The biblical model of Christ's life and death as a sacrifice amounts to an account (in the terms of my Chapter 5) of it as an offering made available to us men to offer as our reparation and penance. There is no need to suppose that life and death to be the equivalent of what men owe to God (or that plus appropriate penance), however that could be measured. It is simply a costly penance and reparation sufficient for a merciful God to let men off the rest.[10] It is a life lived and given voluntarily for that purpose by one who, being God, did not owe God anything, and hence a gift to us. 'I lay down my life,' said Christ, 'no one taketh it from me, but I lay it down of myself.'[11] But Christ did not commit suicide. Rather, living honestly and proclaiming the truth, he was wrongly condemned to death for that. The voluntariness was a matter of Christ doing works of supererogation despite the foreseen consequence that unjust men would kill him.[12] Thereby, allowing his life to be taken as a result of his living it with great sanctity, and given the element of my theological assumption that Christ gave his life for the purpose of removing our sin, Christ's life is then ours for this purpose and so we can offer it to God as the life we ought to have led (our substitute reparation and penance). 'Greater love hath no man than this, that a man lay down his life for his friends.'[13] My account provides an account of how Christ's intention in laying down his life is fulfilled.

'Our life is a failure,' we may now say. 'We have made a mess of the life which you gave us, we have made no reparation of our own for our sins, nor have we helped others to make atonement for their sins.

serious, for example, because it was an objective wrongdoing of which the wrongdoer was unaware, and in that extended sense 'forgive' the wrongdoer.

[10] The centuries between Augustine and Aquinas contained much talk about our sin being of infinite wickedness, and Christ's suffering on our behalf being of infinite intensity. Duns Scotus got away from that exaggerated talk. See Grensted, op. cit., pp. 158 ff. Our sin is awful, but how one measures it is a somewhat arbitrary matter. And since Christ suffered as man, he can only have suffered up to the limit of human capacity, and the worth of his suffering was the worth of human suffering. The Reformers inevitably reverted to infinitistic talk—see Grensted, op. cit., p. 243, for his quotations from Turretin.

[11] John 10: 17 f.

[12] For this as Christ's attitude to his death, see C. F. D. Moule, *The Origin of Christology*, CUP, 1977, 109 f. See the whole of his ch. 4 for a fuller discussion of the New Testament understanding of Redemption.

[13] John 15: 13.

But we have been given a perfect life, not owed to you, O God. We offer you this life instead of the life we should have led, and instead of the lives which others (in whose sins we are involved) should have led. Take its perfection instead of our imperfection. We are serious enough about our sins to repent and apologize and to offer you back an offering of this value as our reparation and penance.'

On the sacrifice model, God's action (until we come to the forgiveness stage) is confined to his action in Christ of allowing himself to suffer as man. On the penal model, God acts also as punishing judge. There is no parallel for that in the sacrifice model, and that is much to its credit.

Although most writers on redemption loosely refer to Christ's (life and) death as a sacrifice, the Jewish understanding of sacrifice was no longer part of the Christian way of thinking after the second century AD, and hence the prevalence of other models. The thinker who brought back into Christian thought what is in essence the sacrifice model was Anselm. He phrases it, however, in terms very close to my own terms. The term he uses most frequently for what is rendered by Christ to God is 'satisfaction'. Anselm makes the point that something beyond reparation is owed, and he uses 'satisfaction' to denote reparation plus penance.[14] Christ effects this atonement as man and it is to God the Father that this atonement is voluntarily rendered by one who is himself God.[15] Anselm is sometimes seen as a precursor of the penal theory, but that seems a mistaken interpretation. Punishment is something imposed by the wronged party (in this case, God); atonement is offered voluntarily. Anselm writes of 'satisfaction, that is . . . voluntary payment of the debt' which overrides the need for 'punishment'.[16]

Anselm's *Cur Deus Homo* is a magnificent achievement, a restoration of some basic New Testament ideas; but it has its faults. It makes the rendering of satisfaction, of an amount of reparation equal to the harm done and penance required, necessary before forgiveness can be given. And it leaves it quite unclear how the benefits of Christ's death come to us. Aquinas takes over Anselm's basic idea, but remedies these deficiencies. Christ's life and death

---

[14] *Cur Deus Homo* 1.12.

[15] On this point see op. cit. 2.8; 2.7 and 1 *passim*.

[16] Op. cit. 1.19. See Grensted, pp. 121 ff.; and p. 129. The Devil is removed from the picture—'Does not the omnipotence of God reign everywhere? What then did God lack that he should descend from Heaven to defeat the Devil?'—*Cur Deus Homo* 1.6. See Grensted, p. 127.

were desirable but not necessary. It provided proper reparation and penance, but it is we who have to repent and apologize.[17] The benefits of Christ's death flow to us through our incorporation into it in baptism.[18] And Aquinas regards his theory as a sacrifice theory.[19]

Granted the purity of the present of Christ's life offered to God, why does it have to be a human life which is offered, why not an angelic life, or why not some private deed in the fifth heaven known only to God? Aquinas, following Augustine, held that indeed there were other ways open by which reparation and penance could be made, but that there was something peculiarly appropriate in the method chosen.[20] Although I do not find Aquinas' account of wherein lies the appropriateness altogether satisfactory, I believe that the basic point is right. The best reparation is that in which the reparation restores the damage done rather than gives something else in compensation. If I damage your wooden fence, I ought to repair it if I can rather than give you a crate of whisky instead. Or if there is no wood with which to repair the fence, perhaps I can do something else which will restore something like the status quo, at any rate in essentials—for example, erect a wire fence instead. This is because the point of reparation is to restore the status quo as nearly as possible. Likewise, the best penance is that which more than makes it up to you in the respect in which I harmed you—for example, perhaps I can finish the fence if it was not completed before; or having damaged the rusty bumper of your car, I can do penance better by giving you a new bumper, rather than restoring the old one and giving you a box of chocolates at the same time. This is because

---

[17] As I quoted in ch. 5, Aquinas, *Summa Theologiae* 3a. 48.2 ad 1, accepts the objection that 'the man who sins must do the repenting and confess', while affirming that 'satisfaction has to do with the exterior act, and here one can make use of instruments, a category under which friends are included.'

[18] Christ by his passion merited salvation, not only for himself, but for all who are his members, as well [i.e. members of his body the Church, which they become by baptism]'—*Summa Theologiae* 3a. 48.3. 'Christ's passion, the universal cause of the forgiveness of sins, has to be applied to individuals if they are to be cleansed from their sins. This is done by baptism and penance and the other sacraments, which derive their power from the passion of Christ'—ibid. 3a. 49.1 ad 4.

[19] 'It is clear that Christ's passion was a true sacrifice'—*Summa Theologiae* 3a. 48.3. For Aquinas, however, it is Christ who offers the sacrifice to the Father. He does not, when developing his ideas in terms of sacrifice, use the point which he himself makes in the quotation in n. 17 that it is the sinner who makes use of 'instruments' provided by another.

[20] See Aquinas, *Summa Theologiae* 3a. 46.1–4. On this point Aquinas quotes Augustine, *De Trinitate* 13.10.

penance, to be good, must evince a concern that the particular harm was done which was done. It must show a sensitivity to that rather than be something which could have been a penance for anything or the repayment of a debt. Thereby it expresses the penitent's awareness of what he has done. Since what needs atonement to God is human sin, men living second-rate lives when they have been given such great opportunities by their creator, appropriate reparation and penance would be made by a perfect human life, given away through being lived perfectly.

Did the sacrifice have to be made by God himself becoming man? Could not any ordinary man have made it? Traditional theology has found two difficulties in the way of the sacrifice of any ordinary man availing, arising from the two aspects of the original sin belonging to ordinary men—their involvement in Adam's guilt and their sinfulness. His involvement in Adam's guilt would make an ordinary man's offering impure. I argued in the last chapter, however, along with many pre-Augustinian theologians, that we present-day men do not bear the guilt of Adam's sin. We are, however, as I argued in the last chapter, 'involved' in the sins of our brethren (including Adam) in that we have an obligation to help them to deal with their sins. If they are alive, we can urge them to repent and apologize. Whether they are alive or dead, we could do something supererogatory which (when they know of it) they could offer as their reparation and penance. However, in virtue of our status as creatures, it is very difficult for ordinary men to make available an atonement for the sins of others. We ordinary men, even if we had not sinned ourselves, would owe so much to God anyway (for reasons given in Chapter 8) that the little extra we could do for our brethren in this way would not amount to very much. Only when I owe you nothing can I give you something. God in taking in Christ a human nature, a body, and a human way of thinking and acting, did not cease to be God. Being God, Christ owed God nothing; and he owed little to man. For no man was responsible for his existence; and in so far as other men provided for him the benefits of bodily life, nurture, and education, they only gave back to him his own and did so only in virtue of being given by God the power to do so. Although God in Christ took our character, he did not inherit our past. Hence, virtually his whole life was available to be given away. His living a life honest and generous unto death, being supererogatory, could be made available for our use.

The other difficulty which traditional theology found in the way of an ordinary man making atonement is his sinfulness. It will be very difficult, well nigh impossible, for one as prone to sin as men are (as we saw in the last chapter) to offer a pure life. That seems correct. But then the problem arises—would not a God who took upon himself in full our nature have been equally prone to sin? Did Christ take upon himself our liability to sin? Theological tradition has been fairly unanimous in affirming not merely that Christ did not sin, but that he was not able to sin. But in that case, surely the perfection of his life would not have resulted from such moral effort as the perfection of a normal human life, and so would not have been so full an offering?

Now certainly Christ could not sin (in my sense of the term), and that for the trivial reason that sin (as I have defined it) is wronging God, and Christ, being God, could not wrong himself. Theology has, however, wished to affirm more substantially by the claim that Christ was incapable of sin, that he was incapable of doing wrong, for example to us men by lying to us or cheating us.[21] That claim, given our theological assumption, must be correct. God is essentially good. It is wrong to put yourself in a position where you are under an influence inclining you to wrong another; it is wrong to drink if you are going to drive, to take drugs if it will make you inclined to fail in your obligations to your family. It would have been wrong of God in becoming incarnate to take upon himself a proneness to do wrong. Thus, being essentially good, he could not have become incarnate in that way.

However, it does not follow from that that it would have been wrong of God in becoming incarnate to take upon himself a proneness (on balance) not to do what is supererogatorily good. There is nothing wrong in doing that; and in certain circumstances it may be the best thing to do an action which involves taking upon yourself such a proneness. Suppose I have no debts but a large regular income out of which I give generously to such good causes as come to my notice. But an even better good cause comes to my notice (e.g. founding a school) which I do not have enough money to undertake. I therefore invest the money which I would normally give to other good causes in a risky venture. If the venture succeeds,

---

[21] For example, the synodical letter of the Council of Nicaea anathematized the view that Christ was capable in virtue of his free will of choosing between virtue (ἀρετή) and vice (κακία) Denzinger, 130.

I shall have enough money to found the school; if it fails, I shall not. Meanwhile, I shall be able to give money to any other good cause only by cutting back on my standard of living, and I shall be strongly inclined (on balance) not to do this. If the great good cause is great enough, investing the money may be the best action; but I thereby subject myself to a balance of desire (that is, inclinations) not to give to lesser good causes, which I would not otherwise have, and which I need to resist if I am to show supererogatory goodness. If God put himself in the situation where he can only do a great supererogatory good by allowing himself to be subject to a balance of inclination not to do lesser supererogatory goods, he does not do an act less-good than he would do if he did not take the risk. (In becoming incarnate under these conditions, he would, of course, have been taking the risk that he would fail to live a saintly life which would have made a pure atonement. But his failure would not have wronged anyone. It would just have left things as they were.)

So I conclude that it would have been compatible with God's perfect goodness to put himself in a situation where he was subject to a balance of inclination not to do the best available act. In order to live a life deriving a goodness from pursuing the good despite a contrary balance of desire to which he had freedom to yield, God could, I suggest, have become incarnate in that way. On the other hand, there would have been great goodness (even if not goodness of the kind which, by the criteria of Chapter 2, deserves moral praise) in God becoming incarnate in such a way as necessarily to do the best action available to him in all the circumstances in which he was placed. He could still have suffered much pain, including the pain of resisting bad desire, although it was a bad desire to which he could not yield, because he always had a stronger contrary desire. The fact that you have so trained yourself that you cannot yield to some bad desire (you have developed a stronger contrary good desire) does not mean that the pain of the frustration of the bad desire is any less. Traditional theology holds that Christ did suffer pain, including pain from the frustration of desire; but it has not always been very clear about the distinction between Christ doing a wrong act and Christ doing less than the best,[22] and so about whether Christ's

---

[22] Aquinas listed 'difficulty in doing good' among the disabilities to which Christ was not prone. See *Summa Theologiae* 3a. 14.4. This disability, together with 'proneness to evil' were, according to Augustine, among the disabilities resulting from original sin. However, neither Aquinas nor Augustine had in mind when discussing

temptations to do less than the best were ones to which he could yield (because free and not subject to a stronger contrary desire) or could not yield (because subject to a stronger contrary desire to do the best).[23] As Eliot wrote, 'the impossible is still temptation'.[24] Either way, given my assumption, Christ did the best and lived an objectively saintly life ending in a foreseen death; and publicly intended that life as a means of removing human sin. Although he was under no obligation to do so, God showed that he accepted the offering as sufficient for the purpose for which it was made by taking it over; for (given my assumption) he intervened in the natural order to bring the embodied Christ to life again in the Resurrection.[25]

I argued in Chapter 5 that it is the victim of wrongdoing—in this case God—who has the right to choose, up to the limit of an equivalent to the harm done and the need for a little more in penance, how much reparation and penance to require before he will forgive. So, despite all of these considerations about man's inability to make substantial reparation and penance, God could have chosen to accept one supererogatory act of an ordinary man as adequate for the sins of the world. Or he could have chosen to accept some angel's act for this purpose.[26] But if it is good that there be reparation and penance, it is good that these be substantial; that the atoning sacrifice be not a

---

Christ's temptations the distinction between the obligatory and the supererogatory; and so Aquinas' 'difficulty in doing good' may be read simply as 'difficulty in doing some good act' rather than as 'difficulty in doing the best'. For all Aquinas says in this place, Christ might not be necessitated to do the best. My own preference among these two theories is for the theory that (at any rate on some occasion or occasions) Christ was subject to a balance of desire not to do the best, and overcame that balance by a voluntary act. That would make his life and death morally praiseworthy, which in effect is surely the biblical and subsequent Christian view. The change of character involved in original sin I have interpreted simply as the 'proneness to evil'. (According to later Latin theology, the mechanism whereby Christ was protected from original sin was his virgin birth, original sin being transmitted by the male semen. See e.g. Augustine, *Enchiridion* 34 and 41; and Aquinas, *Summa Theologiae* 3a. 31.1 ad 3. But there seems no very good reason for adopting that account.)

[23] In one place Pope Leo seems to imply that there were in Christ no discordant desires at all producing inner conflict (Denzinger 299), which seems to fly straight in the face of the biblical affirmation that Christ was tempted.

[24] T. S. Eliot, *Murder in the Cathedral*, 3rd edn., Faber, 1938, 26.

[25] For more detailed argument on the consequences for the human nature of Christ, of Christ being God and so essentially good, see my paper 'Could God Become Man?', forthcoming in a volume of lectures delivered to the Royal Institute of Philosophy on the interactions of philosophy and theology, edited by G. N. A. Vesey.

[26] Scotus saw that very clearly. See Grensted, op. cit., pp. 160 f.

trivial one. And it is good too that our creator should share our lot, and of his generosity make available to us his sacrificial life.

Given my earlier arguments, the way in which we humans can use Christ's life and death as a means of removing sin is by offering it as our reparation and penance. To do so, we must join to it our feeble repentance and halting words of apology. There has to be a formal association with it in the process of our dissassociating ourselves from our own sins and from involvement in those of our ancestors. A further part of the theological assumption which I made was that Christ founded a body to carry on his work. The Christian Church provides a formal ceremony of association in the pledges made by the candidate for admission in its initiation ceremony of baptism and before participation in the Eucharist. These ceremonies are very closely tied to the redeeming death of Christ, and they involve the participants entering into that death. St Paul in Romans writes that 'we who were baptized into Christ Jesus were baptized into his death'; and it is through sharing in that death that we are 'justified from sin'.[27] In the Eucharist, St Paul wrote to the Corinthians, 'we proclaim the Lord's death until he come';[28] and, of course, our participation in that involves receiving Christ's 'body and blood', which, whatever else it means, means at least the benefits of his laid-down life. We plead the sacrifice of Christ in joining and rejoining ourselves to the new humanity, the new and voluntary association of those who accept Christ's offering on their behalf, the Church. In so doing we repent and apologize and offer that sacrifice as our reparation and atonement. But, as it is difficult to repent and utter the words of apology, that too the Church in its evangelistic and pastoral capacity helps men to do. In accepting Christ's offering, God accepted it as an offering which men could offer as their reparation and penance and which he would accept as that. Hence he pledges himself to forgive those who truly repent and apologize for their sins; though the weight of sin requires a thorough repentance and apology, for which initial words of 'I am sorry' might not suffice. However, repeated and sincere repentance, and apology must suffice for God's forgiveness; and those who die, thus forgiven, without fresh sins, die in the traditional terminology, 'in a state of grace'.

If redemption works by Christ providing a sacrifice which we can offer to God, then in the light of that model we can understand how

---

[27] Rom. 6: 1–7.   [28] I Cor. 11: 26.

Christ's life and death is a victory and, in a less literal sense, redeems us. It is a victory over evil because as a result of it we are no longer inevitably guilty; we have only to use it to throw off our guilt. It cuts the shackles which bind us; we have only to throw them away. And, to speak metaphorically, it 'pays off' evil; we have only to walk away from the prison. It is, however, only a punishment in the somewhat remote sense that it replaces the punishment which we would otherwise have deserved (though not one which God would necessarily have inflicted). But on my account, as on all the other accounts which I have considered so far, God in Christ performs an act which makes an objective contribution to removing our guilt which we ourselves were in no position to make. Christ's act is not efficacious solely in virtue of moving us to do something. Abelard's exemplary theory of the atonement, that Christ's life and death work to remove our sins by inspiring us to penitence and good acts, contains no objective transaction.[29] No doubt Christ's life of supererogatory goodness does so move us, and I shall stress this point myself in the next chapter. But it will move us even more if we believe that what he has done for us is to provide our reparation and penance. I have argued that it is good that God should provide that for us. Given that (as I assumed in my theological assumption) Christ publicly made available his life for the purpose of removing our sins, then it is available to us to plead as our reparation and penance.

[29] See Grensted, op. cit., pp. 103–11.

11

Sanctification and Corruption

Sanctification

The man who seeks to do the best will make atonement and use the atonement made available to him by others to purge himself from his past wrongdoing. Above all, he will purge himself from the sins of the past by pleading the sacrifice of Christ. He will also fulfil his obligations and do works of supererogation in the present. We saw in Chapter 8 how my theological assumption changes our understanding of which actions are good; and so of which moral beliefs are correct and of which desires are to be cultivated. It makes a difference to where the boundary lies between the obligatory and the supererogatory. It also adds actions to each list—worship and proclaiming the Gospel, prayer and helping others to pray, and theological study enter both lists in the sense that some worship, etc., becomes obligatory, more worship, etc., becomes supererogatory. Among works of supererogation are taking steps to mould one's character for the future, so that in future doing the good comes to one naturally and spontaneously.

I distinguished in Chapter 1 three kinds of goodness of character. There is the goodness of the agent naturally inclined to do the actions which are good. There is the goodness of the agent whose moral beliefs are correct. And finally, there is the goodness of the agent who is naturally inclined to do the good as he sees it. I called these three kinds of goodness of character goodness of desires, goodness of beliefs, and goodness of will. A truly good character will have all three; and one who has goodness of will will tend to acquire the other two. For he who seeks to do the good is likely to acquire at some time the belief that his moral beliefs are open to question, and so he will look for true beliefs. Among such true moral beliefs, I claimed in Chapter 1, is the belief that it is good that actions which are good be done not just because they are good, but for their own sake. The acquisition of this belief in turn will lead the agent with a good will to seek to have desires to do those actions for their own sake, to have a natural love for particular people and things. Among true moral beliefs also, as I shall argue in the next chapter, is the belief that the supremely worthwhile act for man is the 'beatific vision' of God in Heaven, and he who seeks a good character will cultivate a desire above all for that.

I pointed out in Chapter 1 that a maximally subjectively good act can be done only by someone who has no strong desire to pursue the good; and that the development of a good character makes it less and less open to an agent to do an action of the kind which alone deserves moral praise. Is it not a good reason for not developing a good character that you will deprive yourself of any opportunity for doing morally praiseworthy actions? No, it is not.

For what makes a subjectively good action good is that the agent believes that the action has an objective goodness which exists independently of his beliefs about it. If, despite a contrary desire, I keep a promise because I believe that it is good to do so, then the subjective goodness of my action arises from my conforming to a belief that promise-keeping is objectively good (and remains so whether or not I keep my promises). Actions are objectively good either because of some intrinsic quality (for example, an act of promise-keeping is good just because it is an act of promise-keeping) or because it brings about something beyond itself which is good (giving to Oxfam is good because it brings it about that the hungry are fed); that is they are good either because they constitute or because they forward the good. Now any action or set of actions of mine taking steps (despite present contrary desire) to form my character for good is an act of making myself in future prone to do actions which constitute or forward the good. Any act which (despite contrary desire) contributes to the formation of a good character will therefore be praiseworthy for just the same reason as any other act of forwarding the good (despite contrary desire). It is good because it tends to bring about subsequent acts which themselves contribute to or bring about the good. But by forming my character I am exercising now an agonizing choice of choosing the good despite contrary desire, in consequence of which I shall not need to exercise it later in such an agonizing form. Since pursuing the good despite contrary desire is difficult, if I refuse to develop my character I make it unlikely that I shall in future do the subjectively good action. Indeed, we are so made (see Chapter 1) that any refusal to do a subjectively good act when the opportunity is there makes it less likely that we will do it next time. A refusal to do the act of character-forming when it is available on the grounds that that will restrict the opportunity for subjectively good acts in future, since the good will come so naturally, will have the effect that we are less and less likely to do the subjectively good act when the opportunity does arise. No one who really thinks it good that the poor be fed or that God be honoured will refuse to make himself someone who does these things spontaneously, simply in order to have the opportunity in future to do a supremely morally praiseworthy act. Rather, the truly subjectively good agent seeks to make the good come so naturally that he has little opportunity for conscientious action in future.

Although it is good that I form my own character for good, it does not follow immediately from that that it is good that I should form the characters of others for good, and so deprive them of the opportunity for subjectively good action. It is good that they be able to exercise a serious choice of whether or not to pursue the good. The choice will be serious only if the bad as such is an option which the agent could choose, and that can only be if he is subject to some desire for what he believes to be bad—for reasons given in Chapter 2. If by moulding his character I deprive him of any such contrary desire, I deprive him of the choice of what sort of character he is to have. That deprivation has of course to be weighed against the good of having the good character which I am imposing on him, and the pros and cons of forming another's character are something on which I shall need to say more in due course. My only point here is that there are reasons why it is good that I do not form another's character for good which are not reasons why it is good that I do not form my own character for good.

We saw in Chapter 9 how unnatural it is for man, laden with original sinfulness, to have true moral beliefs, right desires, and a will naturally inclined to pursue the good. How shall his reformation be achieved? The formation of one's beliefs and desires is a process in which both outside forces and the agent himself have parts to play.

Beliefs are involuntary; we cannot choose immediately what to believe about some matter. We acquire evidence through our senses and feel that that evidence supports a certain belief; our beliefs are beliefs only because we believe that they are forced upon us by the world, and do not result from our choice. If we could choose what to 'believe' and our choices were immediately efficacious, we would realize that our 'beliefs' resulted from our choices and were not forced on us by the world. Hence we would realize that our 'beliefs' had no connection with how things were in the world, and so we would have no reason for supposing those 'beliefs' to be true and so we would not really believe them. True, we might condition ourselves over time to hold beliefs which we do not now think likely to be true, but that is a foolish enterprise, and should not be pursued by the rational man. For someone who is setting about forcing himself to believe things which, in his present opinion, are unlikely to be true must regard himself as attempting to force upon himself (probably) false beliefs; and so beliefs which are likely to lead him astray when he is attempting to attain his goals. The rational man allows his beliefs to come to him, and to be moulded by new evidence unsought by him which may change or add to the set of his beliefs. He does not seek to distort the belief-forming process.

What applies to beliefs generally applies in particular to moral beliefs. We may acquire new moral beliefs by being shown the consequences of our actions (being shown what it is like to be insulted, by being insulted ourselves); or by seeing or being shown the internal coherence and adequacy to our moral intuitions of some developed system of morality. While an agent cannot choose which beliefs to have about some matter, he can choose which matter to have beliefs about. He can choose to set out to investigate some area and to acquire better justified beliefs than he currently has. A man who is seeking to do good actions, and above all to form a good character will seek to open himself to argument and experience which will give him a better moral understanding. (At least, he will if he believes it good so to do; and he is likely to acquire that belief in the course of time.) And since general metaphysical and theological considerations crucially affect the content of morality (in the way illustrated in Chapter 8), he will seek to have true metaphysical and theological beliefs.[1] He will seek to discover whether there is a God, and whether he has intervened in history and done various things for us and told us various important truths.[2]

---

[1] For extended argument in defence of positions affirmed in the last two paragraphs, see my *Faith and Reason*, Clarendon Press, 1981, especially chs. 1–3.
[2] I argued in *The Existence of God* that it is within our capacity to reach reasonably well-justified conclusions on these matters.

Circumstances not subject to our control may also strengthen or weaken, add to or subtract from our desires; but an agent can take deliberate steps to form his desires (steps which often have some prospect, though no sure guarantee, of success). The deliberate cultivation of a particular desire, unlike the deliberate cultivation of a particular belief, is a highly rational enterprise. The agent who seeks a good character will seek to make himself desire to do and experience those things which, he anteriorly believes, are good. Desires arise from a mixture of physiological and cultural causes. My desires for food or drink, sleep or sex have largely physiological origins; and there is often some prospect of changing them by simple bodily actions or by chemical means. Eating will often rid me of my desire to eat, but if it doesn't there are drugs which may help. More sophisticated desires can sometimes also be altered by simple bodily or chemical techniques. I can lessen my desire to smash your head in by taking harmless violent exercise instead. Longer term and more sophisticated desires have more in the way of cultural causes. My desire to visit Antarctica may be caused by someone telling me of its beauties. I can seek to control my more sophisticated desires by forcing myself to take seriously things which I believe but haven't faced up to. I can stimulate my desire to give to Oxfam by visiting Bangladesh and viewing the poverty which I know I will find there. And above all, the most frequent method of developing a desire to do actions of some kind is by doing an action of that kind. You get in the habit of doing the action and so you become naturally inclined to do it in future. By forcing yourself to tell the truth when it is difficult, you gradually get into the habit of telling the truth, and then you find truth telling a natural inclination. (I commented in Chapter 1 that habituation of this kind is a characteristic of humans and animals and might not hold for any other rational creatures.)

Similarly, just as an agent may train himself to desire to do certain specific actions, so he may train himself to desire to pursue the good as such. Through reminding himself of the range of goodness, and through the practice of pursuing it, and through the practice of frustrating contrary desires, he may develop a holy will.

In the developing of such a will, as, to a lesser extent, in developing more specific desires, it is important to train oneself to frustrate other desires (however good in themselves) when they show signs of deterring one from pursuit of the better. A major reason for the practice of many ascetic disciplines for limited periods (such as Lent) is for a man to train himself not to indulge such desires as the desire for food except when it is good so to do. A man trains himself for a limited period to resist a desire for food, when otherwise it would be good to indulge it, in order to make it easier for him outside that period to resist that desire when it is not good to indulge it. The Church's 'precepts', of which I wrote in Chapter 8, are advice (and sometimes very tough advice) as to how to mould your desires for good. Further, it is often a useful technique when a man finds it very difficult to do good actions for the balance of right reasons, that he should remind himself or others should remind him of the lesser good purposes which the good action serves. While to avoid the pains of Hell is always a good reason for doing anything at all, including worshipping God or giving to the poor, there are other good and often better reasons for doing the latter things. But if it is very difficult to get yourself to give out of love for the poor, it is good to remind yourself that by giving you avoid the pains of Hell (if you so believe). That will make giving come more easily. The miserly desire for possession, being vanquished on several occasions, will not have such strength in future. That will make it easier to give out of love for the poor on a future occasion; and having done it once, it becomes easier to do it again. Threats are a useful spur to virtue, not because they immediately produce virtuous action, but because they weaken the power of desires which inhibit the pursuit of virtue.

So a man may deliberately choose to mould his character, seeking true beliefs about which actions are good, and seeking to develop desires to do those actions and to pursue the good itself. Or merely through doing actions which he believes to be good, a man may unintentionally make it come naturally to him to do such actions. Virtuous action would thus have its own unsought reward in virtuous character. In view of the enormous influence of habit on desire (doing or failing to do an action once making it easier or harder to do it again), the agent himself is a major influence on his own character.

But, as we have seen, circumstances (upbringing and environment, what one hears and reads, the examples one sees) make it much harder or easier to build up or maintain a good character. Our beliefs are formed very largely by what others tell us, and our desires are much influenced by what others encourage us to do or deter us from doing. Our families and our culture have a large influence, which it is hard for most of us to resist. We saw in particular in Chapter 9 how a corrupt society may give a man wrong moral beliefs, evil desires, and a will with little desire for the good. Conversely, of course, a society may promote good character—goodness of belief and desire by verbal teaching about what is good and by examples of good behaviour which help a child to see its worth; and goodness of will by encouraging and not frustrating the following of conscience.

If circumstances help, a man on earth can make his will so dedicated to the good (i.e. so desirous of the good) that in the normal circumstances of life he will inevitably pursue the good. But even the saints on some occasions have desires which they regard it as wrong to indulge on those occasions. And in particular, however much they train themselves to work hard and do without sleep, there comes to them, as more frequently to all of us, sloth, the desire for rest which seems the one inescapable desire of embodied man; and it will often attack a saint at a time when he judges that there is a task which it is better that he should do than that he should sleep. Such desires will be regarded by the saint as 'extrinsic', external forces to which he is subject, not welcomed or appreciated desires. But he can only be free of such desires when his earthly body is no longer his. So total unchangeable dedication of will cannot belong to man on earth—such is the normal Christian view; it is that of Augustine, Aquinas, and the Council of Trent, and also of Luther and Calvin.[3] What can, however, be formed, is a will dedicated to the good, with true beliefs about which actions are good, naturally pursuing what is believed to be good, subject only to contrary desires which in most normal circumstances of life are far too weak for the agent to need to devote effort to resisting them (i.e. they are normally weaker than his desire for the good, and so he does not need to choose between yielding to them and pursuing the good). One so endowed, we may say, is a saint.

In writing that a man has true beliefs about which actions are good I mean, more precisely, that he has true beliefs about the moral principles which have consequenes for which is the best action for him to do in most normal circumstances of life. Factual error or ignorance may make him unable to apply these moral principles; with the best intentions, the saint may forget that he has made some

---

[3] See J. Passmore, *The Perfectibility of Man*, Duckworth, 1970, ch. 5. See also the Bull of Clement V (Denzinger, 891). For the contrary view, that perfection is attainable on earth, see the views of some Quakers and Methodists (Passmore, op. cit., ch. 7.

promise, and for this reason be ignorant of his obligations on some occasion, and he is no less a saint for that. But there is something morally the matter with someone who does not believe that he ought to keep promises. The phrase 'most normal circumstances of life' has now entered twice into the definition of a saint. He is one who has no difficulty in pursuing the good, except in circumstances where the applicable moral principles are of unusual kinds or he is subject to quite unusually strong desires to act contrary to his moral beliefs. Who counts as a saint thus becomes in some small degree arbitrary; but this will be found not to matter for the uses to which we shall need to put the concept of sanctity in the next chapter. Note that human goodness can always be bettered; it has no maximum. However much we know about moral truths, we may not know the moral principles which apply in some circumstance wildly beyond our understanding. And however firm our dedication to the good, we could become subject to some contrary desire which put it to serious test. Only God can conceive of all conceivable circumstances and so understand the moral principles which apply to them; and only God can ensure that he is not subject to tempting desire.

The acquisition of new moral beliefs is clearly a procedure that often takes some time. No one in the passing of a second can acquire a belief that the most worthwhile thing ever to be sought is the beatific vision of the blessed Trinity; he has to acquire some theological concepts before he can hold that belief. But the formation of a good will, a firm desire for the good as such, can perhaps sometimes (though not, I suspect, normally) be a fairly quick process, and so thorough that it makes actions come quite easily which before were impossible. The acquisition of a good will and the resulting natural pursuit for their own sake of things believed good can be very sudden. Of course there are superficial quick conversions, but there are deep ones as well. Neither 'once-born' nor 'twice-born' should be suspicious of the other.[4]

Although there are many influences on humans, most of them are unintentional—one man often gives another a good example of how to behave without intending thereby to influence his behaviour. Parents, schools, and government, however, sometimes seek intentionally to form the characters of children and even adults. Often their concern is only with fairly low-level goodness; they seek only to

[4] For Calvin's view that approximating to perfection is a very gradual process, see Passmore, op. cit., pp. 157f.

make others naturally inclined to fulfil their obligations. But there is in the world one institution with a primary concern to promote supererogatory goodness of action and character, supererogatory goodness of those kinds which are shown to be such by our theological assumption—including worshipping God and seeking to get others to worship God for his supererogatory goodness shown in our Redemption, by the varied means which he has provided for this purpose. That institution of course is the Church. As we all know, the Church's educational system may be counter-productive; children finding its teaching and example uninspiring, rebel against it. But if my theological assumption is correct and so the Church's ideal of sanctity is a correct one, then the presentation of that ideal by teaching and example ought to encourage that ideal; for that ideal is a good one, and those capable of recognizing a new kind of goodness (as humans generally are) when they are shown this new kind and when they are shown what makes it a kind of goodness (e.g. its similarities to obvious kinds of goodness) will recognize that and so be inclined to pursue it. If that does not happen, then the teaching must be poor, the example weak, or the child must have some contrary desire (e.g. the desire to be different from others) which in the circumstances works against the assimilation of the teaching. Other things being equal, the Church will be the means of sanctification. The supreme example which it presents for imitation is the example of Jesus Christ sacrificing himself to atone for human sins. Also, it was because of Christ's death on the Cross and his Resurrection (given my theological assumption that the latter occurred) that the Church came into being to bring men to sanctity. For these two reasons, Christ's atoning death must be the supreme means of human sanctification—for without it there would be neither the Teacher (the Church) nor the supreme example of sanctity (Christ) for it to present. That atoning death accepted by God in the Resurrection led to the foundation of a church and gave it an ideal which inspires those forgiven through its agency to seek sanctity in imitating it.

The Atonement and so all that flowed from it in the way of the Church, its preaching and sacraments, was, if my theological assumption is correct, due to God's intervention in Christ in history. His gracious action thus helps men on the way to sanctity; and so, to use the theological expression, he provides through the Church means of grace. God's 'grace' is God's gracious action. For many

writers (especially the Greek-speaking Fathers) this is shown in all
God's work of creating the world and forming man and his
environment;[5] other writers write only of God's influence in forming
a specifically Christian character as his 'grace'. But for all Christian
writers God's grace is concentrated and especially manifest in the
latter process whereby God's action in redemption leads men to use
that act to become forgiven and to become holy. A man is in a state
of grace in so far as he has allowed God's gracious action to work in
him. I have described the grace which flows through the Church to
its members as deriving by natural processes from God's original
intervention in history in Christ. However, I do not wish to rule out
subsequent intervention by God into natural processes in order to
forward his gracious work. My argument for the operation of God's
grace through the Church does not, however, require the occurrence
of any such subsequent interventions.

But, of course, men are also helped to virtue in ways distant from
Christian ecclesiastical influence—by the example of a Ghandi or
the teaching of a Mill. Yet, if my theological assumption is correct,
God sustains in men all the abilities which they have and thus keeps
in being the other chains of influence which inspire to virtue.
Although a Ghandi or a Mill have to use their abilities, it is God who
gives them the power to do so, and so (if we use 'grace' in the
extended sense) provides through them also means of grace.

And in so far as man's journey to sanctity requires also his own
effort, that too, given my theological assumption, will only be
possible if God gives him that ability. So God's grace is indeed a
necessary condition for the beginning as well as the completion of
the formation of a good character. In theological terms, man needs
both 'prevenient' grace, i.e. grace which allows a man to make a first
free choice of a God-ward (or perhaps Christ-ward) action, as well as
'co-operating' grace to help him make further choices. Augustine
insisted on the need for prevenient grace; but he seems to have meant
by it irresistible prevenient grace. Later Latin theology also insisted
on the need for prevenient grace; but some of it, culminating in the
formal declarations of the Council of Trent, insisted that man had a
free will to choose whether or not to co-operate with this grace. We
noted this debate at greater length in Chapter 9.

[5] See N. N. Glubokowsky, 'Grace in the Greek Fathers (to St John of Damascus)
and Inter-Church Union' in W. T. Whitley (ed.), *The Doctrine of Grace*, SCM Press,
1932.

At times in theological history there has been dispute about whether a pagan can do ordinary good actions without grace. Among the vast majority of disputants who allowed both that pagans sometimes do perform voluntary good actions and that without God's agency they would have neither the capacity nor the opportunity to do such good actions, it is difficult to see anything except a terminological dispute about which of God's acts of enabling men to do good are to be called acts of providing 'grace'. There have, I suppose, been occasional theists who have not thought through their theism enough to realise that theism is committed to the doctrine that God's action is a necessary condition of men doing good (or evil). And there have been occasional hardliners who have claimed that pagans do not do ordinary good actions. The latter claim is, however, manifestly false. Pagans do perform objective, spontaneous, and subjectively good actions. And, given my theological assumption, God's action is necessary if men are to be able to do such good actions.

Although non-Christian influences can conduce to creating a good will (help a man to form a firm desire for the good), if my theological assumption is correct, Christian influences are necessary for the *final* stage of the formation of a saint. For a man is a saint only if he has true moral beliefs and desires to do those actions which he believes truly to be good. It follows from my assumption that these actions will include worship of God and pleading the atoning of Christ—of the goodness of which latter a man could know, clearly, only as a result of Christian influences. The particular grace which flows from the Church is necessary for the final perfecting of souls; and, since, as we saw earlier, pleading that atoning death is secured through membership of the Church, then, given that only saints are finally saved (an issue which I shall discuss in the next chapter), *extra ecclesiam nulla salus*; there can be no *final* salvation outside the Church. The saint will belong to the Church; to be a saint, either here *or hereafter* a man must be joined to the Church, and its grace must flow through his spiritual veins.

Corruption

Man is born sensitive to moral considerations. Barring a few possible exceptions of those with severe psychological malformities, all children—whatever their intellectual and practical abilities—are open to developing a good character. They are, to start with, capable of having good desires, capable of natural love and loyalty; capable too of believing that certain actions are the right ones to do; capable too of choosing to do actions which they believe right, despite contrary inclinations. But this matrix of belief and desire may be corrupted, as well as sanctified—first, through the agent's own choice. He may yield to desires for what he believes to be wrong. If he does this once, his moral belief will still be there when he faces his next temptation. If, yielding to a desire for money, I steal, contrary to my belief that stealing is wrong, the belief will still be there when the next opportunity to steal arises. But habit which strengthens good desires strengthens bad ones too. And, further, as we know anyway and the psychological study of cognitive dissonance has recently brought to our attention again, men find such a situation of conflict between action and belief intolerable.[6] Gradually, unless a man to some degree pursues the good, one of two things happens. First, the agent may try to persuade himself that the action which he believes to be wrong, say stealing, is not really wrong. He looks for disanalogies between stealing and other wrong acts, and analogies between stealing and acts which are not wrong. 'It's only luck the victim had the watch to start with,' says the thief; 'so I'm just upsetting the balance of luck. Anyway, hardly anyone really loses anything, because almost everybody is insured.' And so on. Or secondly, the agent may say 'I don't care about right and wrong. I'm not going to be a moral man in future.' In one or other of these ways the agent intentionally dulls his conscience, blinds himself to awareness of good and bad, right and wrong. Both of these processes are processes of self-deception, a process whose structure Freud drew so well to our attention. He showed how self-deception was an intentional act of suppressing some belief from consciousness, which also involved the act of suppressing from consciousness the belief that you were performing that act or any other self-deceptive act. In the first case the agent refuses to admit to himself the wrongness of a particular act, and tries to persuade himself that the act is morally indifferent or good. The second case may not initially look like a case of self-deception. Do we not have here a deliberate and honest choice not to be moral? At stage one, yes. But a man will only reach

---

[6] See e.g. R. A. Wicklund and J. W. Brehm, *Perspectives on Cognitive Dissonance*, Lawrence Erlbaum, 1976.

equilibrium, and not be subject to the nagging of conscience, if he persuades himself that those features of actions (e.g. causing pain) which make for their moral goodness or badness is something about them that doesn't matter. But since, on the understanding of moral goodness or badness which I spelled out in Chapter 1, there is involved in an action being morally good or bad that it matters that it be done or be not done, this self-persuasion involves self-persuasion that no actions are morally good or bad. Yet, since it seemed to the agent originally that some actions were good or bad in this way, self-deception is involved.

Each of these processes takes time; conscience is not easy to exterminate. The second process would require repeated acts of brutal repression of conscience finally to exterminate conscience in all areas of its operation. The first process is only designed to make conscience insensitive in a certain area. If the agent suppressed it in other areas too, gradually it would cease to be operative at all; and the final result would be the same as that resulting from initial adoption of the second process. But if the agent accepted the dictates of conscience in another area, his perception of goodness being sharpened thereby, his conscience could reassert itself in the area in which he had chosen to ignore it.

So the corruption of will involved in not following conscience leads to a corruption of belief, ultimately so that there are no moral beliefs. A few good desires may remain; a man who has lost his understanding of morality may still love a particular woman. But that desire will be at the mercy of physiology; it will have no backing from reason. The agent does not see it as a good desire to be cultivated and acted upon, rather than some rival desire (e.g. to torture a child). Corruption has the consequence that a man is no longer open to the influence of reason to guide him to nurture worthwhile desires; he will have become merely an arena of competing desires. Clearly some bad choices help this process along much more than others. If one chooses the bad only in some minor respect, one's will may remain set on the good in respects recognized as more important. But if one deliberately chooses the bad in a respect recognized as all-important, one is setting oneself against the moral world. In theological terms, this is the distinction between venial and mortal sin, whether or not the agent is a theist and recognizes it as such. Repeated venial sin may sometimes be a stage towards a general contempt for the obligatory, and hence towards mortal sin. One mortal sin is not enough to produce total contempt for morality. Conscience will nag again; but repeated mortal sin will produce the state of total corruption. Sin is less serious in so far as the agent's choice is less deliberate (in so far as he is swayed by passion).⁷ The downward path may, of course, as we saw in the last chapter, be greatly helped by corrupt society—bad morals, bad influences. The absence of grace, or, more positively, the presence of evil influences, assist.

Why would a good God allow other men to make it easier or more difficult for a man to be good? Why not give us all an equal chance to acquire good character, instead of putting us at the mercy of our societies? It is good that men should have great responsibilities. A very great responsibility is the responsibility for helping or hindering the growth of souls. God gives me a very great responsibility if he allows me to play a role in the education of my children; but the logical consequence is that whether it is easy or hard for them to attain good character depends in part on me. The inequality of chance to attain good character for some is an inevitable consequence of giving such serious responsibility to others, of God allowing others to share in his creative activity. Secondly, it is good (for different reasons) both that God should make some agents naturally good to begin with (as I shall urge further in the next chapter), and that God give to other agents a serious choice of destiny by giving them many bad desires, against which they need to fight in order to choose the good. If both these actions of God are good, there cannot be anything bad in God creating some agents with just a few bad desires. Up to a point, inequality in the number and strength of bad desires cannot therefore be a bad thing; and that applies whether God allows these bad desires to originate genetically or through a corrupt environment.⁸

---

⁷ All of this is, of course, very Thomist. See Aquinas, *Summa Theologiae*: 'sin and vice occur among men because they follow the inclination of sentient nature, contrary to the order of reason' (Ia. 2ae. 71.2 ad 3); mortal sin occurs 'when the soul is so disordered by sin that it turns away from its ultimate goal, God, to whom it is united by charity . . . When this disorder stops short of turning away from God, then the sin is venial' (Ia. 2ae. 72.5); a single mortal sin still leaves some disposition to virtue, but this is eliminated by multiple mortal sins (1a. 2ae. 73.1 ad 2); causes which 'weaken judgment or interfere with the free movement of the will lessen sinfulness' (1a. 2ae. 73.6).
⁸ Of course God as our creator has the right (no doubt up to some limit) to subject us to bad desires in a way that we do not in general have the right to subject our fellow humans to bad desires. On this see *The Existence of God*, pp. 216 ff.

The man who has blinded himself to the goodness of things is no longer an agent, one who chooses what to do in the light of beliefs about its worth. He has become, as well as a passive subject of sensation and thought, merely an arena of conflicting desires of which the strongest dictates his bodily movements. He no longer chooses between desires. If we think of the soul in its active capacity as the choosing agent, there is no soul left. The man has 'lost his soul'. Although there is no maximum to human goodness, there is a minimum; and this is it.

The man who has lost his soul will have either a miscellaneous collection of desires, to the strongest of which on any occasion he conforms, without any belief about the relative goodness of each; or he will have just one or two desires, unharassed by other desires or by moral beliefs. The former man is the wanton, who has reverted to an animal state; while the latter is the obsessive, urged on by one mastering desire with no moral beliefs or other desires to balance it—a desire perhaps for freedom, or for the extermination of the Jews, which dominates the agent's being. The more obvious examples of wicked men are usually in the latter category.[9] And because the wicked man does not recognize the moral goodness of things, he cannot do actions or enjoy such experiences because of what is morally good about them. And because happiness or pleasure consists in doing what you want to do and experiencing what you want to experience,[10] the wicked cannot be happy in doing actions or experiencing states whose value arises from their moral goodness. He cannot rejoice at the triumph of good over evil, nor be glad at his children doing the best in difficult circumstances, nor reverence a great one for his goodness.

It is evident that a man, through his own choice assisted by external influences, can lose his moral sensitivity. But have we reason to suppose that such corruption may be total and (barring special divine intervention) irreversible, so that the man can no longer have his conscience pricked?[11] My grounds for supposing

---

[9] For a good discussion of the latter category, see Mary Midgley, *Wickedness*, ch. 7. She writes (p. 138) of 'the emptiness at the core of the individual' in such cases.

[10] See my *The Evolution of the Soul*, Clarendon Press, 1986, 106 f.

[11] It was a subject of dispute in medieval philosophical theology, the extent to which a man's ability to recognize the good and bad, which medievals called *synderesis*, could be extinguished. See the extracts from Philip the Chancellor, who seems to think that it could be extinguished in the crucial respect that a man was no longer moved to virtue by his recognition of the good (and that it was so extinguished

that this could happen are, first, what we have, many of us, recognized in ourselves—how easy it is to dull sensitivity to certain aspects of the good. That we could exterminate totally our sensitivity to the good is a natural extrapolation therefrom. Secondly, this is what seems to have happened in some of the evil men of history, such as Nazi butchers. Thirdly, an agent who has over time deliberately suppressed his awareness of the good in all areas will have built up a strong desire, which belongs to the central structure of his soul, to resist all such awareness. In that case, such a total change as a reawakened awareness of goodness would be very difficult to achieve against the agent's will. Yet the agent who had suppressed his awareness of the good would not allow such a reawakening to occur—for he would not desire that it should, nor could he think it good that it should.[12]

Human Free Will

Given that humans have free will (as I have been assuming) and have moral beliefs, they are, I urged in Chapter 3, morally responsible for their actions. Given too that they are subject to desires to do what they believe bad, they find themselves in a situation of temptation, where their free will involves a choice between good and bad. Also as I first noted in Chapter 1, it is characteristic of human free will that our actions affect our character. This chapter has brought out how totally we can affect the sort of people we become, natural saints or totally corrupt. Human free will also involves choice of how to influence other humans, to build up or to neglect or to break down their characters. And it involves a choice of how to influence the environment in which we and future humans will live. Human free will is not just free will; it involves what I may call a choice of destiny.

in the damned), and Aquinas, who seems to think that it could not be extinguished, in T. C. Potts, *Conscience in Medieval Philosophy*, CUP, 1980, 108 f. and 129 f.

[12] 'Evil has a threshold magnitude. Yes, a human being hesitates and bobs back and forth between good and evil all his life. He slips, falls back, clambers up, repents, things begin to darken again. But just so long as the threshold of evil doing is not crossed, the possibility of returning remains, and he himself is still within reach of our hope. But when, through the density of evil actions, the result either of their own extreme degree or of the absoluteness of his power, he suddenly crosses that threshold, he has left humanity behind, and without, perhaps, the possibility of return'—A. Solzhenitsyn, *The Gulag Archipelago* i–ii, trans. T. P. Whitney, Collins and Harvill Press, 1974, 175.

12

Heaven and Hell

Soul and Body

Man consists of soul and body. What makes me me is not this body, for it is conceivable that each part of it be replaced (gradually, or at a stroke) and yet I continue to have experiences. So there must be another part of me, the essential part which makes me me, and to which I give the traditional name of soul. It is the soul which is the initiator of intentional action and is the subject of conscious experience, and is the vehicle of character (i.e. to which beliefs and desires belong). The soul may not be able to function without a body in the normal course of things, but God could give it a new body or keep it temporarily in being without a body.[1] In considering now how a good God who seeks man's eternal well-being in friendship with himself will deal with men of various kinds, I phrase the question (since their earthly bodies will be destroyed) in terms of how he will deal with souls of various kinds. A soul deprived of its body would, however, have no way of expressing itself or influencing the world, and no way of acquiring knowledge of it, and no instrument to give it the energy to organize its mental life. Of course, God could give to a soul new ways of expressing itself and acquiring knowledge and energy from some other source, to enable it so to act. But, as it is at the moment, many of the kinds of desires to act and beliefs about the world which we have acquired during our lives are of a kind naturally expressed and derived through bodily means— viz. many of our desires are desires to do things with our bodies, and many of our beliefs about objects are beliefs about how sensorily they look or feel, viz. about how they present themselves to eyes or hands. Human souls seem fitted for human bodies. For this reason alone I am inclined to accept the normal Christian view that God will give eventually to such souls as he keeps in being after death new

---

[1] I have argued at considerable length for this view of man as consisting of two parts, body and soul, in my book *The Evolution of the Soul*, Clarendon Press, 1986.

bodies, and any continuing existence of the soul without a body is a temporary state. The primary concern of this book is, however, with the most general moral issues, and so the primary concern of this chapter is with whether a good God would keep men in existence after death, and the quality of the kinds of belief and desire which he would give to men (e.g. whether he would give them desires for the good, and true beliefs about what is good) and whether he would satisfy their beliefs and desires. The issue of whether any life after death would be an embodied life seems a relatively subsidiary issue, and so not one to which I shall devote further argument.

During men's life on earth their characters are formed; and, given that he has free will, each man is the final determinant of his own character—though circumstances make it harder for some than for others to form a good character. At the end of life souls are of various kinds.

The Future of the Totally Corrupt

First, there is the totally corrupt (or wicked) soul whom we left at the end of the last chapter. He has allowed there to form in himself a strong desire to resist awareness of the good. How will a perfectly good God deal with him?

Perhaps God could remove from this soul the desire to resist awareness of the good, resensitize it to the good. However, I suggest that it would be wrong of God so to do. He who seeks man's eternal well-being in friendship with himself would respect man's free choice and not force his friendship upon him. In giving to men the gift of free will, a creator is, I suggest, under an obligation not to use force to change it when men's choices are not to his liking. A good God who made creatures with a choice of pursuing the good or pursuing the bad would allow those creatures to become what they deliberately, persistently, and freely in all aspects of their behaviour choose to be. Like a good parent, he would, of course, encourage his children to follow one way rather than another; but in the end he would allow them the consequences of their choice, to become the sort of person they choose to become.

Although a good God could *allow* a man to become totally corrupt, it would surely be wrong of him to *make* an agent who began life with a vision of good eliminate that vision and lose his soul. Surely no good God would take back from a man that most precious of gifts, the gift of the ability to make or mar himself as a person. Christian tradition has been divided over whether God reprobates, i.e. predestines to damnation, any man. For the reason given I side with those who claim that he does not; that a man can only damn *himself*. Since any who do damn themselves will have had an initial vision of a good, and a capacity to choose it freely, they will have been given God's gracious help, enough of it to avoid damnation if they choose (though grace of varying amounts, making it easier for some than for others). Augustine and his classical Protestant successors must be numbered among those who hold that God does reprobate; so, too, alas, must St Thomas Aquinas.[2] But there is a strong tradition before Augustine, and a firm Catholic tradition after Duns Scotus culminating in the clear implication of a firm declaration of the Council of Trent,[3] that God does not reprobate.

What would a good God do with such a totally corrupt being as we have described? This corrupt being has sinned against his creator, and made no atonement for his sins, nor helped others to atone for theirs. He has destroyed his God-given capacity for moral awareness and choice and left himself as an arena of competing desires. He certainly deserves punishment, and God has a right to punish him (and the more his guilt is subjective, as opposed to objective, the greater the punishment deserved). And it is perhaps good that God should exercise that right if, in order to provide men with a disincentive to sin, he has vowed previously that he will punish sinners, in virtue of the general considerations which I adduced in Chapter 6. We saw in the last chapter how the threat of the pains of Hell can be a valuable means to get men to pursue the good, ultimately for better reasons. But God, being good, would not punish a sinner with a punishment beyond what he deserved; and I suggest that, despite majority Christian tradition, literally everlasting pain would be a punishment beyond the deserts of any human who has sinned for a finite time on Earth.[4] To punish a man with such

---

[2] *Summa Theologiae* 1a. 2ae. 23.3.

[3] Denzinger 1556. See also the Second Council of Orange (Denzinger 400). The post-5th-cent. Greek tradition was, of course, largely uninfluenced by Augustine. St John Damascene is therefore to be numbered among those who deny reprobation (see J. Tixeront, *History of Dogmas*, iii. B. Herder, 1923, 478).

[4] For careful discussion of this point, see Marilyn McCord Adams, 'Hell and the

punishment would be horribly vindictive, and a good God would not be that.

On the other hand, what is the point of keeping a totally corrupt being alive? He has lost the centre of his being. There would be no point in giving him the 'vision' of God, for he could not enjoy it. As I noted in the last chapter, the wicked cannot be happy in doing actions or experiencing states whose value arises from their moral goodness. Moral goodness is so central to what God is that only one who valued that would wish to adore God. For the totally corrupt there must be the *poena damni* (i.e. damnation), the penalty of the loss of the vision of God, a penalty of far greater importance than any *poena sensus* (i.e. punishment by means of painful sensations, which I shall call in future sensory punishment), as Augustine, himself a firm advocate of eternal sensory punishment for the wicked, pointed out. The *poena damni* is a loss of good, not an inflicted evil; and it is not so much a punishment inflicted from without as an inevitable consequence of a man allowing himself to lose his moral awareness. Annihilation, the scrap heap, seems an obvious final fate for the corrupt soul. There is an obligation on God not to punish anyone beyond what he deserves, and that, I have suggested, involves an obligation not to punish a man who has sinned on earth with everlasting sensory punishment. But there is no obligation on God to keep any man alive in a world to come. Yet should he keep the totally corrupt man alive for ever, my argument suggests that he will give him only those pleasures whose enjoyment involves no recognition of the moral goodness of what is enjoyed. That the wicked have permanently a status quite other than that enjoyed by the blessed (their subsequent pattern of life, if any, would not be a very good one) seems a crucial central point of the great biblical parables of judgement such as the parable of the sheep and the goats. As Augustine himself put it in response to criticism of his own stern doctrine: 'This perpetual death of the wicked, then, that is their alienation from the life of God, shall abide forever, and shall be common to them all, whatever men, prompted by their human affections, may conjecture as to a variety of punishments, or as to a mitigation or intermission of their woes.'[5]

Justice of God', *Religious Studies* 1975, 1, 433–47. That the wickedness of human sin was not infinite was a claim of Duns Scotus—see Ch. 10.

[5] Augustine, *Enchiridion*, chs. 112 and 113.

The New Testament writings seem to me ambiguous on the issue of whether the punishment of the wicked is an everlasting sensory one. They are fairly unanimous that the end of life marks a permanent division between the good and the wicked, and hence the fate of the wicked is αἰώνιός, not unreasonably translated 'everlasting'. And they claim that the wicked shall be thrown into a fire; this is sometimes described as αἰώνιός, but sometimes rather as ἀσβεστός, 'unquenchable'. But all that the latter implies is that the fire will leave nothing of the wicked unburnt; and indeed, if we take such talk literally, and suppose the wicked to be ordinary embodied men, the consequence of putting them in such a fire will be their elimination. St Paul in one place talks of the fate of the wicked as 'eternal destruction from the face of the Lord'.[6] There are even occasional passages which seem to imply that the division of the sheep and goats is only a temporary one. For example, there is the warning to men to be reconciled quickly with their adversaries lest they be thrown into prison: 'You shall by no means come out from there until you have paid the last penny.'[7] As John Hick comments, 'Since only a finite number of pennies can have a last one, we seem to be in the realm of graded debts and payments, rather than of absolute guilt and infinite penalty.'[8] St John sometimes seems to suggest that sin is its own punishment.[9]

However, most Christian theologians of subsequent centuries have had a fairly definite doctrine of eternal sensory punishment of the wicked. The best-known exception was Origen, who claimed that all men would eventually be saved, and his view remained to exert a considerable influence over the next three centuries. Gregory of Nyssa advocated Origen's view, and Gregory Nazianzen toyed with it. St Basil acknowledged that most ordinary men of his day believed that the sufferings of Hell were only of finite duration; and St Augustine acknowledged the diversity of opinions on this matter which were current in his day.[10] Augustine, however, was firm in his own belief in the eternal sensory punishment of the wicked, and Pope Pelagius I declared that the wicked 'will burn without end'.[11,12]

---

[6] 2 Thess. 1: 8.   [7] Matt. 5: 26.
[8] J. Hick, *Death and Eternal Life*, Collins 1976, 244.
[9] See e.g. John 3: 19.
[10] St Basil, *Rev. Brev. Tract.* 267; St Augustine, *Enchiridion* 113.
[11] Denzinger 443.
[12] For references and discussion of the patristic period, see J. N. D. Kelly, *Early Christian Doctrines*, A. and C. Black, 5th edn., 1977, 473 f. and 483 ff.; Tixeront, op.

Medieval thinkers, however, were united in supporting the view that the wicked would undergo an eternal sensory punishment. The First Council of Lyons (AD 1245) declared that those who died without penitence in mortal sin would be 'crucified forever in the fires of eternal Hell'.[13] Aquinas, however, claimed that this physical punishment was not of infinite intensity; and, like all other thinkers, he also held that it varied in intensity for different sinners.[14] Protestant reformers stoutly defended eternal sensory punishment. But the last two centuries have, of course, witnessed a large-scale rejection of this view, at least among Protestants and Anglicans.

I suspect that one factor which influenced the Fathers and scholastics to affirm eternal sensory punishment was their belief in the natural immortality of the soul. Even if God could eliminate a soul (and some of their arguments have the consequence that he could not), it would in their view require an action of God of a quite extraordinary supernatural kind to eliminate a soul.[15] The extinction of the wicked was therefore seldom entertained as a possibility open to God. The only possibilities being eventual everlasting happiness or everlasting misery, it was not totally unnatural that the Fathers and Scholastics should hold everlasting misery to be the fate of the wicked—for the other options would involve God not taking the wicked free choice of the wicked seriously. Today we think that conservation in existence rather than elimination is what requires special divine action, and so there is in our view an obvious alternative to eternal punishment to which God could consign the wicked— he could eliminate them.

The Future of the Saints

What will a perfectly good God do with a saint? Such a man has a right direction of will so firm that in normal circumstances other desires will be far weaker than his desire for the good. He has true

cit. ii., 193–9, 331–47; and the discussion (in connection with the different topic of Purgatory) in J. Le Goff, *The Birth of Purgatory*, Scholar Press, 1984, ch. 2.

[13] Denzinger 839.

[14] See *Summa Contra Gentiles* III. 145 and *Summa Theologiae* 1a. 2ae. 87.3. ad 4.

[15] See Aquinas, *Summa Contra Gentiles* II. 55 and 79; and the discussion of arguments such as his in my *The Evolution of the Soul*, pp. 305 f.

beliefs about which actions are good, and firm desires to do those actions.

Note one thing about the saint before we consider his subsequent fate. He will be already in part blessed; I understand by a blessed man one who is happy and whose happiness comes from doing good actions and experiencing good experiences. To be happy is to be doing what you want (i.e. desire) to be doing and have happen to you what you want to have happen to you. The man who is happy playing the piano is happy because he is doing what he wants to be doing—playing the piano. The man who is happy listening to the piano being played is happy because he is experiencing what he wants to experience. But happiness may be derived from trivial and wrong pursuits and experiences—from watching TV quiz games incessantly or from torturing one's enemies. Or it may be obtained from doing and having happen to one what is supremely good—from singing the praises of God to the sound of the organ. The latter man is not merely happy but blessed. The wicked may be happy—temporarily, while their desires are satisfied. But the happiness of the wicked is likely to depend totally on circumstances for the fulfilment of their desires. For their desires are not typically to try or purpose to do a certain kind of action, but to succeed—not to try to torture one's enemies, but to succeed. And the fulfilment of such desires depends on factors outside oneself—whether one's enemies have been captured or whether they have escaped. And evidently the fulfilment of desires for experiences are also dependent on factors outside oneself—for experiences are a matter of things being caused in one by outside factors, on the organ being there and in working order, for example. The happiness of the saint also depends on outside factors for his having the right experiences and his actions being successful. But the saint will also value greatly his trying to do what he believes to be good; and he will also desire that he should so try. He will desire to act in accord with his conscience. And the fulfilment of that desire depends on nothing outside himself. Merely having a good will and moral beliefs, he can try to fulfil the moral beliefs, and be happy in being virtuous. That of course is not enough for total happiness. One who tries to help the starving and is frustrated cannot be perfectly happy; nor can one who is being tortured, however well directed his will. Still, some happiness must belong to the saint, simply in virtue of his having such a character.

Having the true moral belief that he owes to God atonement for his sins and to help in the atonement of others, the saint will continually repent, apologize, and plead the atoning sacrifice of Christ. God will therefore have forgiven his sins. In virtue of his good will, true beliefs, and good desires, the saint will be ever doing supererogatory acts, in so far as opportunities are available to him; and chief among such acts will be the worship of God. The saint's moral beliefs will follow in part from his credal beliefs, such as I set out in my theological assumption. He will in consequence have what is called in Catholic terminology 'faith formed by love' (i.e. he is ready to act out of love, guided by faith as to how to do so) or in Protestant terminology 'faith' (which seems to be understood so as to include a good will as well as belief).

It follows from Chapter 4 that the saint has merit, perhaps the merit of having done many supererogatory acts but at least the merit of having acted supererogatorily so as to make himself ready to do them. Hence it is good, though not obligatory, for God to reward the merit which I have claimed that the saint will have as a result of his supererogatory act. Though many Christians in different centuries have claimed that man has no merit through doing good acts, it seems to have been a persistent theme of Christ's teaching that those who have done good deeds will be rewarded in the world to come,[16] and that surely would be good only if they have merit through having done such good deeds.

In such a situation a God who seeks man's eternal well-being in union with himself would surely complete the process of character formation which the saint sought to achieve on earth, and to allow his desires to do good actions and have good experiences to attain their fulfilment—for ever. Because this path to eternal life was made available by Christ's redeeming life and death in the way described in the last chapter, Christ overcame not merely sin but death. As we saw in the last chapter, even the saint on earth is often subject to extrinsic desires, and especially sloth, the desire for rest, against which he has to fight if he is to do the good. A good God who seeks man's eternal well-being in union with himself, will finally remove his imprisonment to desires which he fully rejects by judging them

---

[16] See K. E. Kirk, *The Vision of God*, Longmans, 1931, 143 f. Kirk cites Von Hügel's point that 'Jesus constantly promised reward only to those who were prepared to follow and obey him from some other [good] motive' (e.g. 'for my sake and the Gospel's'), not for the sake of the reward.

bad and fighting against them. God will give him a firmly fixed good will, and firm desires to do what he rightly believes to be good. And so God will make the good actions which even the saint does with difficulty after a fight with his conscience come naturally and easily to him. On earth we can exercise what I called in Chapter 1 subjective goodness, choice of good despite contrary desire. But the exercise of subjective goodness is painful, even if temporarily desirable. And if we are serious in our pursuit of the good, we will seek to remove the risk that we may fail to do the good. And God will respond to our serious choice by granting it. God, in allowing our desires to attain their goals, will grant us to do and experience what we rightly want. Our acts of kindness will bring forth the fruits we seek; and our desire to experience the love of others who choose to love us will be granted. And because they are what we want, we will enjoy our acts of kindness and our experience of the love of others. (There is, however, the qualification to what I have just written that God will not, of course, grant our right desires where he can do so only by doing a wrong act. He will, therefore, not force another free agent to do some act. So God will not give to the saint the love of one who refuses to love him.)

Although the saint merits a reward, he hardly merits by his actions a reward as great as this. A God of perfect goodness must have a further reason to give to the saint such an eternal life than to give it as mere reward. And surely he does have such good reason. A human being of good character is something infinitely precious, worth preserving to eternity. And though there is point, in order to give him a choice of destiny, in subjecting him to pain and frustrated desire, there is no point in continuing so to subject him, once he has through a continued serious choice formed his own character. Heaven seems the appropriate place for the saint—Heaven in the sense of circumstances in which he can do supremely worthwhile acts, and have supremely worthwhile things happen to him, the doing and experiencing of which, since that is what he desires, will make him very happy. Because the saint puts no obstacle in the way of God granting him what God seeks for him—eternal well-being in union with himself—God will surely grant that to him.[17]

The view that God will give to the saint, in the sense of the man who has pleaded the atoning sacrifice of God in penitence for his sins

[17] See Additional Note 9.

and is ever ready to do supererogatory works, the life of Heaven is, I believe, the view of both Catholic and Protestant. Their use of 'faith' in different senses (see Chapter 11) does, however, disguise their agreement. On the Protestant view, 'faith' alone suffices for salvation, in the sense of faith as a good will directed by true belief about central Christian doctrines such as the atonement. In the Catholic view, 'faith formed by love' is what is needed, in the Catholic sense of faith as mere belief in central Christian doctrines and love as a good will.[18] The one who has such 'faith' or 'faith formed by love' stands justified before God. God has imparted to him the status of being justified. But although there is this (disguised) agreement between Catholic and Protestant, there seems to me to remain a difference of emphasis. In the Protestant picture a man can be justified in virtue of his penitential reliance on the sacrifice of Christ without having a greatly reformed character. The 'good will' may be only fairly good. Whereas for the Catholic 'love' has to be substantial for a man to be justified.[19]

I sketched in Chapter 8 the acts and experiences which are of supreme worth. Given my theological assumption, the move from earth to Heaven merely removes obstacles to the fulfilment of the saint's desires to do those acts and have those experiences. In Heaven too the saint will seek to do acts of helping others to be able to do and experience supremely worthwhile things, by praying to God on their behalf and by acting as God's agent. But the saint in Heaven will know in detail for what to pray, and his prayers will be granted. Yet the internal activity of Heaven to which the saint will help others must include, in the widest sense, 'understanding' (both coming to understand, being aware of, and reflecting upon) the deepest truths about the world and rational agents; developing friendship with other rational agents; and responding to the world

[18] For justification of this account of the similarity of Catholic and Protestant views as to the kind of faith needed for salvation, see my *Faith and Reason*, Clarendon Press, 1981, especially ch. 4. Recent reports of interdenominational commissions have recognized this similarity in the present understanding of Roman Catholics and others of the kind of faith needed for salvation. See e.g. the report of the Anglican–Roman Catholic Commission, *Salvation and the Church*, Church House Publishing, 1987, 14 and 19.

[19] McGrath sees it as one of the hallmarks of Reformation theology that it makes a sharp notional distinction between justification and sanctification; and another such hallmark that it sees justification as a forensic justification that the believer is righteous, rather than a process by which he is made righteous. See McGrath, op. cit. ii. 2.

and rational agents in ways appropriate to their beauty, goodness, wisdom, ultimacy, and so on. Given our theological assumption that God, a being of infinite power, wisdom, and goodness, made the world, and given that by his actions in Christ he redeemed the world, then, as we saw in Chapter 8, the deepest friendship would be with God himself, and the most worthwhile response to rational agents would be the worship of God. For the proper response to the necessary being which is the source of all being is endless adoration; and the proper response to him who has so generously and, in our redemption, at such cost given us so much is endless gratitude. Yet in Heaven the desire of the saints to adore 'face to face' will be made possible by experience of the presence of him whom they adore (and who so often seems absent on earth). And the saints' desire to know more of God will be fulfilled by God showing them more and more of himself. Since he alone has an infinite depth of wisdom and goodness to reveal, he can go on for ever yielding more to man's longings and yet leave him unsated. Although by far the most important task for man must be to respond to and enjoy the response of the source of being himself, other friendships and understandings are also of value, including friendships with those who have shared our earthly pilgrimage. Such friendships will be by far the more valuable if they are exercised in co-operative worship of him who alone can satisfy man's deepest longings.

Christian descriptions of Heaven have stressed different facets of the life of experience and action which I have described. There is a long Christian tradition that the saints have work to do by intercession and in other ways acting as God's agents in his work of sanctification.[20] But co-operative worship is certainly the primary activity of the Blessed in the one book of the New Testament which gives much attention to their fate—the Book of Revelation. Much of the new Testament stresses that love is the supreme Christian activity. Love consists in doing things with and for the beloved, seeking to understand the beloved, and showing the beloved the respect which he deserves. The philosophical tradition which had its roots in Plato and Aristotle saw the supremely worthwhile activity for rational creatures as contemplation. The Christianizing of this

[20] See Christ's words to his disciples, 'Ye which have followed me, in the regeneration when the Son of Man shall sit on the throne of his glory, ye also shall sit upon twelve thrones, judging the twelve tribes of Israel' (Matt. 19: 28). 'Judging' may here mean 'ruling over'.

tradition saw the primary activity of the Blessed in Heaven as the contemplation of God; yet a contemplation which was not a mere passive experience, but an active gazing which involved understanding of the object contemplated.[21] We may regard this as the way in which the love of God would be manifested—by showing supreme respect and trying to understand. There have been different views about the extent to which the life of Heaven involves change and growth.[22]

I have written of 'the life of Heaven'. Since the happiness of Heaven can only be had by those who desire to pursue the occupations of Heaven, the life of Heaven can only be enjoyed by saints. For they alone would have the right desires. If there is a place where those and only those who live that life are located (as I am assuming for simplicity of exposition) what is crucial about being in Heaven is not being in that place but living in circumstances where the ideal desires which I have described achieve their fulfilment in the ways which I have described. Although the inhabitants of Heaven retain their free will, the range of choices open to them changes. Having no desires for the bad, they inevitably pursue only what they (correctly) believe to be good (see p. 48). Their choice will lie among a range of equally good actions (a range which, if their knowledge of possible actions and capacity to perform them are much increased, is I suspect, enormous).

The Future of Good Pagans

However good the will of some man on earth, he may have more to learn about what things are good, and more to do to cultivate good

---

[21] 'By a single uninterrupted and continuous act our minds will be united with God'—Aquinas, *Summa Theologiae* 1a. 2ae. 3.2. ad 4.

[22] On different views of the supreme good as attaining or pursuing, see J. Passmore, *The Perfectibility of Man*, Duckworth, 1970, 48 f. and 102 f. See my fuller justification of the claims in the text of what are the most worthwhile actions and experiences in my *Faith and Reason*, op. cit., pp. 131–6.

In so far as there will be little place for acts of charity towards one's fellows in the full life of Heaven, and far more place for worship, that supports what Kirk calls 'the 'valid theory' of the two lives on earth, the 'active life' and the 'contemplative life'. For those who practise the former on earth, that is but a stage towards making themselves ready to practise the latter in Heaven; whereas the heavenly life of those who lead the contemplative life on earth will be more like their earthly life. See Kirk, op. cit., pp. 242–57; and n. 13 to my Ch. 8.

desires. Even though we have some basic understanding of what is morally good, clearly our understanding is limited by our finite nature and environment. Even the best saints on earth, it is reasonable to suppose, have a lot to learn. But there are many on earth who have a lot more to learn than they do. If our theological assumption is correct, there are many men of good will who die lacking crucial moral beliefs (such as that they have a duty to worship God). Nevertheless, the man of good will has his heart in the right place. Despite his lack of good desires and important true beliefs, he deserves reward for the firmness of his good will. And the most appropriate and best reward would be to allow him to acquire the true moral beliefs and right unfrustrated desires which will give full blessedness. Having a good will, he will seek to do the good and, being informed as to its nature, will naturally and readily allow himself to acquire true moral beliefs and form his desires to accord with them. And anyway, such a will is so precious a thing that a God who seeks man's eternal well-being would naturally allow it to be perfected, since that is the agent's basic choice, and allow him after this life through change of belief and desire to plead the atoning sacrifice of Christ and thereby join the Church and enjoy the bliss of Heaven.

In the history of Christian theology there have been different views about the fate in the afterlife of men of good will with false religious beliefs. The view which seems has on the whole finally prevailed is that a man who has tried to pursue the good but through ignorance has failed to do so has implicit faith, *fides in voto* in Catholic terminology, which suffices for salvation. Where the Christian Gospel has not impinged on a man's conscience, such faith is enough. This is, I believe, the view of a majority of Protestants, but it is also now the official Catholic view. The Second Vatican Council officially declared that all men who strive to live a good life and who through no fault of their own 'do not know the Gospel of Christ and his Church . . . can attain to everlasting salvation'. This possibility is open not only to theists but to those who through no fault of their own 'have not yet arrived at an explicit knowledge of God'.[23] Although it has taken a couple of millennia to make the point explicitly clear, it is, I believe, the point which Jesus is reported as making, that the servant which did not know his master's will and

[23] *Lumen Gentium* 16.

did things worthy of a beating 'shall be beaten with few stripes', in contrast with the servant who knew the master's will and still did not do it, who 'shall be beaten with many stripes'.[24] (The point of the saying must lie in the contrast, not in the fact that the ignorant servant would have a small beating.) It is also, I believe, the natural extrapolation from the patristic and scholastic doctrine of *limbus patrum*. According to this doctrine, the Old Testament patriarchs were consigned to an intermediate state, *limbus patrum*, until Christ 'descended into Hell' to preach to them the redemption which he had won for them on Calvary. Once they accepted that (as they were already geared to do in virtue of their good will), they inherited its benefits—Heaven. Their inability, through ignorance, to plead Christ's sacrifice alone barred them from Heaven; when it was remedied, they could avail themselves of that sacrifice and Heaven was theirs. Although most of the Fathers either implicitly assumed or explicitly taught that only the Jews had that privilege, not all did. Both Clement of Alexandria[25] and Augustine[26] taught that this way to Heaven was available for Gentiles also.

Predestination

In so far as salvation is a reward, it can only be given for acts which have some degree of freedom, as we saw in Chapter 4. In such cases, then, the grace which God provides to help man on the road to salvation cannot be irresistible. Man needs to co-operate with grace.[27] That is no argument against salvation being given sometimes

---

[24] Luke 12: 48.

[25] Clement of Alexandria claimed that the Gospel was preached to both Jews and Gentiles in Hades by the Apostles—*Stromateis* 6.6.

[26] Augustine considers the case of Job, a non-Israelite, so praised in the Old Testament 'that no man of his times is put on a level with him as regards justice and piety'; and goes on to affirm: 'I doubt not that it was divinely provided, that from this one case we might know that among other nations also there might be men pertaining to the spiritual Jerusalem who have lived according to God and have pleased him'— *City of God* 18.47. Irenaeus (*Adversus Haereses* 3.23.8) and Anselm (*Cur Deus Homo* 2.16) both held that Adam (who was not, to speak strictly, a Jew) would be saved. Anselm held that at each moment of history there was someone alive who would eventually be saved.

[27] The view that man has to co-operate with God's grace in order for it to be efficacious is known as synergism. It was held by many of the early Fathers (see the essays by N. N. Glaubokowsky and E. W. Watson in W. T. Whitley (ed.), *The Doctrine of Grace*, SCM Press, 1932), by the more moderate opponents of extreme

to those who have not in any way earned it (and not rejected it)—on these more below. But if the grace of God were always sufficient for salvation without human effort, and without that grace none can be saved, then it would follow that all who were not saved were not saved solely as a result of being deprived of grace enough to make salvation possible for them, i.e. God would have reprobated them; and I have argued against that earlier.

What, then, of the doctrine that God predestines all those who are eventually to be saved to that salvation. For Augustine and Aquinas this doctrine means that God foreordains the salvation of certain men chosen for no prior merit of theirs—i.e. he programmes them in advance to do such good works as will merit salvation; they are predestined, to use the technical term, *ante praevisa merita*.[28] But if my arguments are correct, that is not possible. For, first, though those who do not merit it can be saved, salvation through merit is only possible for those who are not programmed. And, secondly, if all and only those who are saved are programmed in advance to be saved, then those who are lost will be so as a result of not being programmed, i.e. they will have been reprobated; and I have argued that a good God will not reprobate.[29]

There are two other ways of understanding the doctrine of predestination. One way, which has had considerable support in

Augustinianism, such as John Cassian, and seems to be affirmed by the Synod of Arles (Denzinger, 339) and eventually affirmed firmly by the Council of Trent (Canon 4 on Justification—Denzinger, 1554). It was also affirmed by Wesley and other Methodists (see the essay by E. D. Soper in W. T. Whitley (ed.), op. cit.). By contrast, Augustine and his classical Protestant successors insist on the irresistibility of grace. For the Reformers the divine grace, once given, inevitably produces faith sufficient for salvation without man's co-operation.

[28] 'Why does he choose some to glory, while others he rejects? His so willing is the sole ground.'—Aquinas, *Summa Theologiae* 1a. 23.5 ad 3.

[29] So many theologians wanted to hold that the saints were predestined to Heaven, while denying that the wicked were predestined to Hell. They wanted, to use the technical term, to deny 'double predestination'. But that position looks self-contradictory for the reason given in the text. For some of the vicissitudes and complexities of the different interpretations of predestination, see McGrath, op. cit. i. 128–45. He discusses, as well as the views which I mention, the view of William of Ockham that a statement about God having predestined someone is, despite its past tense, really a statement about the future; a statement, that is, whose truth conditions lie entirely in the future and in no way in any *past* will of God. Whether God 'has' predestined someone depends entirely on what that person subsequently does. However, although Ockham states this doctrine he subsequently complicates it so that it loses its pristine clarity. See M. M. Adams and N. Kretzmann (eds.), *William Ockham: Predestination, God's Foreknowledge, and Future Contingents*, Appleton-Century-Crofts, 1969.

Christian thought, is that God predestines to salvation only those who, he foresees, will partly of their own free will do good works. Predestination, that is, is *post praevisa merita*.[30] On this view predestination simply amounts to foreknowledge. Although there are no moral objections to this view, there do seem to be substantial philosophical difficulties in supposing that God can have now complete foreknowledge of that which is not yet determined. For if I am freely (i.e. not determinedly) to choose tomorrow what I shall do then, I shall then have it in my power to make false anyone's beliefs of today about what I will do tomorrow. So how can anyone, even God, already know what I will do? Christian theology has often attempted to avoid this difficulty by claiming that God is timeless; he is outside time, and so does not, to speak strictly, *fore*know anything. Nevertheless, he knows (in the one eternal moment of his time) all things that happen in our time. There are difficulties in making sense of this doctrine of God's timelessness. If the doctrine of God's timelessness can be rendered coherent, the doctrine of predestination *post praevisa merita* will thereby also be rendered coherent.[31]

In my view the doctrine of God's timelessness cannot be rendered coherent, and hence I prefer an alternative way of understanding predestination, which has not been very common in the Christian theological tradition. This is to understand it as the doctrine that God predestines in the sense of 'intends as their destiny' the salvation of all men; and he helps them towards that salvation, but he does not force it upon them. Our names may be in the book of life, but it is up to us whether they stay there. That view is the view implicit in the words of Christ which, in the Book of Revelation, St John pictures him as saying to the Church of Sardis: 'He that overcometh, the same shall be clothed in white raiment; and I will in no wise blot his name out of the book of life.'[32]

[30] Among many others who have advocated predestination *post praevisa merita* are St Justin Martyr (*First Apology* 44); St John Chrysostom (*In Epist. ad Rom. Hom.* XVI, 5–8); Cassian, various semi-Pelagian opponents of Augustine, and St Prosper (see Tixeront, op. cit. iii., 268–78); St John Damascene (*De Fide Orthodoxa* II.30).
[31] I discuss these issues in detail in Chapters 10 and 12 of my book *The Coherence of Theism*, Clarendon Press, 1977. Since God wills all men to be saved, but does not determine in advance who will be saved, and since salvation depends on pleading the sacrificial death of Christ, we must say with most theologians and contrary to some hardline Protestant theologians that God died for all, and not just for the elect. See McGrath, op. cit. ii. 48.
[32] Rev. 3: 5.

The Future of Babies

So, then, at the end of their lives there may be men of at least these two kinds. There are, first, those with a good will. They may be morally ill-informed but, when given true information about what is good to do, they are ready geared to assimilate it and act on it. They may have desires for the bad, but they will be ever striving to rein these in, and a good God will give to them the right desires. Then there are the totally corrupt, who have annihilated their perception of the good and made themselves mere arenas of competing desires, of which the strongest wins. The former are ready for the beatific vision, the latter for the scrap heap. But then there are to all appearances also intermediate cases of two kinds, first babies without character, and secondly those who die in childhood or adolescence with inadequately formed character.

Babies are beings capable of a vision of the good, right desires, and a will directed towards it, but they have not yet understood what goodness is nor chosen it. There are various futures which a good God could give to such beings. First, he could give them goodness of character, of will, belief, and desire, without their choice. Although it is good that men have a choice of destiny, there seems to me nothing bad in God making men good without their choice (though there does seem something bad in his giving them a good will when they have chosen not to have one; and above all something bad in his making them totally corrupt without them so choosing). Traditional theology has maintained that this is the fate of baptized babies who die before they have the opportunity to sin. They are given moral perfection and go straight to Heaven. However, although, I suggest, there would be nothing bad in God making men good without their choice, there would also be nothing bad in his not making men good without their choice. He who seeks man's eternal well-being in friendship with himself might regard babies as not fully enough men to seek this for them; or, although regarding them as fully men, might choose not to impose his friendship for eternity on any who have not chosen it for themselves. There are in that case other futures which God could give to babies. Secondly, he could make them incarnate again in this world or some other world and allow them there the choice of destiny of which they were deprived on this earth; though few Christian theologians have supposed that this will happen. Thirdly, God could give them some goodness of desire and a worthwhile life without goodness of belief and will and the opportunity to enjoy the Heaven of the Blessed. Just as there is nothing wrong in God making goldfish,[33] so there is nothing wrong in God not making the souls of human babies to develop into the fully human souls of adults. The normal Catholic doctrine since the early Middle Ages has been that those who die suffering only from original sin and not actual sin, viz. unbaptized babies, suffer only the *poena damni*, the loss of the vision of God, and no *poena sensus*.[34] Medieval theologians spelled that out in terms of such babies going to *Limbus Puerorum*, where they led an undemanding but not unpleasant existence.[35] Since neither sending babies to Heaven nor sending them to Limbo is morally bad, a good God could indeed send the baptized ones to heaven and the unbaptized to Limbo. A fourth possibility, by no means inconsistent with divine goodness, would be simply elimination—on the grounds that here there is no formed character worth keeping to eternity, nor good deeds to be rewarded. God certainly does not owe every human soul an eternal life. Many Christian theologians, however (and among them, notoriously, Augustine),[36] have held that God sends many babies, viz. the unbaptized, humans who have done no wrong, to eternal sensory pain in Hell. That view seems to me profoundly and

---

[33] See Robert M. Adams, 'Must God Create the Best?', *Philosophical Review*, 1972, 81, 317–32.

[34] Pope Innocent III wrote (AD ·1201) that 'the penalty for original sin is deprivation of the vision of God, but the penalty for actual sin is the torments of everlasting Hell' (Denzinger 780).

[35] Aquinas did not write the intended section of the *Summa Theologiae* on the afterlife. His disciples compiled a supplement on matters· which Aquinas left undiscussed in the *Summa*, largely on the basis of his other writings. In Q.70 of this, Aquinas wonders whether children in Limbo suffer not so much punishment as a 'delay of glory'—see Le Goff, op. cit., p. 270. For Albert the Great (IV Sent. Dist. XLIV, 45) as in Dante's *Inferno*, the *Limbus Puerorum* is the most pleasant part of Hell (and a permanent receptacle, in which the inhabitants remain for eternity; by contrast the *Limbus Patrum* and Purgatory are only temporary receptacles, in the normal medieval picture). And later Catholic thought opposed the view that Limbo was a separate 'place' beyond Heaven, Hell, and Purgatory—the view was opposed in a Bull of Pius VI in AD 1788 (Denzinger 2626).

[36] 'Little ones are sent either to the kingdom [of heaven] or to eternal fire' (PL 38. 1337). There is, he holds, no third possibility. In the fire the unbaptized infants suffer pain. See also PL 33, 727. Canon iii of the Council of Carthage (AD 418) firmly advocated the Augustinian position in this respect (Denzinger 224). N. P. Williams, *The Ideas of the Fall and of Original Sin*, Longmans, 1927, 348 and 391, affirms the authenticity of this canon against some who have cast doubt on this. '

obviously false. A being who did that obviously would not be morally good, and so would not be God.

The Future of those of Unsettled Character

What, finally, of those who die in childhood or adolescence or even later with inadequately formed character and with some good deeds and some bad deeds behind them? He who seeks men's eternal well-being in friendship with himself would, I suggest, not impose that friendship on those who had only half-heartedly opted for the good. Once again elimination seems not an unjust fate, again on the grounds that there is no formed character worth preserving to eternity, nor enough good deeds worthy of reward. Or, secondly, God could allow them reincarnation in a world where they could finally form their characters one way or the other. Or, thirdly, God could allow them, or perhaps those of them whose will was more settled towards the good, but who remained beset with bad desires, the benefit of the doubt, by making them such that they could never lose their good will, but such that the perfecting of character remained in their own hands. In that way God would, as it were, respect the extent of their prior choice of the good by giving it permanent significance, but also respect their freedom by leaving open to them how much they would build upon that choice. The Catholic doctrine of Purgatory affirms that such is the fate of those whose will is basically good, but who have still an imperfect character and have done much evil for which they have made but half-hearted apology. Once you get to Purgatory, you cannot finally lose the possibility of Heaven, but it is up to you how long it takes you to get there. The doctrine, as normally expounded, does entail that those in Purgatory will get to Heaven some time, but it would require little amendment to it to allow someone to refuse ever to be reformed sufficiently to make himself suited for Heaven.[37]

---

[37] For a history of the doctrine of Purgatory, see Le Goff, op. cit. Eastern Orthodox thought has preserved some agnosticism about the state of the departed between death and the Last Judgement. It has allowed the propriety of prayer for the departed, but on the whole opposed the view that Purgatory is a place. Purgatory was an issue disputed between Eastern Orthodox and Roman Catholics at the Council of Florence, which sought to bring about reunion in AD 1439. David Brown has argued that moulding an imperfect character into a holy one requires time and pain, and so a purgatorial process is required before the imperfect are fitted for Heaven. See his 'No Heaven Without Purgatory', *Religious Studies*, 1985, **21**, 447–56.

Those who die having pleaded the sacrifice of Christ with true repentance and apology, die forgiven by God. Although they do not merit the life of Heaven, God, who seeks man's eternal well-being in friendship with himself, would surely recognize their basic inclination of will towards the good manifested in that pleading, either by taking them straight to Heaven (removing from them in the process their bad desires) or by allowing them to reform their own character further, e.g. in Purgatory. That God does with them one or other of these things is of course the view of both Catholic and classical Protestant. He who is ready for Heaven stands justified before God. But, as we saw earlier, on the Protestant picture justification can be attained with less in the way of reformation of character than on the Catholic picture. The Protestant sees God as prepared to recognize a man as suited for Heaven in virtue of his penitential reliance on the sacrifice of Christ, and so as prepared to reform his character for him in an instant of time before taking him to Heaven. Whereas the Catholic sees many such a man as needing to reform his own character more before he could be justified; and hence as needing a Purgatory in which this can be achieved. Although the classical Protestant account of how a good God might deal with men of this kind has some plausibility, it seems clear that there are so many who die with some Christian faith and some half-sincere penitence for their sins, and others who die with no Christian faith and a mixture of deeds good and bad behind them and a half-formed character for whom some sort of intermediate state seems highly appropriate.

Conclusion

I have been concerned in this chapter with what follows from my detailed theological assumption about how God created men, with respect to the futures which it would be good or obligatory for God to allocate to men after their death. I have argued that some allocations of fate (e.g. eternal *sensory* punishment to anyone) would be wrong, and so God would not allocate such a fate to any-one. I have suggested, somewhat hesitantly, that certain allocations of fate to certain categories of men would be the best for them, and hence God would give them those fates. But I feel less confident about some of these moral intuitions than about others. As I have illustrated by examples, the Christian tradition has been far from unanimous in its view of the fate of different categories of men in the afterlife. But, with all its variations, some of which seem to me to suffer from serious moral error, that tradition has had two central guiding intuitions to which almost all writers have subscribed and which seem to me profoundly correct. The first is that the fate of man for eternity can and often does depend on his own choices in this life. And the second is that no man in the end is ever deprived of that fate (among those fates on offer) which he really seeks. Aquinas vigorously affirmed that if ever the wicked in Hell were to be truly penitent for their sins and to seek reconciliation with the Creator, he would be quick to forgive them and end their alienation from him.[38] Of course, he also held that the wicked were so fixed in their impenitence that they never would choose to be reconciled to their creator. But my point is the positive one that he held that in the end we always get what we choose.

These two guiding intuitions of the tradition seem to me profound intuitions into what a generous God will do. God has something marvellous to give us—the beatific vision of himself in Heaven. But to have that vision you need a certain sort of character, and no one who firmly seeks to have that character will be finally frustrated. But God does not force our nature or our destiny upon us. He gives us an unformed character and free will sufficient to allow us over a few years of earthly life to commit ourselves to the process of forming it so as to become saintly—and if we do, he gives the reward and the life appropriate to that commitment. But he allows us also the freedom to reject the pursuit of the good, and through our choices to acquire a bad character, and, if we do, he gives us the punishment and the future appropriate to that choice. And once our will is fixed for bad, we shall never desire or seek to get what we have missed.

But, although what I have described might be the best way to deal with us men, made as we are so that our choices affect our subsequent character, would it not be better if we were so made that we had always available to us a third kind of choice—to be able to do wrong without that affecting our character, leading to the destruction of our souls? If we had that sort of choice, we could always postpone any irrevocable choice of character.

---

[38] 'There would be no everlasting punishment of the souls of the damned if they were able to change their will for a better will'—*Summa Contra Gentiles* 4. 93. 2.

We choose, but God chooses which choices to give us. And it is good that our bad choices and good choices should not form our characters with instantaneous effect. We need to show the resoluteness of our commitment over a short period. For a year or two we can change our minds and postpone any irrevocable choice. But sooner or later, whether we like it or not, our refusal to choose the good begins to have a permanent effect on our nature. Our freedom to choose between good and bad has a heavy cost. We may choose the bad, and cause much suffering to our fellow men, and in other ways also wrong them and our Creator. The longer the period of time for which God allows us this kind of freedom, the heavier the suffering to our fellow men may be. There are limits to God's right to allow others to suffer for the sake of our having this kind of freedom. Further, if God allowed us always to be able to postpone any irrevocable formation of character he would be putting in our way a very strong temptation never to face up to things, to trivialize our lives and forever to waste God's gift, and to avoid ever making ourselves worthy to enjoy Heaven. It is good that God should allow us to be tempted over a brief period to do evil, for that gives us a real choice. But to allow us to be subjected forever to a temptation to avoid any ultimate commitment would make it very difficult for us ever to make that commitment; and a good God might well avoid putting us in that position. He will do this by giving us a limited period of earthly life in which by our actions we can choose our character; he will leave us free to choose, and he will give to each with his resulting character the kind of life appropriate to such a character. What more could we want?

Additional Notes

1 [ch. 3 n. 12]. Peter Van Inwagen has recently given an initially very plausible argument against compatibilism. (See his 'The Incompatibility of Free Will and Determinism', *Philosophical Studies*, 1975, 27, 185–99. The paper is reprinted in G. Watson (ed.), *Free Will*, OUP, 1982. The argument is developed at greater length in P. van Inwagen, *An Essay on Free Will*, Clarendon Press, 1983). He argues as follows: Consider any action A which at some time t an agent J does not do. If determinism is true, then there are laws of nature L, and there is a state of the Universe at a time t_0 before J's birth, described by a proposition P_0, such that L and P_0 logically entail the state of the Universe at t, described by a proposition P. P (what does happen at t) entails that J does not do A. (I understand by the laws of nature non-derivative, ultimate universally operative laws determining of physical necessity what happens—not laws which operate only under certain physical circumstances.) Now if J could have done A at t, then at t J could have rendered P false. Since P_0 and L entail P, not-P entails not (both P_0 and L). So if J could have done A at t, he could have rendered false P and so rendered false the conjunction of P_0 and L. But it is not possible for men to affect causally states of the Universe before their birth. So J could not have rendered P_0 false. Nor is it possible for men to change the laws of nature. For something would not be a law of nature if men could change it. So J could not at t have rendered false the conjunction of P_0 and L. Hence J could not have rendered false anything entailed by P_0 and L; hence he could not have rendered P false; hence he could not have done A. So determinism would seem to entail that men cannot ever do other than they do do and so that they are not morally responsible for their actions.

Determinism does indeed entail that men cannot ever do other than they do do—if this latter phrase is understood in the incompatibilist sense of 'given all the circumstances, they do not have uncaused freedom to act one way or to act the other way'. But Van Inwagen's argument does not work if we understand 'could' in the compatibilist sense of 'would, if he had chosen'. Even though (P_0 and L) entails P, it does not follow from 'A could have rendered P false' that 'A could have rendered (P_0 and L) false' if we understand 'could' in the compatibilist sense of 'would if he had chosen'. For in a deterministic world, if A had chosen to render P false, he would not thereby have rendered (P_0 and L) false. They would already have been false, as a result of which he would have been caused to choose to render P false. Van Inwagen claims that this particular compatibilist analysis does not give a plausible account of the meaning of some cases of 'could have done otherwise', that a more complicated analysis of a compatibilist type might be correct, but that it is less plausible to suppose that such an analysis is correct than to suppose that 'A could have rendered P false' and 'P entails $(P_0$ and $L)$' entails 'P could have rendered $(P_0$ and $L)$ false'; whence it follows that the balance of evidence suggests that any compatibilist analysis is false. (I understand by a compatibilist analysis of 'could have done otherwise' one on which 'S could have done other than he did' does not entail the falsity of determinism.) Van Inwagen's argument depends on the assumption that 'could' is used in just one sense, at any rate in the context of discussions about moral responsibility. In view of the variety of senses in which we use 'could' and connected modal notions in various contexts, I find it implausible to suppose that it is used in just one sense in this context. Whether Van Inwagen's principle of inference is correct is going to depend on the sense of 'could'. The conclusion most likely to follow from careful analysis of the meanings of 'could' in this context, in my view, is that determinism entails that in one sense of 'could' used in this context men can do other than they do and in another sense they can't. Whether it would follow from the fact that in the latter sense they cannot do other than they do that they are not morally responsible can only be settled by the kind of discussion exemplified in the text, and not by arguments of the type discussed in this note.

I am grateful to Peter Van Inwagen for discussing his view with me at some length, and thus helping me to formulate this criticism of it.

2 [ch. 6 n. 1]. On the aspect of punishment as expressing moral abhorrence, see Joel Feinberg, 'The Expressive Function of Punishment', *Monist*, 1965, **49**, 397–423, repr. in his *Doing and Deserving*, Princeton University Press, 1970. See also J. R. Lucas, *On Justice*, Clarendon Press, 1980, pp. 133–44; and R. A. Duff, *Trials and Punishments*, CUP, 1986, *passim*. Duff sees punishment as essentially communicative, communicating society's abhorrence of the crime. I agree that punishment ought to announce itself as the forcible taking of reparation for wrong done, and thus to communicate abhorrence (of the victim or of society on his behalf). For otherwise the one 'punished' would rightly suppose himself to have been wronged, and so seek reparation in return. But this must not be confused with the moral education theory of punishment which Duff argues is a major point of punishment. The moral education theory is ably expounded in Jean Hampton, 'The Moral Education Theory of Punishment', *Philosophy and Public Affairs*, 1984, **13**, 203–38. (See also Herbert Morris, 'A Paternalistic Theory of Punishment', *American Philosophical Quarterly*, 1981, **18**, 263–71, and R. Nozick, *Philosophical Explanations*, Clarendon Press, 1981, 203–38, and 363–97.) According to this the purpose of punishment is moral education (to be distinguished from mere rehabilitation; the rehabilitated

criminal will do the right acts, the reformed one will do them because he believes them to be morally right). The expression of abhorrence is on this view a tool of moral reform. Both Duff and Hampton emphasize how punishment, unlike manipulative or preventive treatment, respects the agent as a person, as one to whom society is responding as one who has freely chosen to do wrong and can be persuaded by seeing society's abhorrence thereof to do right for moral reasons. While agreeing that this is a good use to which punishment may be put, I shall be arguing that the right of retribution alone makes punishment permissible; and integral to retribution is the expression of abhorrence. Moral education is then one of several good utilitarian purposes which may be served by punishment, and may indeed be initiated by the expression of abhorrence. (In later discussion in this chapter I include both 'moral education' and 'rehabilitation' under the heading of 'reform'.)

3 [ch. 6 n. 3]. See e.g. G. W. F. Hegel, *The Philosophy of Right*, trans. T. M. Knox, Clarendon Press, 1942. Reparation may be made for outward harm done, but the bad will also needs in the same way to be cancelled out, claims Hegel (p. 69). To cancel this will is 'to annul the crime, which otherwise would have been held valid, and to restore the right . . . When the right against crime has the form of revenge, it is only right implicit, not in the form of right' (p. 141), i.e. it is done by the victim for his own sake, not by an impartial authority to instantiate a universal law, and only some people have the power to execute revenge. But when justice becomes no longer revenge but punishment, it is 'no longer contingent on might' (p. 73). 'Instead of the injured party, the injured universal comes on the scene, and has its proper actuality in the court of law . . . Objectively, this is the reconciliation of the law with itself, subjectively it is the reconciliation of the criminal with himself, i.e. with the law known by him as his own and as valid for him and his protection.' Kant's approach seems to be on the same lines as Hegel's and its consequences are very clear. Kant writes that even if a community is disbanding and its members scattering abroad, they must execute the last murderer left in gaol, 'for otherwise they might all be regarded as participators in the murder'. (See I. Kant, *The Philosophy of Law*, trans. W. Hastie, T. and T. Clark, Edinburgh, 1887, pp. 195–8). Although both writers hold that in general the state has not merely the right but the duty to punish, they do both allow that the state has the right sometimes to pardon and then not execute the right to punish. Kant holds that the state ought only to pardon crimes directly against itself, e.g. treason, and not 'crimes of subjects against each other'. (See Kant, op. cit., pp. 204 f. and Hegel, op. cit., p. 186.)

4 [ch. 6 n. 5]. Some of the few modern philosophers who have written on mercy have urged (in effect) that mercy is simply an aspect of justice. Thus for Claudia Card ('On Mercy', *Philosophical Review*, 1972, **81**, 182–207)

mercy is the remission of penalty simply in virtue of aspects of the situation (e.g. the criminal's current misfortunes, or his contribution to society) which cannot adequately be captured by laws; such remission is not merely permissible but obligatory. That view of mercy, however, seems less satisfactory when we consider not the state showing 'mercy' to criminals but one individual showing 'mercy' to another—e.g. my not punishing my child who has deliberately broken a window or not insisting on your repaying money which you have stolen from me. Here, it seems to me, there is clearly an area of possible cases where it would not be obligatory to show mercy, and not wrong either. I have a right to punish my child for deliberately breaking a window; but there is nothing wrong if I refrain (barring the consideration to be mentioned on pp. 102 f.) and often it is good if I refrain (if I am generous in not insisting on my rights). When we come to the state letting criminals off the punishment prescribed by law the situation becomes very different, because the state's officials are acting on behalf of the people in this respect and so they have a duty to execute any instructions given— whether always to enforce a mandatory punishment or in certain circum- stances to remit it. As we shall see, the people may have given very detailed instructions to officials as to the kind of punishment to be used in different kinds of case, or simply have instructed the officials to award the punishment they judge best for the community and/or the wrongdoer. But either way, the officials have a duty with respect to the punishment which they award—to give the one prescribed or the one judged best; and there is, in consequence, no scope for supererogatory goodness. Yet when the victim and not his agents are deciding whether or not to punish, there is plenty of scope for supererogatory mercy.

5 [ch. 6 n. 6]. A further difficulty for the view that the victim has the right to take, as the major part of retribution, reparation for the harm done arises from those cases where restoration of the status quo would be extremely costly for the wrongdoer, but not at all costly for the victim (given his resources and powers). This kind of case is often one where the harm done is unintentional; a poor man by accident breaks a rich man's expensive vase. It would cost the poor man years of unremitting toil to pay for the damage at market prices, yet for the rich man the loss is not of great importance and it is replaceable without too much difficulty. Does the rich victim really have the right to full repayment? This kind of case can be dealt with in more than one way without denying the general principle of punishment as retribution. When the harm done is unintentional, one could regard the wrongdoer as only a partial cause of it—his action would not have had its effect but for other factors ('bad luck') of which he was unaware; and so he can only be held responsible for a proportion of the damage. Further, the requirement that the reparation should be of 'equivalent' value could be understood not as 'of equivalent value to the victim' of the loss caused

(a value which might need to be determined by objective examination by others), but be understood rather in relation to the wrongdoer's ability to pay, as the requirement that he pay the same proportion of his resources as the victim has lost of his. Or perhaps some compromise between these understandings of 'equivalent' would be the right solution.

6 [ch. 6 n. 10]. A modified utilitarianism about punishment is expounded by Jonathan Bennett ('Towards a Theory of Punishment', *Philosophic Exchange*, 1980, **3**, 43–54. I am most grateful to Jonathan Bennett for detailed discussions with him about his theory and mine. For Bennett, how and when punishment is imposed should be determined not merely by the normal utilitarian considerations of deterrence, prevention, and reform, but by our basic reactive attitudes, to which P. F. Strawson drew attention in his essay 'Freedom and Resentment', in his book *Freedom and Resentment*, Methuen, 1974. The attitudes of 'blame', 'gratitude', 'praise', 'forgiveness', which I have been examining in the last three chapters and saw, given that we have (in my sense) free will, as deserved by agents in virtue of their conduct, Strawson sees merely as attitudes, probably undeserved, but nevertheless indispensable for worthwhile human interaction. Likewise, according to Bennett, punishing the guilty and not the innocent with a punishment of a kind and amount proper to the crime is part of this whole web of reactive attitudes which is indispensable for worthwhile human interaction—quite apart from whether humans have free will (in my sense). The justification for so doing is ultimately the utilitarian one of promoting such interaction, Bennett holds; and there may be rare occasions when utilitarian considerations other than the benefits of living within this web of reactive attitudes, of a more traditional kind (prevention, deterrence, and reform) rightly lead us to punish the innocent or punish excessively, despite the general utilitarian advantage for normal human interaction of doing otherwise. However, I argued in chs. 2 and 3, agents who do not have free will are not blameworthy, and hence, in the terminology of ch. 5, the only guilt will be objective guilt. If men do not have free will, the reactive attitudes including those involved in punishment for subjective guilt depend for their application on a false assumption. Punishment beyond that appropriate to objective guilt (or, if men have free will, to subjective guilt as well) does seem to run contrary to our normal understanding of justice. If there is some pay-off for personal relationships in going beyond these limits, it is not one which we are justified in pursuing by trampling on individual rights—barring the considerations mentioned in the last paragraph of this chapter.

7 [ch. 9 n. 26]. St Paul wrote that through Adam's sin 'death came into the world' (Rom. 5: 12), and it is a natural implication to suppose that he is claiming that, had Adam not sinned, he would have lived forever. If the claim is that this would have occurred as a natural process (i.e. without

God's special intervention), it seems a claim very unlikely to be true, given man's close kinship with the apes and the close similarity of his powers to theirs (and also one which Williams reasonably claims to be in contradiction to the Genesis account—see Williams, p. 53). If the claim rather is that if Adam had not sinned, God would have intervened in the natural process to preserve him from death, that seems to me to have some plausibility. For Adam would have been greatly worth preserving if he had acted on his feeble moral beliefs despite strong contrary desires. My argument in ch. 12 that God has abundant reason to preserve the good eternally would apply to Adam. If, thirdly, the claim that the death which 'came into the world' concerns not physical death, but a spiritual death of the soul (i.e., its guilt or being dominated by bad desires), then the claim is obviously correct.

The Council of Carthage (AD 417) anathematized the view that Adam was created mortal (Denzinger 222). Aquinas understands Adam's immortality to amount to the fact that God gave him a special supernatural grace which would have kept him from death, but which was withdrawn when Adam sinned (*Summa Theologiae* 1a. 97.1). This in effect is the first view above. Some other Fathers and scholastics were more qualified in their claims. Irenaeus wrote in one place that although 'human nature was indeed capable of immortality and incorruptibility, at the beginning it was not actually possessed of these gifts' (see N. P. Williams, *The Ideas of the Fall and Original Sin* (Longmans, 1927), 194). Duns Scotus held that unfallen Adam's 'immortality' consisted, not in the impossibility of dying, but in the possibility of not dying (Williams, op. cit., pp. 409 f.) (and, oddly enough, there are traces of that view in Augustine too—Williams, op. cit., p. 361 n. 2).

8 [ch. 9 n. 36]. Clearly the biblical source of the doctrine of original guilt is one passage—Rom. 5: 12–21—and without that passage there would to my mind be no biblical support for the doctrine. But even that passage read carefully does not in my view give any support to that doctrine. Certainly it says that Adam began the process of sinning and so the process of dying. And it also says (v. 15) that 'by the trespass of the one, the many died'. But it makes clear that the reason for this is that Adam's successors themselves sinned, through acquiring his tendency to sin—'death passed unto all men, for all sinned' (v. 12); the many did not die directly in consequence of Adam's sin. Hence when it says that 'through one trespass the judgement came unto all men to condemnation' (v. 18, echoing v. 16) and 'through one man's disobedience the many were made sinners' (v. 19), these passages can be read at most as supporting the second component of the doctrine of original sin—that Adam's sin caused our sinfulness—and not the third, that we are guilty for Adam's sin. I write 'at most' because St Paul qualifies the doctrine just stated. Strictly speaking, he holds, there is no sin without a law against which to rebel, and there was no such law before Moses—'until the

law sin was in the world, but sin is not imputed where there is no law. Nevertheless, death reigned from Adam until Moses, even over them that had not sinned after the likeness of Adam's transgression' (vv. 13 f.). Paul may hold, as he holds in effect elsewhere (Rom. 1: 18–22), that men did have a law of which they were aware between Adam and Moses, only an unwritten and undetailed one, and it was against that that they were sinning. Or he may hold that their sin was merely objective (i.e. done in ignorance) and so not to be 'imputed', merely penalized by death. Either way, he held that sin does not belong 'to those who had not sinned after the likeness of Adam's transgression' in the way it does to Adam; and the suggestion that they were guilty for sin in the way that Adam was, let alone guilty for Adam's sin, seems clearly out of line with the tone of the passage. See the analysis of this passage in Williams, op. cit., pp. 124–34.

9 [ch. 12 n. 17]. Awareness of the point that it would not be good that God should 'reward' us unless we had acquired through our deeds 'merit' in some sense led to the medieval distinction between *meritum de condigno*, condign merit, and *meritum de congruo*, congruous merit. An agent acquires condign merit if his beneficiary is put thereby under an obligation to reward him. An agent acquires congruous merit if it is 'congruous' or appropriate for his beneficiary to reward him, but not obligatory. As I introduced the term 'merit' in ch. 4, it was in the sense of congruous merit. I did however argue that there were some cases where there was an obligation to reward, in the sense of do some favour in return for the benefactor. I argued that in general any obligation to benefactors arises only from the voluntary acceptance of benefits, except in cases where the recipient of benefit is unable to choose to accept or reject the benefit (e.g. because he is too young). Now in cases where God is the recipient in virtue of creatures having used well his gifts to them of life and ability, it must be that God, by choosing to give them gifts of life and ability, thereby chooses to accept any good use they make of them. So, were we not to sin but use his gifts only to do supererogatory good acts, we would acquire not merely congruous merit but condign merit. But in fact we all sin and our sins cancel out any condign merit. God is under no obligation to forgive human sins even when humans plead the atoning sacrifice of Christ, but he has chosen to do so and to reward their supererogatory good acts. God's action is thus a recognition of congruous merit. Or at least that is so, unless God has already promised us humans to forgive us if we plead the atoning sacrifice of Christ and then to reward our supererogatory good acts. In that case, the reward being obligatory, the merit is condign. Theologians of the late medieval and Reformation periods argued about whether the man who goes to Heaven goes there in virtue of condign or only congruous merit. But those who argued for condign merit usually claimed that it arose only from God's gracious decision to put himself under an obligation to reward saints with

Heaven. That being so, it will be seen that there is not much at issue in this dispute. Whether we acquire merit in a certain situation depends on our free choice, aided by grace; whether it is condign or congruous depends on whether God has previously bound himself by a promise.

However, all those from Scotus onwards who argued that humans acquired either condign or congruous merit, assumed that the life of Heaven was a reward for that merit, and since God was not obliged to give such a reward, he determined the amount of our merit. Scotus emphasized strongly that the meritorious quality of an act might be quite out of proportion to its moral quality. Given my understanding of merit spelled out in ch. 4, this is an unsatisfactory way of putting the matter. How much we deserve our congruous merit, depends on us; but whether God gives us what we deserve (which he is not obliged to do unless he has promised) or more than we deserve depends on him. He cannot determine our merit, but he can determine his response to it. And, given my theological assumptions, that response is a generous one. But if you think of an action as having as much merit as it gets recognized by reward or gift beyond reward, then Scotus' point holds.

The congruous/condign merit distinction had application not only to the giving of Heaven to those who do good acts, but to Mary's 'merit' in being chosen as the mother of Jesus, and to the 'merit' of Christ's sacrifice. The distinction also got confused at one stage with the distinction between good acts done with, and good acts done without grace.

However, since the life of Heaven was more than men deserve, the Reformers were surely right to claim that, in my sense, that life is an unmerited gift. Where they were wrong is to claim that the *whole* value of good works comes from God's grace (J. Calvin, *Institutes of the Christian Religion*, iii. 15.3).

On the vicissitudes of the distinction between condign and congruous merit, see A. McGrath, *Iustitia Dei, A History of the Christian Doctrine of Justification*, CUP, 1986, i. 110–19 and ii. 83–90. On Scotus' view that our 'merit' depends on the will of God, see also Allan B. Wolter (ed.), *Duns Scotus on the Will and Morality*, Catholic University of America Press, 1986, 48–51 and the extract from Scotus' *Ordinatio* II (dict. 7, nn. 28–39) contained therein (on pp. 218–25).

Index

212   *Index*